Conference Papers Series
No. 10

Beyond *Guernica* and the Guggenheim

Art and Politics from a Comparative Perspective

Edited by Zoe Bray

Center for Basque Studies
University of Nevada Reno

This book was published with generous financial assistance from the Basque government

Conference Papers Series, no. 9

Series editor: Joseba Zulaika
Center for Basque Studies
University of Nevada, Reno
Reno, NV 89557
basque.unr.edu

Cover illustration: Autonomia, 2008, lacerated posters on board, by Josette Dacosta. Courtesy of the artist.

Library of Congress Cataloging-in-Publication Data

Beyond Guernica and the Guggenheim (Conference) (2013 : University of Nevada, Reno)
Beyond Guernica and the Guggenheim : art and politics from a comparative perspective / Edited by Zoe Bray.
pages cm. -- (The Center for Basque studies conference papers series ; No. 10)
Summary: "Art and politics are viewed from a comparative perspective in this book that goes from the Picasso's Guernica to the modern Bilbao Guggenheim"-- Provided by publisher.
ISBN 978-1-935709-56-5 (pbk.)
1. Art--Political aspects--Congresses. 2. Art--Political aspects--France--Pays Basque--Congresses. 3. Art--Political aspects--Spain--Pa?s Vasco--Congresses. I. Bray, Zoe, 1974- editor. II. University of Nevada, Reno. Center for Basque Studies. III. Title.

N72.P6B49 2013
701'.03--dc23

2014032386

Contents

Introduction

Art, Politics, and Identity

Zoe Bray

Politics is about the struggle of human beings for different kinds of power.[1] Power comes in a myriad of different forms, as influence, control, domination, or violence.[2] These can be expressed and exerted physically, directly, indirectly, and symbolically. The French philosopher Michel Foucault reminds us that what we take to be reality is itself a construct of power.[3] In coming into being, a reality stifles others and legitimizes itself. And at the same time, thanks to relations of power, this reality facilitates other power relationships that reinforce it.

The assumption of this book is that art is part and parcel of this process. The works of Foucault and of French sociologist Pierre Bourdieu help us understand how art is given social and political significance, and can be controlled and/or controlling.[4] Defining something as art, for example, is an act of politics, in that 'art' assigns a value to a 'thing' while it at the same time excludes other things from attaining this value. Whatever this art may be, it is produced and acquires significance in context. Those who create things considered art do so in social, cultural, and political situations that influence them both consciously and unconsciously, directly and in-

---

1. See also Lewellen, *Political Anthropology: An Introduction*; Kurtz, *Political Anthropology: Power and Paradigms*, 175.
2. Lukes, *Power: A Radical View*.
3. Foucault, "The Subject and Power," in *Michel Foucault: Beyond Structuralism and Hermeneutics*, ed. Dreyfus and Rabinow. 208-226.
4. Bourdieu, *Distinction: A Social Critique of the Judgement of Taste*.

directly. And their audiences perceive the work in context, too, also processing them wittingly or unwittingly according to social and cultural norms and the direct and indirect power relationships enshrined in them. Through their work, artists may wish to communicate something that has deliberate political aims. In some situations, however, the artwork or the artist may be appreciated or politicized in a way not intended by the artist.

Artists may also play specific roles in society. They may be dilettantes, provocateurs, harbingers of change, ambassadors, critics, or representatives. These roles may be self-assigned, or assigned to them by other people. Such roles may be welcomed by the artists, or they may be roles played in spite of themselves, despite some artists' desire for privacy and a discreet profile, or aspiration to neutrality.[5] Artists may also be fetishized, glorified, or used as scapegoats. Or they may be simply ignored. And the reason may not simply be because their work is 'bad' or 'mediocre' or 'uninteresting', whatever that may mean in a particular context. As British social anthropologist Jeremy MacClancy points out, "the question 'But is it art?' is not a hoary chestnut to be ignored but a politically-motivated interrogatory to be studied."[6] Indeed, art is the site of contestations in which different people place meaning and values that are themselves socially and politically related. While the assumption underlying this book is that art is politics, its aim is to inquire into how people play this out.

Since works of art deal with aspects of the reality(ies) upheld in the social context in which it is created, they also essentially embody that social context's power relationships.[7] This is true irrespective of whether the artist is critical toward or affirmative of the prevailing power relationships—or, as often is the case, critical toward a certain constellation of power relationships while affirming another one. So, to different degrees, every work of art reflects and encodes power relationships, irrespective of whether that was the intention of its creator.

But interpretation of art is also wrought with power relations. Art history, for instance, is itself based on certain philosophical and epistemological assumptions. Art historians have traditionally studied the way form and content convey aesthetic meaning. However,

---

5. See for example Bray, "Sculptures of Discord: Public Art and the Politics of Commemoration in the Basque Country."

6. MacClancy, "Anthropology, Art and Contest," in *Contesting Art: Art, Politics and Identity in the Modern World*, ed. MacClancy, 4.

7. See also Day, *Power: Its Myths and Mores in American Art, 1961-1991.*

meaning that is assigned to form and content is constructed from cultural values based on certain norms and understandings of reality. One can also misinterpret a work of art, or read too much into it.[8] And its significance may change with the times and political situations. The gendered readings of artwork come to mind, that is, the different interpretations, opportunities, and importance given to works of art made by people of different sexes and sexual identities.[9] For example, the Mexican artist Frida Kahlo, whose profile and work go hand in hand, is given today more attention than her husband, Diego Rivera, who was once much more revered and known.[10] This has much to do with changing sensibilities and taste, and with the art market, which is affected by who purchases what and at what price.[11]

While artists might make conscious choices regarding the medium and message, and how to frame their work meaningfully, the work might not be received in its social environment in the way the artist intended. That is to say, artwork may very well take on a life of its own.[12] It could take on other meanings and importance to different people depending on their political context. In the case of Picasso's painting, *Guernica*, for example, people may love it, despite not having any appreciation of art, because of their sensibility to issues of discrimination and human suffering, or to Basque national pride. With these sensibilities, they pick up on the values associated with the painting and learn to love it, thereby also reinforcing the power of the painting and the values and relationships related with it. The appreciation of a work of art will depend on a multiplicity of things: who made it, with what intention, for whom, under whose patronage, in what context, with what conceptual framework, what has already been said about it, the social and political network of its creator, and the cultural, emotional, aesthetic, and political dispositions of the audience.[13] Each of these aspects will have different degrees of importance depending on the situation.

---

8. Waller, "Foreword," in *Power: Its Myths and Mores in American Art, 1961-1991.*

9. See also Nochlin, "Why Have There Been No Great Women Artists?; Méndez, "From the Trap of Difference to That of Excellence: The Women Artists, Their Works and the Artistic Field."

10. Van Laar and Diepeveen, *Active Sights: Art As Social Interaction*, 93.

11. See also Lindauer, *Devouring Frida: The Art History and Popular Celebrity of Frida Kahlo.*

12. See also Appadurai, *The Social Life of Things: Commodities in Cultural Perspective.*

13. See also Becker, *Art Worlds.*

Art, as British social anthropologist Alfred Gell has argued, can also have agency.[14] It influences social perception and interaction. As American art professor Timothy Van Laar and Canadian English professor Leonard Diepeveen point out, "the best way one can understand, produce, and critique art is by paying attention to what a work does: the beliefs it embodies, the social roles it assumes, and its interactions with its audience."[15] So, just as politics can influence art and perception of art, art can influence politics. Art provides "ways of seeing," to paraphrase British art historian John Berger.[16]

Picasso's *Guernica* is paradigmatic in relation to all of these aspects of art and politics. Picasso painted this canvas, measuring 11 by 25.6 feet, in May 1937, to commemorate the horror of the aerial bombing of the Spanish Basque town of Guernica-Gernika (in Spanish and Basque respectively). The bombing had taken place less than one month earlier by Hitler's Condor Legion with the authorization of General Francisco Franco's Falange forces. Since then, the importance and reputation of this painting have grown enormously, to establish it as not only a masterpiece of twentieth-century art but also as a politically significant work. It is common today to hear people exalt the power in *Guernica* to communicate suffering, pathos, and a cry for justice.[17] The painting has entered our imagination as an indisputably great work, with a huge symbolic status.

As such, Picasso's *Guernica* is often brandished in situations of protest across the world. In the Basque Country, it is additionally a key symbol of Basque identity.[18] Reproductions of the painting are often found in the homes of people who identify themselves as Basque, especially Basque nationalists. Many artists in the Basque Country with Basque nationalist leanings also produce works, which they call Gernika (the Basque spelling) often imitating or drawing direct reference to Picasso's depiction. Regularly, participants in the *Aberri Eguna*, the annual Day of the Basque Nation, hold up banners prominently featuring sections of Picasso's

14. Gell, *Art and Agency: An Anthropological Theory*.

15. Van Laar and Diepeveen, *Active Sights: Art As Social Interaction*, 9-10.

16. Berger, *Ways of Seeing*. See also Bray, "Anthropology with a Paintbrush: naturalist-realist painting as 'thick description'."

17. For example: https://www.commondreams.org/views03/0209-04.htm. Last accessed May 1, 2014.

18. See also Raento and Watson, "Gernika, Guernica, Guernica?: Contested meanings of a Basque place; Sebastián García, "Guernica, Cuna del Gobierno Vasco. De Símbolo Foral a Símbolo Autonómico," in *Gernika y la Guerra Civil*, ed. Granja and Etxaniz.

Guernica. When the violent left-wing Basque separatist group ETA finally declared a ceasefire in October 2011, the left-wing Basque nationalist newspaper, *Gara*, announced the news on its front page and featured a painting entitled *Gernika* that bore many similarities to Picasso's famous work. The painting had been produced by a locally celebrated artist, José Luis Zumeta. Many other political uses of the *Guernica* painting are common in the Basque Country. For example, in October 2012, ecologists and other activists rallied to resist government and corporate plans to cut down Zilbeti, a forest of aspens in the region of Navarre, Spain. The most effective way that they found to stage their protest was to paint the trees as one big reproduction of Picasso's *Guernica*.

The symbolic importance attached to Picasso's *Guernica* is surprising, given the initial tepid response of the public to the work. When it was first exhibited in the summer of 1937, in the pavilion of the exiled Spanish Republican government at the Paris World Exhibition, its reception was on the whole cold and critical.[19] Criticism revolved around its alleged ugliness, blandness, obscurity, and even inability to convey the tragedy of the bombing. For many Basque people at the time, the relevance of the painting to their tragedy was not clear. Some, for instance, were unable to relate to the bull and horse featured in the painting, which have more to do with Spanish culture than with their own.[20]

But soon after its exhibition in Paris, the painting went on a world tour and, on the eve of World War II, it began to acquire both further symbolic meaning and recognition.[21] Picasso had given the painting to the Spanish Republican government-in-exile during General Franco's dictatorship and stated that it should not go to Spain until the country became a democracy again. Over the years, the painting became a universal symbol of the general devastation of war and a protest against oppression.[22] Even General Franco wished

---

19. Witham, *Picasso and the Chess Player: Pablo Picasso, Marcel Duchamp, and the Battle for the Soul of Modern Art*, 175-76; Greenberg and O'Brian, *The Collected Essays and Criticism, Volume 4: Modernism with a Vengeance, 1957-1969*; Van Hensbergen, *Guernica: The Biography of a Twentieth-century Icon*, 5.

20. See also for instance www.independent.co.uk/travel/europe/guernica-a-brush-with-history-7675829.html. Last accessed May 27 2014.

21. Sebastián García, "Guernica, Cuna del Gobierno Vasco. De Símbolo Foral a Símbolo Autonómico; Van Hensbergen, *Guernica: The Biography of a Twentieth-century Icon*; Greeley, *Surrealism and the Spanish Civil War*, 146-55.

22. See www.museoreinasofia.es/sites/default/files/salas/informacion/

to secure the painting, as part of his own propaganda. Its powerful symbolism reached a zenith, when, in the late 1970s, Spain's first democratic government repeatedly tried to bring the painting 'home', thereby evocatively demonstrating its own credentials.[23] The government's effort to bring the painting to Madrid was challenged by both the Basque autonomous government and the town council of Guernica-Gernika, which both claimed the painting for themselves. More recently, the continuing power of the painting was revealed in 2003, when US authorities had Rockefeller's tapestry reproduction of *Guernica* removed from its usual place at the United Nations headquarters in New York. In their view, the tapestry provided an inconvenient backdrop for Secretary of State Colin Powell as he presented his case for war with Iraq. Today, only few people with basic knowledge of the painting would admit to not seeing what is so great about *Guernica.*

In the 2005 edition of the magazine *Art in America*, US art critic Kim Bradley sub-headed her "Basque report" with the positive statement: "Eight years after the opening of the Guggenheim Museum Bilbao, the art scene in the Basque Country is thriving."[24] In various ways, the collection of essays in this book expands upon and reassesses Bradley's report ten years later. The collection also examines the politics of this art scene. The book is titled *Beyond* Guernica *and the Guggenheim* to invite reflection beyond the general discourses on Picasso's *Guernica* as a political chef-d'oeuvre and the conventional success story of the Guggenheim Museum Bilbao. The book also explores the ways in which art, power, and identity relate to each other in the Basque Country, empirically and comparatively.

What role do Basque institutions and authorities play in this process? What are artists doing and what political relevance does their work have? How are artists and artworks appreciated and given meaning by its different audiences? How does the social, cultural, and political context affect how art is produced and given significance? Conversely, how does art affect the context in which it exists? These are all questions addressed, in one way or another, by the contributors to this book. While some authors touch upon identity politics in the art world, others question what it means to be an artist engaged in politics and how such engagement is perceived

---

206_6_eng.pdf Last accessed May 23 2014.

23. Martin, *Picasso's War*. Van Hensbergen, *Guernica: The Biography of a Twentieth-Century Icon*, 297-307.

24. Bradley, "Basque Report."

by different audiences. Some contributors discuss the political simplification of artists' profiles and their work, while others explore the political process of curating and exhibiting art. The range and variety of this book's contents reflect the multiple ways in which we can think about politics in relation to art—politics as something involving conventions and control, or party politics and conflicting ideologies. Some scholars look at the expectations, influence, or censorship that people have over an artist or an artwork, while others determine how a work is valued, and how different audiences ascribe different meanings to a particular work. Some scholars inquire into structural power, how some artists get favored, or disfavored, or ignored, according to inherent values, such as gender, cultural or political affiliation, and market forces. Other scholars investigate how the artist works and what he or she seeks to say, and through what choice of medium—which itself is the product and agent of power relations.

The Basque Country presents an interesting array of phenomena linking art and politics. Following industrialization in the nineteenth century that led to a crisis of modernity, especially in what is today the autonomous region of Euskadi, which brings together institutionally three of the seven Basque provinces, the Basque Country was shaped over the course of the twentieth century by conflicting political agendas, with direct consequences for artistic expression.[25] Some artists played an important role in influencing certain political and cultural developments. During the years of General Franco's dictatorship (1939–1975), a group of (essentially male) avant-garde artists in the Spanish part of the Basque Country were celebrated by self-identifying Basques as standard-bearers of a distinctive Basque culture—in the words of one veteran, they were "the *ikurriña* (Basque flag) that we could not fly."[26] Their influence was so strong, particularly that of the artists Eduardo Chillida and Jorge Oteiza, that younger Basque artists found it difficult to assert themselves and their work independently from this heritage.

With Spain's return to democracy in 1977, Euskadi developed autonomous institutions. These served to normalize a notion of Basque national identity, with a consequent impact on the production and appreciation of a specific type of art in the Basque Country.[27] Since the 1980s, the Faculty of Fine Arts at the University of the

25. MacClancy, "Negotiating Basque Art"; Guasch, *Arte e Ideologia en el Pais Vasco: 1940-1980*.

26. Interview with art collector, Hondarribia, Euskadi, June 9, 2013.

27. See MacClancy, "Negotiating Basque Art," 209.

Basque Country in Bilbao, and prestigious art prizes such as *Gure Artea* (significantly meaning 'Our Art' in Basque) have been established as fundamental collective reference points for local artists. In the first three decades of its existence, the government of Euskadi devoted an important part of its budget to culture and specifically to the arts. Investments in the arts also included the creation of institutional collections and subsidies to artists. The twin processes of the institutionalization of art and globalization in Euskadi combined to produce a new generation of artists who engage both with national and regional references, as well as with contemporary art on an international level.[28] Many of these artists have investigated different kinds of issues in their art that are deemed political, from questions of form and content to feminism.

A key symbol of the new institutional and global trend is the Guggenheim Bilbao Museum (GMB), opened in 1997. It provides a combination of seduction and spectacle that is quite the opposite of the Basque avant-garde's aspirations. It was initially criticized as a "McDonaldization"[29] of Basque culture; and, according to the artist Jorge Oteiza, "something worthy of Disney, totally anti-Basque."[30] Yet, nearly twenty years later, the Guggenheim Bilbao is a source of pride to most Basques: it has helped to lift the former industrial city of Bilbao out of its postindustrial depression and put both Bilbao and the Basque Country on the map of international aesthetics in a manner totally distinct from past images of the region linked to separatist violence and folkloristic tradition.[31] As part of the international complex of the Guggenheim Foundation, the GMB now represents a key reference for the global art world. The 'Bilbao effect' that it is credited with producing has inspired other cities and regions across the world to consider art as a way to revitalize their economies.[32] Ironically, however, during its first decade

28. On the importance that Arteleku, the art residency established by the department of culture of the provincial council of Gipuzkoa in San Sebastián-Donostia in 1986, had on the art scene in Euskadi until early 2000, see http://santieraso.wordpress.com/2014/05/15/ultimos-dias-de-arteleku/ (accessed June 19 2041) and Jaio, "Tout va bien/Garai Txarrak: Una Mirada a Treinta," *Mugalari*, October 30 2009.

29. Zulaika, *Guggenheim Bilbao Museoa: Museums, Architecture, and City Renewal*, 109-33.

30. MacClancy, "Negotiating Basque Art," 208.

31. Guasch and Zulaika, *Learning from the Bilbao Guggenheim*; Zulaika, *Guggenheim Bilbao Museoa: Museums, Architecture, and City Renewal*, 117-20.

32. See www.forbes.com/2002/02/20/0220conn.html. Last accessed

of existence, the GMB paid relatively little attention to local artists, focusing instead on international blockbuster shows. The museum has also had the reputation of catering to a certain privileged local and global elite; only recently, its exclusivity and elitism was heightened by the role the GMB played as the prestigious venue for the Global Forum Spain 2014.[33] The Forum brought together leaders in the world of banking and top officials from international organizations such as the International Monetary Fund and the OECD, whose wealth, power, and status contrasted uneasily with local, less privileged citizens who suffer the still acute effects of the current economic recession, including eviction from their homes.

Meanwhile, in the French part of the Basque Country (*Pays Basque*), artistic expression has remained comparatively discreet and on the whole rather traditional, in tune with the more rural, politically and institutionally marginal nature of this region. From the 1970s, a modern Basque nationalist consciousness, specific to the French Basque Country, spread. This development, together with increasing urbanization, encouraged artists to experiment further in the visual and plastic arts and to explore their relationship with this emerging collective identity. Nonetheless, local Basque expression in these arts has tended to look to the Spanish side of the Basque Country for reference, and it has been a challenge for many younger artists to situate themselves significantly.[34] They often find themselves sandwiched between two dominating discourses: those of Spanish Basque nationalism and French nationalism, respectively.[35] Lacking institutions of its own, the *Pays Basque* remains weak in terms of an autochthonous development of the arts. It was only, for instance, in 2011 that the first young contemporary art prize of its kind (*Gazte Saria*) was launched in the region. A small group of cultured outliers from the inland provinces collaborated with the association *Itzal Aktiboa* (which means "Active Shadow," an expression taken, not fortuitously, from a poem by Jorge Oteiza) and *Euskal Kultur Erakundea* (the Basque Cultural Institute of the *Pays Basque*) to create the prize.

ETA's ongoing ceasefire has radically eased the identity polarization existing in the Basque Country. Nevertheless, tensions over different ideologies and correspondingly differing interpre-

---

May 22 2014.

33. See www.globalforumspain.com/en/prensa/. Last accessed May 27, 2014.

34. See for example De Jaureguiberry, *Escultura Vasca, Euskal Eskultoreak*.

35. Bray, "Interviews with French Basque Artists: Identity and Politics, and Art for Art's Sake."

tations of personal and collective identity still characterize the region in its geographical, institutional, political, and cultural diversity. Traditional identities and power structures are also being broken down to a certain extent, with new challenges coming, for instance, from different gender and life experiences.[36] These have consequences for the kind of art that is produced, the motivations of its creators, and the receptivity of art amateurs and investors, all of whom, however, may not necessarily be in tune with each other, as is often the case.

Contributions to this book are grounded in varying disciplines: the history of art, art criticism, sociology, philosophy, and the anthropology of art. The book is the fruit of a conference held at the Center for Basque Studies, University of Nevada, Reno, in May 2013, which brought together scholars, curators, art critics, and artists from different countries to share their thoughts and research on the relationship between art and politics. This means that each contributor has been guided by different epistemological and ontological premises, as well as by different personal sensibilities and preoccupations. Each author has consequently engaged on different critical levels. Some are concerned with providing further empirical data, while others focus more on pursuing philosophical questions or normative agendas. Because of the diversity of foci and approaches, the chapters are also characterized by varying styles. The reader will notice that the authors sometimes take quite different positions and perspectives and do not necessarily agree with each other. This in itself highlights the politics of art. By touching in their own way on the relationship between politics and art, they all contribute to the topic that concerns us here.

The sequence of chapters is structured to relate to three general topics in which art and politics are connected: Valuing Art; Artistic Political Engagement; and Exhibitions and Curating. All together, the chapters included under each of these headings do not claim to treat the themes exhaustively. Many dimensions and critical viewpoints are not considered or represented. This may be a frustration for the reader who expects to follow a cohesive and critically self-reflexive debate on the relationships between art and politics. However, an open-minded reader will be able not only to discover new ways of exploring the topic, but also to reflect on the politics inherent to the arguments made by each of the authors. These opportunities derive from the very fact that the contributors

---

36. See for example Bray, "Interviews with Two Basque Artists: Ana Laura Alaez and Azucena Vieites."

speak from different disciplinary standpoints, concerns, and aspirations. Again, this in itself is a central aspect of politics in art.

In Part 1, Valuing Art, the authors broadly treat the following questions: who gives value to art? how does this occur? and what value is given to art? They also consider how these phenomena change with time and circumstance, including political interest.

In chapter 1, sociologist Nathalie Heinich discusses how appreciation of an artwork is subject to the cognitive context of valuation, that is, the individual's capacity to use one paradigm or another. Heinich observes how contemporary art is often valued in terms of its relationship to politics. She notes the prevalence of a critical stance in contemporary art, which seems now to be part of the conventionally required repertoire of singularity. She observes that engagement with politics, rejection of institutions, and ostensible solidarity with the 'dominated' have become common postures for artists. Heinich pinpoints what artistic criteria are valued today, and how the value of political commitment relates to this set of values. In this vein, Heinich explains why *Guernica* is considered an icon of our modern culture, as it fits all these criteria.

In chapter 2, sociologist Jesus Arpal discusses the art world in the Spanish Basque Country during Franco's dictatorship, with a specific focus on the artistic project of the Sanctuary of Aranzazu in the 1950s. This project was a significant benchmark in the region for change in artistic form and the political role of the artist. The artists commissioned to work on the Sanctuary were deeply aware that their art had the potential to challenge the political establishment and to contribute to the construction of a modern Basque identity. The project brought together three artists now celebrated in the Basque Country as the pioneers of Basque modern art—Jorge Oteiza, Eduardo Chillida, and Nestor Basterretxea. The project gave them the opportunity to produce a combination of non-conventional monumental sculpture and painting. Their work marked a clear break in aesthetics and served to the Basque nationalist liberation movement. Arpal explains why the project was so highly controversial and a challenge to the Franco regime.

In chapter 3, Juan Arana describes how the transition from General Franco's regime to a democratic state in Spain contributed to a paradigm shift in the local production and appreciation of art. Arana notes how a culture of consensus developed that rejected the revolutionary sacrificial art advocated by the artist Jorge Oteiza. Instead, Arana claims that the culture of consensus favored art as an object of decoration, consumption, and status. He describes the most renowned artistic movement of the Spanish transition, the *movida*, as chiefly non-historical and apolitical. With its Pop aesthetics, Arana argues that it could be classified as the beginning of the end of meaningful—political—art in Spain. In the Basque Country, the epitome of this perceived decadence has been the art-as-spectacle also promoted with the Guggenheim Bilbao Museum. On a positive note, Arana observes that, with the recent shift in the Basque political establishment, new reflections on the past and the development of new paradigms in art could be underway.

Art historian Adelina Moya focuses closely on the significance of the Guggenheim Bilbao Museum in its local Basque context. In chapter 4, she explains the origins of the project, the initial local opposition and the more recent integration of this institution in the art world of Euskadi. Moya describes how the GMB eventually began hosting exhibitions that feature Basque artists. Its curators and management seemingly recognized the need to socially legitimize its existence in the region. She notes how the museum also eventually included works of the younger generation of Basque artists, including many women, in its private collection. Finally, she points out a fundamental irony: an essential aspect of contemporary art is to criticize "the system," yet at the same time, contemporary art needs the system to recognize it.

In the chapter 5, artist Txomin Badiola—a major figure in the Basque contemporary art scene—reflects on artists' engagement with politics, their decisions to interact with it, challenge it, or ignore it. The author cautions that too many artists rely too heavily on politics. Badiola speaks from his personal experience. He was a student of art at the Faculty of Fine Art in the early years of the University of the Basque Country. He sought emancipation from the expectations of the art world, including the overbearing influence of the celebrated avant-garde Basque artist Jorge Oteiza, the extremes of Basque politics, and the pressures of giving value and meaning to art. Badiola's work has focused on putting into question the very idea of content, and exposing the language with which reality is produced. So his work takes the shape of "bad form" so to speak, *Malas Formas* (which was also the title of one of his major exhibitions).[37] His concern is with medium rather than meaning, which, he reminds us, cannot be controlled.

In chapter 6, art historian Ismael Manterola discusses the transmission of certain values and traditions in Basque art over time. Manterola notes that, since the late nineteenth century, a clearly

37. Badiola et al., "Malas formas: Txomin Badiola 1990–2002."

distinct Basque consciousness has been passed on from generation to generation of Basque artists. While other scholars consider this transmission to have ended with the close of the twentieth century, Manterola observes a transformation in Basque art at the turn of the twenty-first century that clearly links with a sense of Basque heritage. This transformation came in the form of what he calls the New Basque Sculpture movement. Some of the artists associated with this movement included Txomin Badiola who, while expanding their horizons and references on the international scene, clearly still worked in communication with previous artists, including the ideas propagated by Oteiza concerning the essence of art and the artist's connection with her or his environment. Manterola states that younger artists have in turn continued on from the work of this New Basque Sculpture Movement.

In the chapter 7, as a social anthropologist and artist, I reflect on the value that art, and more specifically "Basque art," is given in the French part of the Basque Country. I explore how this art is further interpreted in the context of rural village politics. I focus on the case of *Haize Berri*, an association created by a group of local inhabitants concerned with providing culture and art to the rural hinterland of the region. *Haize Berri* succeeded in bringing about a cultural renaissance in the locality by attracting numerous key artists, including from the Spanish side of the Basque Country. However, the association remained at the heart of local controversy throughout its existence: while the mission of *Haize Berri* was not publicly stated as political, many of its organizers saw culture and art as part of politics, and part of a specific nationalist agenda with which local inhabitants disdained to associate. The case of *Haize Berri* serves as a lens through which to explore the political values placed on art as elements in the drawing of identity boundaries.

Part 2, concerned with Artistic Political Engagement, leads us to reflect on another dimension of art and politics: how artists may actually be engaged with politics, either through themselves and/or through their art.

Chapter 8, written by art historian Brett Van Hoesen, explores an example of how artists might go down in history in relation to their political associations. Van Hoesen focuses on the case of Max Pechstein, a German artist who spent time painting on the South Pacific islands of Palau after World War I. Van Hoesen discusses the work of Pechstein in its time and invites the reader to reevaluate how Pechstein has been placed in history. She notes that Pechstein, on the whole, has been deemed non-political by many scholars because of his seemingly apolitical subject matter and his traditional use of painting and sculpture. The author goes on to show how he was actually engaged and reflected on his work within the politics of his time, at the intersection between colonial and postcolonial discourses.

In chapter 9, art historian Catherine Dossin reflects on the work of Gérard Fromanger, a French artist who emerged significantly during the 1960s, a politically critical time in France. Fromanger created works that invoked the limits of the French Republican values of liberty, equality, and fraternity. Using paint, which was at that time dismissed as a traditionalist medium, he depicted established codes of representation to reveal their vacancy. Dossin examines Fromanger's work over the years, and how he sought to engage with current affairs through his painting, including the resurgence of Fascism in France in the 1970s and the Gulf Wars in the 1990s. For Dossin, Fromanger is a clear example of an artist who does the revolution through art, and, more specifically, who succeeded through the formalistic medium of paint.

In chapter 10, curator and researcher Aimar Arriola looks at the Spanish artist Pepe Espaliú, conventionally known for his artistic performances relating to AIDS, the disease that afflicted him. In 1992, Espaliú spent a few months in the Spanish Basque city of San Sebastián-Donostia to teach a course at Arteleku, the contemporary art center set up by the provincial government of Gipuzkoa only a few years earlier. Arteleku was then an important hub for innovative artistic experiments. At Arteleku, Espaliú conceived the powerful art-action "Carrying" in collaboration with other artists, just a few months before dying. Arriola argues that the significance of Espaliú and his art needs to be understood in a broader and more complex network of practices and thought that existed in the 1990s, and of which Arteleku was an important part.

In the chapter 11, Azucena Vieites, another key artist in the contemporary art scene of the Basque Country, reflects on the development and evolution of artistic practices in relation to feminism and gender in the Basque Country from the mid-1980s to the present. She speaks from her personal experience, as a member of the generation that began studying Fine Arts in Bilbao at the University of the Basque Country in its first years of existence, and continued on at Arteleku. Together with the artist Estibaliz Sádaba, she founded the pioneering Basque feminist artist group Erreakzioa-Reacción in 1994 to develop the production of activist feminist and queer art projects, thereby increasing the visibility of women artists, and promoting feminist debate in a hitherto narrow and male-centered art world.

In chapter 12, art historian Peter Selz discusses the work of two contemporary artists, Mexican born Enrique Chagoya and the American William T. Wiley. According to Selz, these artists are clearly political in the sense of being explicitly engaged on matters of politics at the same time as being totally committed to the creation of art. Both men created art with political content in a way that was both skilled and gracious, factors that, according to Selz, have helped them both to be appreciated by the general public.

Chapter 13, by curator and art critic Fernando Golvano, reflects on how, over the years, different artistic expressions have served a variety of functions: as critique, the creation of new subjectivities, a means of emancipation, as magic, and the creation of new communities. However, given there is no art without *telos*, the political dimension is present in all artistic practices in some way or other. Golvano brings attention to the fact that the ultimate finality of any art resides in its social-historical context. He draws on the writings of thinkers such as Stéphane Mallarmé, Theodor W. Adorno, Walter Benjamin, Hal Foster, and Félix Guattari, and the artist Jorge Oteiza.

In Part 3, Exhibitions and Curating, contributors focus on another dimension of the relationship between art and politics: what gets exhibited, how and why, and to what effect. The authors tackle these issues from different perspectives and standpoints.

In chapter 14, art historian Selma Holo discusses the process undergone by her students at the University of Southern California to conceive and curate an exhibition of posters from the collection held in the Center for the Study of Political Graphics. Working on the general theme of mass violence and genocide, the students soon realized the need to make pragmatic choices and finally focused on the specific topic of violence against women. As they selected posters exclusively on this topic, they became conscious of the different ways that art (including posters) communicates ideas and messages, and how their way of exhibiting this art could guide the public's reflexive process.

In chapter 15, curator Xabier Arakistain (Arakis) describes the conceptual process by which the Cultural Center Montehermoso was established in Euskadi's capital city, Vitoria-Gasteiz, as the first cultural institution in all of Spain to incorporate feminist thought in its organizational structure and programming. Arakis was at the heart of the feminist debates taking place in Spain in mid-2000 to ensure equal opportunities regarding gender in the art world. He served as Montehermoso's director until it closed down in 2011. He explains how this pioneering center was able to include women on an equal basis to men in its artistic and cultural programs and to increase the quality of these programs. Montehermoso became a key reference within a network of renowned national and international institutions. The center also succeeded locally by successfully connecting contemporary art with the general public.

Finally, in chapter 16, art historian, critic, and activist Susan Noyes Platt reviews "Newtopia, the State of Human Rights." Katerina Gregos curated the exhibition in Mechelen, a Belgian city that was once a major participant in the deportation of Nazi victims to concentration camps during World War II. In Platt's opinion, this exhibition was groundbreaking in gathering a variety of artists, all deeply engaged in political and social activism, to work on the common theme of Human Rights. Platt believes that every work of art in the exhibition accomplished its intention, either to get a message across or to make the visitor reflect. Finally, she claims these artists should be celebrated for engaging with crucial social issues through their art, especially at a time when, in Platt's opinion, the art world still tends to honor aesthetics more than content.

Bibliography

Appadurai, Arjun. *The Social Life of Things: Commodities in Cultural Perspective*. Cambridge: Cambridge University Press, 1988.

Badiola, Txomin, Peio Aguirre, Manuel Clot, et al. "Malas Formas: Txomin Badiola 1990–2002." Bilbao: Museo de Bellas Artes de Bilbao, 2002.

Becker, Howie S. *Art Worlds*. Berkeley: University of California Press, 1982.

Berger, John. *Ways of Seeing*. London: Penguin, 2008.

Bourdieu, Pierre. *Distinction: A Social Critique of the Judgement of Taste*. Translated by Richard Nice. London: Routledge, 1984.

Bradley, Kim. "Basque Report." *Art in America* 93, no. 10 (2005): 83-89.

Bray, Zoe. "Anthropology with a Paintbrush: Naturalist-Realist Painting as 'Thick Description'." *Visual Anthropology Review*, 31: 2 (2015).

———. "Interviews with French Basque Artists: Identity and Politics, and Art for Art's Sake." (forthcoming).

———. "Interviews with Two Basque Artists: Ana Laura Alaez and Azucena Vieites." *N:paradoxa, International Feminist Journal* 34 July (2014): 5-15.

———. "Sculptures of Discord: Public Art and the Politics of Commemoration in the Basque Country." *Public Art Dialogue* 4, no. 2 (2014): 221-48.

Day, Holliday T. *Power: Its Myths and Mores in American Art, 1961-1991.* Indianapolis: Indianapolis Museum of Art, 1991.

De Jaureguiberry, Michel. *Escultura Vasca, Euskal Eskultoreak.* Saint Jean de Luz: Arteaz, 2011.

Eraso Beloki, Santiago. "Los Últimos Días Del Arteleku De Loiola." In http://santieraso.wordpress.com/2014/05/15/ultimos-dias-de-arteleku/, 2014.

Foucault, Michel. "The Subject and Power." In *Michel Foucault: Beyond Structuralism and Hermeneutics*, edited by L. Hubert Dreyfus and Paul Rabinow, Chicago: The University of Chicago Press, 1983.

Gell, Alfred. *Art and Agency: An Anthropological Theory*. Oxford: Clarendon Press, 1998.

Greeley, Robin Adèle. *Surrealism and the Spanish Civil War*. New Haven: Yale University Press, 2006.

Greenberg, Clement, and John O'Brian. *The Collected Essays and Criticism, Volume 4: Modernism with a Vengeance, 1957-1969*. Chicago: University of Chicago Press, 1995.

Guasch, Ana Maria. *Arte E Ideologia En El Pais Vasco: 1940-1980*. Madrid: Akal, 1985.

Guasch, Ana Maria, and Joseba Zulaika. *Learning from the Bilbao Guggenheim*. Reno: Center for Basque Studies Press, University of Nevada Reno, 2005.

Jaio, Miren. "Tout Va Bien/Garai Txarrak: Una Mirada a Treinta." *Mugalari*, October 30 2009.

Kurtz, Donald V. *Political Anthropology: Power and Paradigms*. Boulder, CO: Westview Press, 2001.

Lewellen, Ted C. *Political Anthropology: An Introduction*. Westport, CONN: Praeger, 2003.

Lindauer, Margaret A. *Devouring Frida: The Art History and Popular Celebrity of Frida Kahlo*. Middletown, CT: Wesleyan University Press, 2011.

Lukes, Steven. *Power: A Radical View*. New York: Palgrave Macmillan, 2005.

MacClancy, Jeremy. "Anthropology, Art and Contest." Chap. 1 In *Contesting Art: Art, Politics and Identity in the Modern World*, edited by Jeremy MacClancy, Oxford: Berg, 1997.

———. "Negotiating Basque Art." Chap. 7 In *Contesting Art: Art, Politics and Identity in the Modern World*, Oxford: Berg, 1997.

Martin, Russell. *Picasso's War*. London: Hol Art Books, 2012.

Méndez, Lourdes. "From the Trap of Difference to That of Excellence: The Women Artists, Their Works and the Artistic Field." *Art and Design Review* 2, no. 1 (2014): 1-5.

Nochlin, Linda. "Why Have There Been No Great Women Artists?" *ArtNews* 69 January (1971): 22-39.

Raento, Pauliina, and Cameron Watson. "Gernika, Guernica, Guernica?: Contested Meanings of a Basque Place." *Political Geography* 19, no. 6 (2000): 707-36.

Sebastián García, Lorenzo. "Guernica, Cuna Del Gobierno Vasco. De Símbolo Foral a Símbolo Autonómico." In *Gernika Y La Guerra Civil*, edited by Jose-Luis Granja and Jose-Angel Etxaniz, Gernika: Gernikazarra Historia Taldea, 1998.

Van Hensbergen, Gijs. *Guernica: The Biography of a Twentieth-Century Icon*. London: Bloomsbury, 2005.

Van Laar, Timothy, and Leonard Diepeveen. *Active Sights: Art as Social Interaction*. Mountain View, CA: Mayfield, 1998.

Waller, Bret. "Foreword." In *Power: Its Myths and Mores in American Art, 1961-1991.*, Indianapolis: Indianopolis Museum of Art, 1991.

Witham, Larry. *Picasso and the Chess Player: Pablo Picasso, Marcel Duchamp, and the Battle for the Soul of Modern Art*. Lebanon: University Press of New England, 2013.

Zulaika, Joseba. *Guggenheim Bilbao Museoa: Museums, Architecture, and City Renewal*. Reno: Center for Basque Studies Press, University of Nevada Reno, 2003.

Part 1

Valuing Art

1

Guernica and the Bond between Art and Politics According to a Sociology of Values

Nathalie Heinich

Fact or Value? "Engagement" as a Modern Art Value

Aesthetic radicalism and political radicalism are largely contradictory, despite all the denials accumulated through the multiple forms of idealization of the avant-garde. According to Pierre Bourdieu's definition of autonomy in art,[1] the aesthetical avant-garde can be defined as focusing on autonomous, specifically artistic issues. These inevitably pull toward elitism[2] while the political avant-garde focuses on heteronomous issues, which tend to privilege common welfare or even popular requirements. Faced with this objective contradiction between two equally antibourgeois but unfortunately conflicting definitions of the ideal artist, denial is a rather frequent way to cope with it, whether by artists, by art specialists, or by art amateurs: a denial supported by the idealization of a largely imaginary avant-garde, calling for a critical stand that is all the more present in words than it is poorly present in practice.[3]

The idea to combine the most advanced artists with the most progressive defenders of a highly idealized people comes from the Saint-Simonian tradition, which paved the way for what was to become avant-garde as an ideal, from the mid-nineteenth century down to the present. Such a combination has been only rarely or ephemerally achieved: the Bolshevik Revolution and its aftermath

1. Bourdieu, *Les Règles de l'art*.
2. Poggioli, *The Theory of the Avant-Garde*.
3. All this is developed in Heinich, *L'Elite artiste*.

provided exceptionally favorable conditions for it, with the Suprematist movement in painting and its leader Kazimir Malevich, and the Surrealist movement and its leader André Breton. Later on, the 1968 movement reactivated this idea that pro-working class political involvement should be accompanied by the most cutting-edge artistic experiences (Heinich, 2005).[4] This idealized link between art and politics is of course relative to spatial and historical contexts, as is any value system: here it is especially relevant for the Western world of basically educated people as it developed from the mid-nineteenth century to the present, as evidenced by the increasing number of contemporary conferences and publications dealing with "art and politics."

But, against such an ideal, reality sometimes reveals the contradiction between artistic experiment and political involvement. See the case of Picasso as a "*compagnon de route*"—a fellow traveler—of the French communist party: after having been dismissed as too distant from the concerns of the People, that is, as being a bourgeois artist, he was presented after World War II as an anti-bourgeois artist, an ally of the People. Indeed, the contradiction is irreducible: since innovations in art require a certain amount of cultural capital, one can hardly enhance both originality, according to what I call the "*régime de singularité*" or the "realm of singularity," and conformity to traditional and popular tastes, according to the "*régime de communité*" or "community realm."[5] Both share a common affinity with social margins, but inside the social elite as regards artists, and outside the elite as regards workers or poor people—what is termed "*le peuple*" in French. As an example of this contradiction, one can mention the case of Emile Zola, a model of the committed writer but not a writer who revolutionized the art of the novel—as did Marcel Proust shortly after, although from the most elitist world. One can hardly expect the people to appreciate the value of experiments requiring a high level of culture, and one cannot expect good artists to endorse stereotyped forms of expression submitted to ideological aims.

Faced with such a bitter statement, which would require a fairy tale to reconcile such fundamental and conflicting values as avant-garde aesthetics and the political vanguard, we can understand why so many intellectuals, faithfully applying the well-known ostrich policy, prefer to mistake the exception for the rule, and the "norm" for the "standard." This very denial and its imaginary reso-

---

4. Ibid.

5. Heinich, *The Glory of Van Gogh*.

lution keep on sustaining the old myth of the avant-garde, and the idea that advanced art should go hand-in-hand with progressive political action.

The first generation after the French Revolution developed a new relationship to the arts based on the values of vocation, marginality, and singularity.[6] Why are modern artists and art specialists still so involved in this idea of a necessary connection between arts and politics? We could interpret it as a form of romanticism, according to the definition provided by Norbert Elias: a kind of escape out of the real world, resulting from a situation of dependence on social privileges that cannot be accepted or idealized, as was the case for the young heirs of aristocratic or bourgeois elites after the French Revolution and the relative delegitimization of traditional elitism based on birth or wealth.[7] This probably explains the prevalence of the critical stance in contemporary art, which is now part of the required repertoire of singularity: political commitment, rejection of institutions, and ostensible solidarity with the "dominated" have become required or at least fairly common postures, especially for young artists in need of recognition.

"Only revolt is creative," proclaimed André Breton in 1926: this is indeed a poet's word, but should not be seriously endorsed by social scientists. However, some major philosophers and sociologists used to mix up their political and aesthetical claims, insisting both on art and on politics as sustaining an emancipatory virtue: think of the Frankfurt School (especially Theodor Adorno[8]); then Pierre Bourdieu (especially in his dialogue with Hans Haacke, emphasizing criticality as a major path to avant-garde positions[9]); and today Jacques Rancière, sustaining the idealization of art as possessing intrinsic democratic qualities.[10] In all these cases, the drive of these social scientists to defend ideals outweighs their will to produce genuine knowledge.

So, we have to accept that the bond between arts and politics—at least avant-garde art and progressive politics—is mostly a matter of value rather than a matter of fact. Now, what kind of other values are there in our present artistic world, and how does the value of "engagement" (or political commitment) relate to this whole set of values? This is what I will briefly expose as a second part of my ar-

---

6. Heinich, *L'Elite Artiste.*
7. Elias, *La Dynamique de l'Occident.*
8. Adorno, *Aesthetic Theory.*
9. Bourdieu and Haacke, *Libre échange.*
10. Rancière, *Le Partage du sensible.*

gument, before applying this axiological frame to the special case of *Guernica*, as a third and final part.

The Plurality of Artistic Values

Let us now briefly consider the set of values that are relevant in the relationship to art—that is, what I call artistic values. My perspective is that of the sociology of values, or axiology—that is, knowledge regarding valuations. I call "value" the principle sustaining a valuation, or value judgment, observed through empirical investigation.[11] My aim is to build up knowledge of ordinary people's values, and not to defend any kind of values—which is not, in my opinion, the researcher's task.[12]

The list of the main values pertaining to art will be organized according to the axis of their degree of autonomy or heteronomy, that is, their degree of artistic specificity:[13] I will go from the least to the more autonomous.

Thus, as for the most heteronomous values used to evaluate artists or art works, we meet this value of "engagement," or political commitment, which I mentioned before as a major requirement in modern and contemporary culture. It has to do with the value of *responsibility*, pertaining to a family of values—or "value register" in my vocabulary—that I call "*civic*," that is, it is concerned with the general interest; those who know Luc Boltanski and Laurent Thévenot's book on justification will recognize part of the vocabulary they build up in order to address the plurality of value systems used by people to justify their actions.[14] Responsibility is the very value sustaining claims about "*l'art engagé*" or politically committed art. It is heteronomous since it is not specific to the art world.

Still heteronomous is the value of *morality*, pertaining to the "*ethical*" register. It is used when requiring either that art should be concerned with people's sufferings, or that it should respect the social conventions of decency, or that it should foster virtue and appropriate behavior.[15]

---

11. For a more philosophical approach to this issue, see Dewey, *Theory of Valuation*.

12. Heinich, "Is There a Scientific Beauty?"

13. Bourdieu, *Les Règles de l'art*.

14. Boltanski and Thévenot, *De la justification*.

15. Heinich, "Framing the Bullfight," "Aesthetics, Symbolics, Sensibility," and "From Rejection of Contemporary Art to Culture War."

In between heteronomy and autonomy is a third value: the one I call "*significativity*" or meaning. It pertains to the "*hermeneutic*" register, valorizing the capacity to sustain an interpretation, to be credited of a meaning. Such a requirement is particularly strong in contemporary art, where one can often hear judgments such as "it is interesting in that it is a symptom of our present society," "a symbol of modern condition," and "a questioning about our contemporary world."

A fourth and more autonomous value is the value of *authenticity*, which I define as the continuity and length of the bond between a present object and its origin—be it a wine with a quality label, an animal with a pedigree, or a painting. This requirement of authenticity has been present in art since antiquity, and has increased in importance down to modern times, when it is now a basic artistic value. It is partly challenged by contemporary artists when displaying a distance to seriousness, a kind of irony, but it is still very active when it comes to the evaluation of artworks.

We now come to the most autonomous value, the most akin to the art world: namely, *beauty*. It pertains to the "*aesthetic*" register, together with the artistic nature of an object, or else with the notion of "sublime." No doubt the criteria used to qualify beauty are highly relative to historical and spatial contexts, and thus often change; but beauty still remains a basic requirement in art, as least for the general public. It is strongly challenged in contemporary art, though, where it has lost importance to the profit of the value of meaning or significativity.[16]

The last value to be mentioned is *singularity*: a value that emerged in the second half of the nineteenth century as a major requirement in modern art, where it means originality, innovation, and uncommon practices. It may also be a negative value for the tenants of classical aesthetics, who valorize the capacity to implement standards, conventions, and widely accepted ways of making and conceiving art; and who, conversely, dismiss originality as an incapacity to master such "normal" practices, or as a means of being "bizarre." Of course, the avant-garde is strongly bound to singularity as a positive value. It is still the current way of judging art, be it modern or contemporary: phrases such as "not even original" and "it has already been done" are forms of criticism we know very well and easily practice; and the first task of an art critic is to be able to identify to what extent a work of art is original. Indeed, this value of singularity is so strong in modern and contemporary culture that it tends to surpass beauty as the major artistic value.

16. Heinich, "Is There a Scientific Beauty?"

Responsibility, morality, significativity, authenticity, beauty, and singularity: here are the major values in art, from the less to the more autonomous. Other values are also at stake in art, such as originality, spirituality, responsibility, durability, universality, rarity, autonomy, celebrity, pleasure, truth, expensiveness, work, virtuosity, and so on.[17] Let us now turn to the case of *Guernica* considered according to its place in this artistic axiology.

Guernica's Axiology

Which values have underpinned the evaluation of *Guernica*? I will list them now from the most autonomous to the most heteronomous pole.

What about the value of *singularity*? In the case of *Guernica*, it clearly implements an important cleavage line between "pro" and "con": those who valorize the "*régime de communauté*"—that is, obedience to traditional codes and conventions in line with classical art—are in no doubt that this painting *is* singular; but instead of using this property as a reason to valorize it, for them it is a major reason to dismiss it, as the work appears to them as "bizarre" and a reflection of the notion that "*n'importe quoi*" (anything goes). By contrast, those familiar with modern art, and for whom singularity is a positive value, celebrate the innovative character of the painting, its originality. Both camps admit the singularity of the work, but use this idea of singularity either to dismiss or to valorize it positively.

After singularity comes *beauty* as a major value in modern art. In the case of *Guernica*, its quality has been very much discussed and disputed according to this value, between the "pros," who praise the modern beauty of cubism, and the "cons," who dismiss its ugliness in regard to the classical standards of aesthetics, or even deny its very artistic nature. The result of such discussions depends on the kind of paradigm according to which people judge an artwork: here, the classical or the modern paradigm. In other words, the axiological fate of *Guernica*—its capacity to be valorized for its beauty, according to the aesthetical register—is strongly vulnerable to the cognitive context of valuation, that is, the actors' capacity to use the modern rather than the classical artistic paradigm.

The third value used about *Guernica*—a little less autonomous than singularity and beauty—is *authenticity*. Here, the authenticity is not that of the painting itself—it has never been suspected of being a fake—but the authenticity of its author, that is, Picasso him-

17. See Heinich, Schaeffer, and Talon-Hugon, *Par-delà le beau et le laid.*

self. His opponents might doubt Picasso's sincerity or inspiration, and suspect him of having made this painting only to "challenge" common taste, to provoke negative reactions. By contrast, his defenders would assume that he was deeply involved when painting it, and that he sincerely expressed his indignation, his solidarity with his people, transforming a commission from the French Communist Party into an authentically personal creation, by choosing the subject according to his own "interior necessity," as Kandinsky would have put it.

As for the value of *significativity* or *meaning*, it is of great use for those who want to justify their valorization of the work, since the latter offers a number of affordances for implementing what I call the *hermeneutic* register: for example, the work may be seen as a claim against war and for peace, a protest against suffering and chaos, a lamentation on the people's defeat. Just read this comment on Wikipedia: "Far from being a mere political painting, *Guernica* should be seen as Picasso's comment on what art can actually contribute towards the self-assertion that liberates every human being and protects the individual against overwhelming forces such as political crime, war, and death." No one could dream of a more symbolic way to comment on an art work. On the other side, those who want to dismiss the work may argue that it is "meaningless" in that it stands out of any reasonable standard of figuration.

Still lower on the scale between autonomy and heteronomy is the value of *morality*, which is also very present in the valuations of *Guernica*, especially when they come from non-specialized viewers, or lay people, whose culture of modern art is poor but who are willing to use this work to affirm their own progressive credentials, not so much on the aesthetic but rather on social grounds. It is particularly easy to read *Guernica* as an expression of art serving the oppressed, the poor people, the weakest of all. This *ethical* register is thus quite present in value judgments about the work.

The fifth value expected about *Guernica* is the value of *responsibility*, which is at stake every time some kind of political involvement is required of the artist, who is expected to demonstrate his/her concern with collective and public claims about common welfare. Then again, the heteronomous issue of politics is quite present in the work, since it can easily be read not so much as a work of art dealing with plastic issues but as a manifesto committed to combatting fascism, in favor of republican forces or even communism. This *civic* register is thus, together with its *ethical* counterpart, a major means of valorizing the work when singularity, aesthetics, authenticity, or meaning are not the actors' favorite issues.

Conclusion

The notion of the committed artist is invoked so much as a model of what any artist should be that it is rarely realized, at least with a work of high artistic value. Picasso's *Guernica* is one of the rare art works that cumulates the three axiological dimensions of the avant-garde: *aesthetic*, through the radicality of its plastic experiment; *political*, through the defense of a civic ideal supported by a political party; and *social*, through its denunciation of the sufferings inflicted on the people. Besides, it also satisfies more specialized requirements of authenticity, meaning, and singularity, which particularly concern art historians and art theorists.

Guernica is thus one of the very few art works that brings together the most autonomous and the most heteronomous poles in art, that is, as both avant-garde artistic achievement and sociopolitical involvement. It thus provides the actual implementation of what usually remains but an ideal: the alliance of art and politics in their most progressive state. This is why I believe *Guernica* is an icon of our modern Western culture.

Bibliography

Adorno, Theodor. *Aesthetic Theory*. Translated by C. Lendhardt. Edited by Gretel Adorno and Rolf Tiedemann. London and Boston: Routledge and K. Paul, 1984.

Boltanski, Luc, and Laurent Thévenot. *De la justification. Les économies de la grandeur*. Paris: Gallimard, 2011.

Bourdieu, Pierre, and Hans Haacke. *Libre échange*. Paris: Seuil-Les Presses du réel, 1994. English: *Free Exchange*. Translated by Randal Johnson and Hans Haacke. Stanford: Stanford University Press, 1995.

Bourdieu, Pierre. *Les Règles de l'art. Genèse et structure du champ littéraire*. Paris: Seuil, 1992. English: *The Rules of Art: Genesis and Structure of the Literary Field*. Translated by Susan Emanuel. Cambridge: Polity Press, 1996.

Dewey, John. *Theory of Valuation*. Chicago: Chicago University Press, 1939.

Elias, Norbert. *The Civilizing Process*. Translated by Edmund Jephcott. New York: Urizen Books, 1978.

Heinich, Nathalie. *The Glory of Van Gogh: An Essay on Admiration*. Translated by Paul Leduc Browne. 1991. Princeton: Princeton University Press, 1996.

———. "Framing the Bullfight: Aesthetics versus Ethics." *The Brit-*

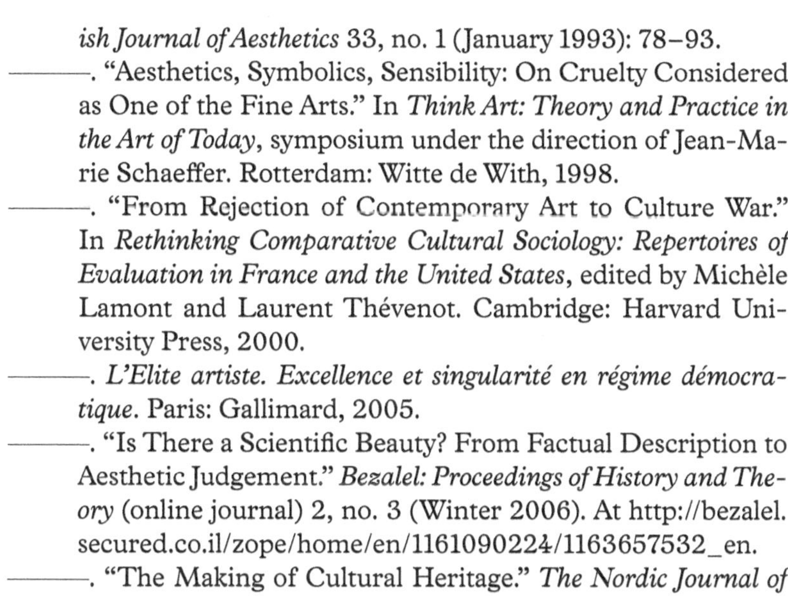

ish Journal of Aesthetics 33, no. 1 (January 1993): 78–93.

———. "Aesthetics, Symbolics, Sensibility: On Cruelty Considered as One of the Fine Arts." In *Think Art: Theory and Practice in the Art of Today*, symposium under the direction of Jean-Marie Schaeffer. Rotterdam: Witte de With, 1998.

———. "From Rejection of Contemporary Art to Culture War." In *Rethinking Comparative Cultural Sociology: Repertoires of Evaluation in France and the United States*, edited by Michèle Lamont and Laurent Thévenot. Cambridge: Harvard University Press, 2000.

———. *L'Elite artiste. Excellence et singularité en régime démocratique*. Paris: Gallimard, 2005.

———. "Is There a Scientific Beauty? From Factual Description to Aesthetic Judgement." *Bezalel: Proceedings of History and Theory* (online journal) 2, no. 3 (Winter 2006). At http://bezalel.secured.co.il/zope/home/en/1161090224/1163657532_en.

———. "The Making of Cultural Heritage." *The Nordic Journal of Aesthetics* 22, nos. 40–41 (2011): 12–25.

Heinich, Nathalie, Jean-Marie Schaeffer, and Carole Talon-Hugon, eds. *Par-delà le beau et le laid: les valeurs artistiques*. Forthcoming.

Poggioli, Renato. *The Theory of the Avant-Garde*. Translated from the Italian by Gerald Fitzgerald. 1962. Cambridge, MA: Harvard University Press, 1968.

Rancière, Jacques. *Le Partage du sensible: esthétique et politique*. Paris: La Fabrique, 2001. English: *The Politics of Aesthetics: The Distribution of the Sensible*. Translated with an introduction by Gabriel Rockhill. London and New York: Continuum, 2004.

2

"Worlds of Art" in the Basque Country: The Aranzazu Period

Jesus Arpal Poblador

By "worlds of art" in the title I mean those persons or groups that, in their actions and interrelations, produce recognition and evaluation of artists and their works. During the Aranzazu period (the 1950s and 1960s), a great artistic project of deep social and cultural significance became a point of reference. It was managed and received in certain "worlds of art" in which the aesthetic got involved with the political in terms of ideology, context (the Franco regime and the anti-Franco movements), and the political-cultural practices of local institutions.

Aranzazu is a sanctuary of the Virgin Mary in the mountains of the Basque province of Gipuzkoa, and has great religious significance for its widespread devotion throughout the Basque Country and Hispanic America. During the 1950s the Franciscan order, which had been governing the sanctuary for a long period of time, made plans to renovate and extend it through a wholesale reconstruction of the site including its architecture, sculpture, painting, and glasswork. The initiative and the twenty-year-long work took place during the Franco dictatorship (1939–1975), at a moment when the regime was trying to leave behind the autarky and isolation of the 1940s by seeking international recognition and by espousing a certain degree of modernization, both of which would perpetuate the dictatorship during the Cold War. The regime also set economic recovery as a main objective, which required the assistance of western democracies and most particularly that of the United States. President Eisenhower's visit and the Concordat with the Holy See were landmark events of the early 1950s.

The Catholic Church had been a bastion of social and cultural conservatism and had a Spanish hierarchy that legitimized Franco's political regime in return for important privileges in the control of education and social morality. Gradually, though, the Church started to show signs of change. On the one hand, this change was affected by the new positions taken by the Vatican, which were clearly visible in the 1960s through the figure of Cardinal Montini following Paul VI, who took a stance against the excesses of the Franco dictatorship. On the other hand, a certain "internationalism" emerged in some religious orders, and this influenced the architecture and art that they supported.

Moreover, a certain delegitimization of the Franco dictatorship took place on the part of various social and political movements, especially in the Basque Country, where they emerged as defendants of a Basque cultural identity and political emancipation. They aligned with the dynamics of violent action and reaction, spiraling back and forth between the measures taken by the state and the subversion initiated by the actions of ETA (from the late 1960s on). These movements encountered growing public support and in certain sectors of the Church, which had suffered the Spanish nationalist repressions of the regime. At the same time, workers rose up and challenged the official trade unionism of the state, and employers' organizations allied with an anti-democratic regime. The critiques and confrontations were particularly visible in the domains of culture, art, and academia. While these domains had been reluctant to open up to new cultural and artistic forms and leftist ideologies in the immediate post-Spanish Civil War years, they now efficiently devised and represented disagreement with a regime that persecuted the freedom of (ideological and linguistic) expression.

On the other hand, the necessity to modernize and improve the image of the regime, along with the inclusion of Christian Democrats and technocrats in the government, enabled an institutional change with a certain degree of tolerance toward cultural and artistic expressions. And these changes had the objective of improving the external image of the country. For example, the Donostia-San Sebastián Film Festival showed some tolerance to such expressions by featuring films from communist Eastern Europe. With regards to architecture, after 1952 state-approved architects began to move away from (neo-Escorial) historicist and fascist models and embrace more contemporary ideas. While the more official art maintained its traditional models, abstraction was not viewed as confronting Franco's ideology too explicitly. Artistic groups and critics who initiated aesthetic changes, as well as new publishing houses and showrooms, however, could well have been under suspicion. In 1957, the group *El Paso* emerged that, despite resistance and lack of understanding, managed to exhibit outside of Spain. The same year the *Equipo 57* group was formed that, from its base in Paris, opened the way for developing movements with a more explicit ideological content (for example, *Estampa Popular*). Several Basque artists had a significant role in these new directions. The Biennials and international contests and shows, which recognized the new Spanish and Basque art, had to be considered as successes in a Spain that finally knew how to be modern.

In August 1960, the Museum of Modern Art in New York featured the exhibition "New Spanish Painting and Sculpture," which then toured the United States and Canada. The exhibition included works by Pablo Serrano, Martin Chirino, Antoni Tàpies, Rafael Canogar, Antonio Saura, Joan Josep Tharrats, Manuel Viola, Luis Feito—and Jorge Oteiza and Eduardo Chillida, who presented informalisms, abstractions, and materialistic art that were not free of political significances, and which were opposed to and positioned themselves on the margins of the Franco regime. This did not change the fact that the major Spanish awards or certain official representations at international forums favored artists who were politically more congenial to the regime, and who represented a conservative or restorative modernity. Similar criteria were implemented in the San Fernando Academy, in the direction of the El Prado museum, and with official monuments. The 1960s were representative of these vacillations in conceptions of how art was perceived in Spain.

In the Basque Country (as in other parts of the state), a sense of cultural uniqueness affected the vindication of liberties and even political independence, based on the idea of a differentiated ethnic identity recreated through confrontation with the Francoist state. This lent special importance to the symbolic capacity of art to represent a people and a culture, to the point of revolutionizing traditional Basque nationalism.

Similar confrontations surfaced around the works of Aranzazu, an ambitious project open to artistic innovation that, besides those innovative aspects, became a site of artistic actions that had great institutional and popular impact: specifically, there emerged an avant-garde that understood art as rupture and that promoted a new aesthetic that expressed a desire for political and cultural change. This happened through the respective reactions of artists, critics, public opinion, and institutions—we must not forget that Aranzazu was a sanctuary of popular devotion, and an important center of the Franciscan order. It also became a site of confrontation with the Francoist ideology of National Catholicism that aimed to reduce culture to a role of legitimizing the dominant political order, and enforced strong political and religious censorship in all walks of life.[1]

The Aranzazu sanctuary also became a point of reference for the development of Basque culture for experts in local Romanesque art (the Andramaris, or icons of the Virgin Mother), such as Father Lizarralde in the 1930s; for experts in the Basque language and literature, such as Father Villasante; poets like Bitoriano Gandiaga (in the 1950s); and the group that formed around the journal *Jakin*, a progressive publication in the 1960s with political, historical, and linguistic essays. Together with other Aranzazu journals (*Goiz-Argo*, or the bulletin of the monastery), these publications were widely circulated not only in religious circles, but also in the cultural and political realm as well. Father Lete, who came from Cuba and had been the guardian of the monastery since 1949, clearly opted for a project of renovation, and even supported Oteiza's innovative propositions in a joint lecture on the new works in Aranzazu in 1952 in Donostia-San Sebastián. His death, together with that of Father Lizarralde in an airplane crash as they traveled to Cuba to raise funds for the work, negatively affected the support that, together with other friars (such as Anasagasti, as well as the painter Xabier Alvarez de Eulate) they had given to the groundbreaking, culturally Basque project personified by Oteiza. The cultural and innovative importance of the project was especially obvious in 1967, when it came to Aranzazu hosting the Basque language unification conference convoked by Euskaltzaindia (the Basque Language Academy), whose president at the time was the Franciscan Father Villasante.

The Aranzazu project (1950–52), presented by the architects Francisco Javier Sáenz de Oiza and Luis Laorga, together with the sculptor Jorge Oteiza and the painter Carlos Pascual de Lara, would grow from its original aim of a being a modernizing form of architecture, painting, and sculpture to become an iconographic and formal revolution (especially in sculpture and painting) due

1. For the construction of Aranzazu, see Gonzalez de Durana, *Arquitectura y Escultura en la Basilica de Aranzazu and Eraso, Oteiza y Vanguardia*. The archives of the Oteiza Museum-Foundation provide us with important direct and indirect documents.

to its unconventional figuration and abstraction. It is thus that the controversies surrounding it, as well as aesthetic and political censorship involved, became polarized along the lines of the sculpture, theories, and leadership of Oteiza, the murals of Nestor Basterretxea, and the political positions expressed by Agustín Ibarrola. Even Pascual de Lara would be included in these diatribes. In a 1954 letter published in an IVAM (Instituto Valenciano de Arte Moderno, the Valencian Institute of Modern Art) catalog on Pascual de Lara and his work, he himself defined the conflict as not only artistic, but also clearly political. Besides the impact of its artistic innovation, unconventional religiosity, and the affirmation of Basque culture, the popular, religious, and monumental dimensions of the sanctuary resulted in widespread public debate.

A scandal led to a decision by the Pontifical Commission for Art to interrupt the work of Oteiza, Pascual de Lara, and Basterretxea in 1955. However, a late rectification enabled the sculptural work to be finalized in 1964. This is what Father Goitia enthusiastically communicated to Jorge Oteiza, who was living in Madrid at the time, in a letter from the Aranzazu monastery urging him to forget about what happened, and only to think of the future. He asked him for a work plan, and that he return to Aranzazu. As the Franciscan put it, a worthy revenge and triumph had been achieved after a tough battle of more than one and a half years, finally overcoming those obscure, forgettable years. Otieza did not respond immediately, and made compensatory demands.

The paralysis of the Aranzazu project through the censoring intervention of the ecclesiastic authority (coming from the bishopric of Donostia-San Sebastián to the Vatican), which local artists of the more conservative kind supported, was symptomatic of the tensions at the time. It must be emphasized that the debates about the "decoration" of Aranzazu were partly encouraged by then art critic Carlos Ribera, an artist who had participated in Franco's rebellion by promoting an educational project for the new Francoist state. But opponents of the Aranzazu projects were equally supported, at least at the beginning, by other artists like Jose Sarriegi, who had been imprisoned for his Basque nationalist ideas, and who was denied the chance to participate in the Aranzazu project by his friend Oteiza; and Joaquín Irizar, a restorer-architect who had long belonged to the commission for the restoration of Aranzazu, and who wrote the bishopric's report that was sent to Rome. In the report, he viciously attacked the abstract character of the representations, accusing the art of being anti-religious.

Certainly, against the enemies of the project and the conspiracies that affected its delay, the personal support toward Oteiza confirmed who the "alma mater" was behind it and, especially, who the censor was. The writer José de Artetxe, in newspaper articles, and the mayor of Oñate, Reyes Corcostegui, in a 1957 letter to the sculptor, both expressed their personal support in this confrontation of artistic, political, and religious circles that aimed to reverse the work. Iñaki Zumalde, an entrepreneur and historian of Oñate who participated in the Errante Academy, discreetly but firmly described in a simple chronicle in *El Bidasoa* (1959) how admirable the project was in every respect for a visitor who came to see the sanctuary, and expressed his hope that the misunderstanding that halted the work would be resolved. In 1963 the unfinished Aranzazu basilica won the José Manuel de Aizpurua Award of the *Colegio Vasconavarro* for its achievements.

The elaboration of the sculpture collection on the façade of the sanctuary that Oteiza completed, together with the innovative interpretation of canonical themes in the murals of the crypt realized by Basterretxea, and even the replacing of the deceased Pascual de Lara with Lucio Muñoz (who was more involved in the avant-garde) for the great central arch, represented the experimental transformations that took place in art and culture from the 1950s to the 1960s especially in the Basque Country, which witnessed the birth of progressive political movements against the Franco regime and its state. The Virgin of Aranzazu that Oteiza seemed to take on in the 1950s for the façade of the temple was still within the iconographic tradition, completed with the hagiographic narratives of the sanctuary—it was going to be placed above the frieze of the apostolate. Instead, the Virgin was finally elevated and transfigured in "Pietà" at the high end of the empty wall, which the sculptor himself would consider as a symbol of pain at the death of the son in the new Basque political culture: the death of Txabi Etxebarrieta, the first "fallen" ETA activist in 1967. This decision about the Virgin was a move that synthetized the political implication of artistic movements of the decade.

The confrontations in the world of art, as well as the anti-innovation reactions in the media and other sectors "of order" intensified against the development of abstraction and the revolutionary proposals spearheaded by Oteiza. They provoked debates, exhibitions, and groups that moved a great many of the artists that formed the so-called "Basque School." During the 1950s and with the active participation of Oteiza, the Stvdio gallery in Bilbao (1948–1952) gave room for works and artists that clearly represented innovation. The "Exhibition of the 10" in Donostia-San Sebastián (1958) positioned itself against the official awards of the city: initiated by the radical anti-Francoist artist Amable Arias in a basement in which he had his workshop, a group of artists presented themselves in front of a (scarce) audience and the (generally unsympathetic) media with the desire to affect a turn in the artistic life of the city. In the 1960s the presence of the new art intensified through the exhibitions of emblematic Spanish groups such as the *El Paso*, groups with a significant Basque presence (*Equipo 57*), the exhibition in the Bilbao Fine Arts Museum of the works of Canogar, Manolo Millares, Francisco Farreras, Antonio Suarez, and Chillida, as well as the exhibitions of *Arte Actual* in the City Hall of Donostia-San Sebastián with shows by local artists. In Vitoria-Gasteiz, the informalism of Joaquín Frailes was exhibited in the Salon of Art in 1963. All these events provoked controversies and movements that, at the same time, prompted new galleries and inspired new art critics. In Vitoria-Gasteiz, Javier Serrano supported innovative art in his writings and through his temporary direction of an exhibition hall (of the industrial company IMOSA). In Bilbao in 1964, the opening of the Grises Hall with the work of Millares meant the incorporation of an important cultural promoter and art critic of the city, José Luis Merino, and the presence of expert critics of the Spanish art of rupture, like José Moreno Galván in this hall, or Carlos Arena in Donostia-San Sebastián. By the end of the decade the critic Santiago Amón was one of the main defenders of Basque art.

This is not to say that the public institutions did not announce their contests and scholarships with very conservative proposals: the *Gran Premio de Pintura Vasca* ("Grand Prize for Basque Painting") of Donostia-San Sebastián, convoked by the Tourism Center (a typical agency of this city and this era) for artists born in the "Basque-Navarrese and French Basque Country" had this as the theme of its first call (1965): "the Basque landscape." There was an eclectic presence of artists and critics on the jury, and in the secondary awards and mentions they did recognize artists of the new generation that introduced the innovative art of those years: figures like Vicente Ameztoy or José Luis Zumeta in Gipuzkoa. At the same time, the politics of scholarships or grants awarded by the administrative bodies of the Basque Country continued to be tied to a very conventional vision of the training of artists.

In any case, and as proof of the difficult acceptance of works with political or religious implications, the 1965 exhibition by Lucio Muñoz (creator of the great central arch of Aranzazu, who enjoyed Oteiza's passionate support) in the Bilbao Fine Arts Museum was condemned by the critic Pedro Javaloyes, one of the detractors of the new art: *religious art is invaded by decorators*.

In another sense, the work and political left-wing militancy of the painter Ibarrola, who had been backed by Oteiza since the times of the Stvdio gallery in Bilbao, and who had trained with Daniel Vázquez Díaz in Madrid until his inclusion in the Aranzazu project, was moving toward a figuration of geometrical synthesis and political content, which would reach its height in the years of the *Estampa Popular* and Basque School. Ibarrola's work was marked by the struggles of the Basque proletariat.

In 1966, the markedly innovative movement presented as the Basque School of Contemporary Art featured as one of its milestone achievements the opening of the Barandiarán Gallery in Donostia-San Sebastián. The painter Amable Arias, promoter of abstraction in Donostia-San Sebastián (along with Mª Paz Jiménez and José Antonio Sistiaga), and Oteiza himself had an important role in the opening of this exhibition hall. This was a place where, besides exhibitions, innovative pedagogical experiments like independent art workshops found a base under the leadership of Sistiaga and Esther Ferrer. It was a place for the creation and the diffusion of culture and art, had an elaborate project in terms of its cultural and political objectives, and clearly espoused the role of promoting new art.

The Basque School is an Oteizian project inspired by his Latin American experience (1935–48), although the idea was conceived even earlier through his previous research for the 1934 exhibition with Nicolás de Lekuona and Narkis Balenciaga. As an avant-garde group, they were seeking an alternative to the ways the culturally tardy Basque Renaissance was politically implanted. Through his research in the village of San Agustín in Colombia, Oteiza developed his project of a (secular-religious) art that forms a people. Upon his return in 1948, he participated in the ethic and aesthetic leadership of young artists in the Stvdio gallery of Bilbao, contributed with his theoretical and artistic work to the innovating worlds of Spanish art, and provided his intense and conflicting contribution to the development of the Aranzazu project as a center of avant-garde art at a time of political and cultural subordination. Thus his decisive interventions led to the selection of artists like Basterretxea and Ibarrola, without a doubt the most qualified young painters in the Basque Country at that time. (Basterretxea was from a family that had been exiled in the civil war, and came from Buenos Aires, where he met Oteiza).

Oteiza's sculpture, which he called statue, had taken a turn toward abstraction from the 1950s on, experimenting with the hyperboloid and the empty space of the cromlech. In 1951 he participated in the innovative exhibition "Four Abstract Sculptures" (with Ángel Ferrant, Carlos Ferreira, and Eudaldo Serra), which moved from Barcelona (Layctanas Galleries) to the Stvdio gallery in Bilbao and to Madrid (Buchholz) despite the minimal attention given to these advanced proposals by institutions and gallery owners. These were the years when the innovating currents of the young avant-garde could find some kind of representation, even if thwarted with frequent paradoxes and lack of understanding, in certain "official" exhibitions like the *Salón de los 11* ("Salon of the 11") in Madrid.

Oteiza's proposal of salvation through art, characteristic of the messianic impulses of historical avant-garde movements, outlined a route or an aesthetic process with a certain mythical-religious meaning. It purported to "recover" a Basque culture and aesthetics, "the soul" of a people, as he proposed in the monument to Father Donostia (1957). This work represented a crossroads of aesthetic and political dimensions, of his research into the origins of the Basque culture and soul, and of the religious feelings of the artist. It is a ritual, a commemorative work that has multiple meanings. It resonates with the impact of Father Donostia on Basque culture. (Donostia was a musicologist, folklorist, and a friar in the Capuchin order of Lekaroz, another central point of Basque culture among the country's religious orders. This is where Oteiza was trained, a place with which he identified (in the 1950s), and where he even made a temporary retreat when he was older. The work reflects his summons to a mountain peak (in Agina), marking out sacred places (especially the empty space, charged with the spirituality of the cromlech), and even the incident of an attempted act of destruction in an obscure attack in which the artistic and the political seemed to get mixed up.

In 1959 Oteiza deemed that his "Experimental Proposal" with sculpture was concluded, shortly after receiving the Sao Paolo Award. The project was enabled by the patronage of Juan Huarte in Madrid after the frustration with Aranzazu. Oteiza settled in Irun close to Basterretxea in 1958. It is there that intense activity started for his aesthetic and cultural leadership, featured in the local magazine *El Bidasoa* under the direction of artist and editor Antonio Valverde. *El Bidasoa* reflected the vitality of the incipient group, with reference to a Basque Renaissance. It is where Oteiza's key text was published in June 1959, titled "The Basque Cromlech as Empty

Statue."[2] His presence in the Errante Academy, which operated in the second half of the 1950s and attracted writers, scientists, and artists with an open approach, placed him among the protagonists of a culture that offered an alternative to the context inherited from the Spanish Civil War (that is, local supporters as well as invited guests such as Julio Caro Baroja, José Miguel Barandiarán, Gregorio Marañón, and Luis Martín Santos).

Meanwhile, Oteiza continued with his trajectory of poetic and formal investigation as a means of knowledge to bring about a new Basque art. This entailed an exploration into origins (of the Basque language and megalithic constructions), and a cultural practice and politics that could render those origins visible in a people. The 1963 publication of *Quousque Tandem: An Essay on the Interpretation of the Basque Soul* summarizes this trajectory.[3]

Oteiza was dedicated to projects that integrated art, culture, and politics with a dimension of education that focused on new generations, who he believed should be the purveyors of a new society. In this regard, his writings and activities were incessant, and his leadership often controversial: through his many publications and public interventions of cultural agitation in international forums of art, through the planning of centers for the training of artists, and through his interference with the construction of cities as cultural spaces.

In the second half of the 1960s western cultural and political confrontation emerged as a generational issue indicating new forms of social reproduction that wanted to break with the previous generations. This was manifest in various forms of youth movements and sexual responses that also reached Spain by the end of that decade. Here they were further fueled by the opposition to Francoist totalitarianism in workers' and nationalist movements, and in the new understanding of art and its social function: from Abstraction, "Socialist Realism" or Pop to "subversive" artistic manifestations expressed by committed anti-Francoist artists.

The role of the artist changed with their presence as subjects and corporeal actors of art, with the new creative centers, new criticism, and new relationships with the public. This took place in tandem with the acceleration and spatial-temporal mobility that characterize movements in progressive modernity. Esther Ferrer, who initiated the experiments of the Free Workshops (*Talleres Libres*)

2. See Oteiza, "The Basque Cromlech as Empty Statue," in *Oteiza's Selected Writings*.

3. Extracts from which can be found in Oteiza, *Oteiza's Selected Writings*.

with Sistiaga in Donostia-San Sebastián, merged with the group ZAJ in 1967, which gained international importance with an artistic work that closely followed John Cage's proposals. No woman participated in the main group of the Basque School (Gaur), although Mª Paz Jiménez, who completely dedicated herself to art by taking on distinctive trends of abstraction, was invited by Oteiza to join them. In Emen (in the province of Bizkaia) Maria Francesca Dapena was the only female artist. Women, although excellent artists, had "no place" in these groups. The widely acknowledged Menchu Gal, who was originally from Irun, worked outside of the Basque Country. In the 1950s, Flores Kaperotxipi merely named female artists in his history of Basque art; the cultural and political ruptures of the 1960s were necessary for the emergence of key female personalities in the art movements.

From Aranzazu to the Basque School, the series of initiatives and activities that took place did not constitute a formalized movement or a "school" in the proper sense of the word—this would be antithetical to the character of the avant-garde. In this case, however, the designation was used in a tactical way to identify a group of territorial dimensions (like other cases of the same epoch from the School of Vallecas to the School of Altamira), and due to its pedagogical aspirations. With the leadership of Oteiza, whose impact affected an entire generation, its activities represented a time and place for art and, subsequently, had long-term effects.

This artistic sequence stretched from the order that aimed to reproduce itself through "modernization" (in art, in society and, with greater difficulty, in the politics of the Francoist regime), to the avant-garde movements that emerged in the Basque Country as a continuation of the work and the group of artists who gathered around the Aranzazu project. The activities and projects of the Basque School ambitiously planned the creation of an art that broke with the past, which was representative of all the territories of the Basque Country, and which integrated artistic and cultural groups with a vision of affirming Basque identity, while it promoted modern art in all its diversity (Gaur in Gipuzkoa, Emen in Bizkaia, and Orain in Araba were the most active of these. Danok in Navarre was less important and there was just a plan that never came to fruition for such a group in the French Basque Country).

These processes invigorated the art world in the Basque Country in the second half of the 1960s and the early 1970s. They had important repercussions abroad not only because of international recognition of the major Basque figures, but also because of the emergence of an increasingly delineable Basque experimental project. This new

Basque art focused on novel forms and contents, and expressed a renewed cultural identity with strong political connotations especially at the end of the Franco dictatorship. In literature, theater, and music, the recuperation of the Basque language went along with the reception of critical debates over political and popular issues (from the poetry of Gabriel Aresti to the multiple musical and theatrical performances of the cultural collective *Ez Dok Amairu*).

Just like Oteiza's sculpture award of the Biennial of Sao Paolo in 1957, the 1965 exhibition by Eduardo Chillida in London was another important recognition of "the artists of Aranzazu."

In the tribute that was paid to Chillida for his success in London and for the reception that same year of an international sculpture award (the Wilhelm Lehmbruck Award), Oteiza gave a talk in which he stressed that this was an art of collective affirmation, a Basque aesthetic and cultural identity that was able to gain artistic and social recognition. Trained in Paris from the 1940s on, Chillida returned to the Basque Country in late 1951, when work on Aranzazu was just starting. Back then he was working on stone sculptures that represented torsos in the style of the classical world. But on his return, he set out to recuperate sensations, sounds, and murmurs, and the iron processed by the old ironmongers in pieces of piercing and pointed shapes. Very soon his work, which he carried out with the collaboration of industries specialized in iron production, emulated nature in its processes of organic development, creating forms like tree trunks that open their arms to space, only to twist by turning around an interior space. The same way as Oteiza placed Basque art in the empty space of the prehistoric cromlech, Chillida's voice was featured in the film *Ama Lur* (Mother Earth) by Nestor Basterretxea, as he gave Basque names to his iron sculptures and declared that his work belonged to Euskara, the Basque language. Later, his monumental work titled "Comb of the Winds" would be presented as a vindication of liberty for the Basque people.

The work of Chillida as sculptor (and later engraver) initiated a course of international success in institutions, galleries, and among art theorists. So much so that, while it maintained a link with Europe, the recognition of its trajectory, the materiality and spirit of the work was identified as part of a "Basque School" that was prototypically sculptural. But going beyond the mere representation of a school, Chillida's work became a point of reference for identity. What definitely established his work as avant-garde was the western recognition of its singularity due to its anti-Francoist positions, its mythical molding in the materiality of iron, wood, and stone, and its spirit of abstraction that more or less explicitly expressed a Basque culture.

Besides emerging in radical ways in the writings of Oteiza, the frequent affirmations of artists also exuded ideologies of identity. They were much evident in the work of the artist Basterretxea. His paintings of the Aranzazu crypt, the eleven murals that had required "a conscientious study of the dismemberment and the process that leads from the figurative to the abstract" had been destroyed one night. In 1966, Basterretxea produced the film *Ama Lur* with José Maria Larruquert, which achieved widespread popular acclaim. Getting around the problem of censorship, it was featured and even recognized at the Donostia-San Sebastián film festival in 1968. Years later, he produced the series *Basque Cosmogony*, which featured sculptural totems, and was inspired by Basque mythology as collected by the ethnographer José Miguel Barandiarán. Its objective was to provide images for collective memory.

In Gipuzkoa, the woodwork of Remigio Mendiburu was a vindication of traditional Basque rural culture, which revolved around the mountains and the farmstead. Instead of nostalgic representations, however, his work was existential. His sculptures, which were produced by collecting and putting together parts of trees, reclaim free spaces, or evoke mythical places such as the cave.

On the other hand, Rafael Ruiz Balerdi, Jose Antonio Sistiaga, Amable Arias, and Jose Luis Zumeta maintained the informalist approach, although each one of them developed their own solutions. They too were involved in various cultural activities and political-didactic intentions.

The other two groups of the Basque School, Emen (Here) and Orain (Now) had a relatively short lifespan, and responded to opposing aspirations. In Bizkaia, Emen significantly dominated by the communist militant Ibarrola, aimed to unite all kinds of participants. In Araba, Orain established a rigorous selection: Carmelo Ortiz de Elguea, Joaquín Fraile, Juan Mieg, and the photographer Alberto Schommer. The sculptor and resident of Kanbo (Cambo-les-Bains) in Iparralde, Jesús Echevarría, periodically joined them. The creation of a non-discriminating collective of Compound Art was not an easy task in spite—and partly because—of the totalizing and paradoxical aspirations of a Basque culture essentialized by Oteiza.

For the sake of a complete analysis of the worlds of art, we have to note the sponsor and entrepreneur Juan Huarte from Navarre. He was an early supporter of Oteiza who, with a well-formed interest in the new art, financed and encouraged many projects of

Basque artists. The Huartes (Juan, Jesús, and Mª Josefa) developed an enterprise on the basis of construction companies and businesses that supported public works in the state. This enabled many institutional relationships, a significant financial capacity, and a relevant intervention in the world of construction and architecture, which was a very significant social and cultural space for the development of art. Their homes and offices became a meeting place for artists, writers, and critics. The family paid special attention to the world of culture, and especially art collections. Juan Huarte founded *X films* productions for the projects of Oteiza and Basterretxea, and promoted the music of the avant-garde, which was led by Luis de Pablo and the *Alea* group. It was an innovative movement that followed the new trends of European music, and which had a special trajectory of development in the Basque Country (Carmelo Bernaola was one of the most multi-faceted personalities). Above all, Juan Harte supported artists and projects (Ruiz Balerdi and other artists of this generation), and would become the promoter of singular works with the participation of Sáenz de Oiza, Rafael Moneo, and Juan Daniel Fullaondo.

Someone so linked to Oteiza as the architect Fullaondo from Bilbao could count on his support to launch the magazine *Nueva Forma* ("New Form," as well as the publishing house Kain), a key publication of Basque architecture and culture in these years. Fullaondo, this great admirer of Chillida and enthusiastic collaborator of Oteiza, participated in architectonic projects with an overall development of arts. Through the magazine *Nueva Forma* he facilitated the work of many Basque and Spanish artists and critics, and fomented the study of architecture. In 1967, together with the critic Santiago Amón—another proponent of new art—he organized in Madrid an exhibition that later traveled to the Jenssen Museum in Denmark, with the participation of Oteiza, Chillida, Ruiz Balerdi, and the architects Saenz de Oiza and Fullaondo, among others. The role of the Huarte family in the development and evaluation of the work of Oteiza would lead to the establishment of the Jorge Oteiza Museum Foundation in the 1990s.

Aranzazu was a key work for Oteiza and a group of Basque artists. It was a meeting place for people, works, and expressions that revolved around the meaning of its art due to the controversies that it created. But beyond these functions, Aranzazu also became the very realization of a wholesale and monumental project, a foundational point of reference for a new Basque art. For the public, it was a monument, a center of popular devotion, and a tourist attraction, which provoked a reaction of having to face up to and process an unusual artistic project. Without a doubt, the defense of "our own" (one local community, one ethnos, one culture) against a "foreign" political regime (imposed, and denying an ideological and cultural identity); the new cultural and political propositions of the 1960s and 1970s in a "revolutionized" Basque Country; the growing artistic personality of Aranzazu's actors; and the very magnificence of the basilica facilitated the reception of an art of rupture. This art would identify itself as emblematically Basque.

Bibliography

Alvarez, Soledad. *Oteiza: Pasión y Razón*. Iruñea-Pamplona: Fundación Museo Jorge Oteiza, 2003.

Arribas, Mª José (1979). Cuarenta años de Arte Vasco 1937-1997. Historia y Documentos. San Sebastián (Erein).

Badiola, Txomin. *Oteiza: Mito y Modernidad*. Bilbao: Museo Guggenheim, 2004.

Barañano, Kosme, dir. *Chillida: Escala Humana*. Gijón: C.A. De Asturias, 1991.

Carandente, G. *Eduardo Chillida*. Venice: XLIV Biennale, 1991.

Eraso, Miren. *Oteiza y Vanguardia*. Cuadernos Sección Arte No. 6. Donostia-San Sebastián: Eusko Ikaskuntza, 1989.

Flores Kaperotxipi, M. *Arte Vasco: Pintura. Escultura. Dibujo*. Buenos Aires: Ekin, 1956.

Fullaondo, J. D. *Doble Retrato: Conversaciones en torno a Jorge Oteiza*. Madrid: Kain, 1993.

———. *Oteiza y Chillida en la Moderna Historiografía del Arte*. Bilbao: La Gran Enciclopedia Vasca, 1976.

Guasch, Ana María. *Arte e Ideología en el País Vasco 1949-1980*. Madrid: Akal, 1985.

Golvano, Fernando, ed. *Poéticas: Políticas y Crisis de la Modernidad en el contexto vasco*. Bilbao: Rekalde, 2009.

González de Durana, J. *Arquitectura y escultura en la Basílica de Aranzazu*. Vitoria-Gasteiz: Artium, 2006.

———. "Revisión del Arte Vasco entre 1939 y 1975." *Ondare: Cuaderno de Artes Plásticas y Monumentales* 25 (2006).

Manterola, Pedro. *El Jardín de un caballero: La escultura Vasca de la Posguerra en la obra y el pensamiento de Mendiburu, Oteiza y Chillida*. Donostia-San Sebastián: Arteleku, 1993.

Manterola, Pedro et al. *Escultores Vascos: Oteiza, Basterretxea, Ugarte*. Oviedo/Gijón: C. A. de Asturias, 1991.

Mas, Elías. *Cincuenta años de arquitectura en Euskadi*. Bilbao:

CAVN, 1990.

Moya, Adelina. "Rupturas y Restauraciones: Jorge Oteiza en la Tradición Moderna." In *Oteiza y la Crisis de la Modernidad/ Oteiza eta Modernitatearen Krisia*. Iruñea-Pamplona: Fundación Museo J. Oteiza, 2010.

Oteiza, Jorge. *Oteiza's Selected Writings*. Edited by Joseba Zulaika, translated by Frederick Fornoff. Reno: Center for Basque Studies, 2003.

Paz, Octavio. *Chillida entre el Hierro y la Luz*. New York: Guggenheim Museum, 1974.

Rosales, A., ed. *Jorge Oteiza. Creador Integral*. Iruñea-Pamplona: Universidad Pública de Navarra/Fundación Museo Jorge Oteiza, 1999.

San Martín, Javier, ed. *Euskal Artea eta Artistak 60 K /Arte y Artistas Vascos en los años 60*. Donostia-San Sebastián: KM Kulturenea, 1995.

Unsain, José María, ed. *Haritzaren Negua: Ama Lur y el País Vasco en los años 60*. Donostia-San Sebastián: Filmoteca Vasca/Euskadiko Filmotegia, 1993.

Zulaika, Joseba. "Oteiza y el Espacio Estético Vasco." In *Oteiza, Esteta y Mitologizador/Oteiza, Euskal Esteta eta Mitologitzaille*. Donostia-San Sebastián: CAM, 1986.

3

Revolutionary Artistic Sacrifice versus Totalitarian Artistic Entertainment

Juan Arana

There is a well-known fallacy ironically called *reductio ad Hitlerum.* Its proponent was philosopher Leo Smith, and it is basically a variant of the fallacy of association and the fallacy ad nauseam. It is customarily applied as follows: X situation resembles what the Nazis did, thus X is part of a Nazi-like program. The user of this pseudo-argument is normally aware of its lack of rigor, and at the same time implements it as if Schopenhauer's compendium of misleading rhetorical weapons, *Thirty Eight Ways to Win an Argument*, was missing a contemporary appendix; the goal of the fallacy would be to win the discussion at all costs. By using the r*eduction ad Hitlerum* the debater tries to detach the conversation from its main point.

Most Basques and anybody with an interest in the politics of the Basque Country understand that although prolific, the reduction *ad Hitlerum* is not so generously applied in their political context as its Iberian counterpart, which I would call the *reductio ad ETArum.* As I write this, in recent weeks defenders of the Spanish *status quo* have made frequent use of the fallacy: these include Dolores de Cospedal, secretary general of the governing PP (Partido Popular, People's Party) and president of the Autonomous Community of Castile La Mancha; Antonio Basagoiti, leader of the same party in the Basque Country; renowned Basque politician and Secretary General of UPyD (Unión Progreso y Democracia, Union, Progress and Democracy) Rosa Díez, and Cristina Cifuentes, delegate of the Spanish government in Madrid (among others). They have all resorted to equating mainly peaceful protests with the Nazis, ETA, or similar violent political expressions.[1]

This widely accepted assimilation of protests with historical violence has to do with a shared vision on the structure and limits of the Spanish political system. The *reduction ad ETArum* provides the dialectic borders of what counts as ethical for what has already been called the Culture of Transition or CT by some critics.[2]

In the 1970s, ETA was arguably the most relevant political player to be absent from the historical reconciliation that supposedly took place during the Spanish Transition to democracy. ETA is thus the mark of what goes beyond the so-called consensus politics that have dominated Spanish institutional culture since the mid-1970s. Among the most important intellectual contributions that shaped the worldview of the majority of today's Spanish citizens, the Culture of Transition interpreted the Spanish Civil War and the criminal dictatorship that followed it as the evolution of a natural dialectical process. Following that narrative, the two sides of the war would be linked by their shared *intrahistoria*[3] of Spain and their fratricidal clash would have been the main driving force of Spanish history. Two *Spains* would thus fight for life or death in a Hegelian dialectic process until the reconciliation of the transition made Spain a paradigmatic country in which the end of history as proclaimed by Fukuyama was reached in the 1970s.

Goya's painting *Fight With Cudgels,* later reproduced for museum exhibition, dramatically portrays this everlasting struggle. In the work, two Spaniards buried up to their knees in their arid land

---

1. Manetto, "Cospedal tilda los escraches de 'nazismo puro' propio de antes de la guerra civil," *El País*, April 13, 2013; Basagoiti affirmed that the grassroots movement Stop Desahucios (Stop Evictions) was "contaminated by Batasuna [the radical Basque nationalist party]" on Eitb.com: "Entrevista: Antonio Basagoiti, sobre deshaucios y escraches." For anthropologists, being labelled as contaminated is, on occasion, tantamount to becoming taboo. For a study on political violence as a taboo subject, see Douglass and Zulaika, *Terror and Taboo*; "Rosa Díez ve 'vil y cobarde' protestar ante la vivienda de los diputados," *Público*, March 23, 2013; Pérez-Lanzac, "Cifuentes afirma que la PAH ha mostrado su apoyo al entorno de ETA," *El País*, March 26, 2003.

2. See Acebedo et al., *CT o la Cultura de la Transición* and Vilarós, *El mono del desencanto*.

3. *Intrahistoria* is a concept created by Spanish-Basque philosopher Miguel de Unamuno, and it refers to a supposed shared historical subconscious that configures the national character. It could be equated to what popular culture refers to today as a country's DNA. Unamuno introduces the term in his book *En torno al casticismo*.

cannot avoid war against their mirror image. And, according to the popular narrative, so it went until they reached the transitional agreement that has in the Spanish Constitution its most symbolic document.

The culture created by this end-of-history Spain draws some clear lines beyond which ETA stands as the combination of a real terrorist group with the fantasy that its image projects. In other words, ETA not only commits horrible crimes, but its actions are also widely publicized. As a consequence, the mainstream media create a demonic aura around its cause, actors, ideology, and methods without distinction, and render any rational approach to the problems ETA pose as morally unacceptable. ETA is thus not only a terrorist group, but also the boogieman that awaits anybody who dares to criticize the Culture of the Spanish Transition and the current sociopolitical establishment.

Those who try to shed light upon the recent history of Spain, anybody interested in the memory of the victims of Francoism or in the concessions that today's institutional Left made during the transitional period could refer to the single most meaningful event of the twentieth century, that is, the Spanish Civil War, and is advised not to *reopen old wounds*. Along the same lines, those who question or peacefully contest hegemonic symbols such as the Monarchy, the actual party system, the financial oligarchic powers, the inviolability of the unity of the nation,[4] or the Constitution as a whole are regularly disregarded by their opponents, who claim that such questions will only encourage those same historical fratricidal differences and lead to destabilizing the current political system.

It has been seventy-five years since the end of the *Spanish Holocaust*, as Paul Preston refers to the Spanish Civil War, and the memory of the disaster and its perpetrators is already dying out along with its remaining survivors. Nowadays, the political subject that remembers the tragic consequences of radical politics is epitomized by the real and imaginary ETA. Thus, ETA has not only created the perfect alibi used by the hegemonic powers to avoid addressing specific issues in the Basque Country; it has also made it extremely unpopular to defend radical politics in Spain. ETA functioned as a means of recalling the culture of fratricidal killing characteristic

4. Section 2 of the Spanish Constitution of 1978 states the following: The Constitution is based on the indissoluble unity of the Spanish Nation, the common and indivisible homeland of all Spaniards; it recognizes and guarantees the right to self-government of the nationalities and regions of which it is composed and the solidarity among them all.

of the Spanish Civil War. The irrational, fantastic, or real Iberian innate urge to slaughter the political opponent was still alive in ETA.

Until now, and by equating the cultures of ETA and the Spanish Civil War, the mere mention of the *reductio ad ETArum* sufficed as a valid argument to end all discussion. The international discourse on terrorism has also, especially since 9/11, helped to establish the *reductio ad ETArum* as a valid argument. Indeed, the fallacy is used with such propensity that its sophistry is being unveiled little by little. Nevertheless, its use is still so common—and grotesque—that we could apply Godwin's Law[5] to the Spanish political arena: *as a discussion about Spanish politics grows longer, the probability of a comparison involving ETA and/or the Spanish Civil War increases.* Of course, the problems that Spain is facing at the moment require long discussions and alternative readings to the transition's *pacto de silencio*[6] that blocks any access to knowledge about the fundamental issues of recent Spanish history. And what do ETA and the Spanish Civil War have in common? Undoubtedly, the culture of sacrifice that was put to an end with the transitional reconciliation. By the term "culture of sacrifice" I mean a culture that advocates killing and dying for a cause. Of course, that culture recalls the supposed millenarian Spanish *guerracivilismo* or propensity to fratricidal confrontation so well represented by Goya's painting *Fight with Cudgels.*

In the Spanish context, after the death of Francisco Franco in 1975 and the later implementation of a parliamentary democracy, ETA was the only influential surviving organization that professed a culture of sacrifice. Since its origins, ETA made much use of Picasso's *Guernica* for its propaganda, as well as other artistic expressions of the civil war such as the song *Eusko gudari* (Basque soldier), thereby symbolically linking its struggle with that of the Spanish Civil War. One of ETA's founders, Julen Madariaga, was also one of those child refugees condemned to exile after the bombing of Guernica. The connection was not only symbolic, but also intergenerational. The first incarnation of ETA emerged as a result of a split in the youth wing of the traditional EAJ-PNV (Eusko Alderdi Jelt-

5. Godwin's Law: "A facetious aphorism maintaining that as an online debate increases in length, it becomes inevitable that someone will eventually compare someone or something to Adolf Hitler or the Nazis." *Oxford English Dictionary.*

6. Also known as *pacto del olvido* (Pact of Forgetting) assumed by political participants in the transition to forget the legacy of Franco's regime. This pact made possible the *Amnesty Law* of 1977 whereby ETA members were released from prison, but, by the same token, any investigation into crimes committed by the Franco regime was considered unacceptable.

zalea-Partido Nacionalista Vasco, Basque Nationalist Party), whose experience in the war had prevented it from using political violence during its exile. These younger nationalists, however, thought they needed to go a step further in their political implication and founded ETA in 1959.

Besides, most Basque nationalists have always envisioned ETA's actions as the outcome of two centuries of conflict against Spain. Those struggles they refer to are the three Carlist Wars, the first of which broke out in 1833. The truth is that, because the Carlist Wars represented struggles between ideologies and not countries—that is, they were civil wars—they do serve as an argument for the alleged innate tendency to fratricidal killing. In all, the Culture of Transition contended that ETA recalled the dangers of radical politics, which in response needed to be avoided for the sake of civilization in the form of a liberal-parliamentary democracy against barbarism.

After the war and the dictatorship, the Spanish Transition equated its democracy to any other. From within Franco's regime, since the 1950s reformists and technocrats had understood that isolation would undermine their wealth and power. Recently, leaked cables from the American Embassy in Madrid show the shared interest of both countries in making Spain an ally within NATO and the former European Economic Community.[7] Interestingly, the transition has been especially celebrated and very seldom—if ever—criticized by English-speaking Hispanists and political scientists who, paradoxically, have been much more accurate in their analysis of the Spanish Civil War and the dictatorship.[8] Those interpreters fail to admit the terrible consequences resulting from the fact that those people who were involved in or have links to the winning side in the Spanish Civil War had a privileged position when it came to negotiating the transition. Consequently, with their interpretations of the transition and Spanish Civil War they added intellectual support to the popular tale of constant domestic struggle, which ended with peace and reconciliation and the "end" of Spanish history.

In truth, fuelled by the *pacto de silencio,* the transition marked the beginning of an era devoid of its historical past. Future genera-

---

7. See www.wikileaks.org/plus/cables 1973NATO06185_b.html *Dec 19 NAC: FRG Statement on Spain and Atlantic Declaration.*

8. Along these lines, Paul Preston's panegyric account of King Juan Carlos (*Juan Carlos: Steering Spain from Dictatorship to Democracy*) can be contrasted with his work on the civil war, *The Spanish Holocaust.* For an Anglo-American and almost official account of the Spanish transition see Maxwell, *The New Spain.*

tions would be defined—as they would be, too, in other parts of the world—with mathematical variables that lack any meaning and that suggest an absence of identity. The most popular of these is *Generation X*, following Douglas Coupland's book of the same title,[9] but this has also been extended to embrace the terms generation Y or Z in order to define younger people. More recently, and in an added cruel fashion, the Spanish press has been labelling today's younger adolescents the *ninis* (*ni estudian ni trabajan*, they neither study nor work) generation. They are, then, living proof of the failure of the policy of silence and so-called consensus and reconciliation, without any rigorous evaluation of the history of Spain in the past century.

The transition also shaped a paradigmatic type of art. Post-transitional generations have grown up within the culture of consensus that rejected the idea of revolutionary sacrificial art and substituted it for art as an object of decoration, consumption, irreverence, or social status. It is not by chance that the most renowned artistic movement of the Spanish transition, the *movida*, was chiefly non-historical and apolitical[10] and intended to subvert moral values and awaken consciences in a similar way similar to what the Dadaist and Surrealist movements had tried during the early twentieth century. In that regard, the Dadaist movement and especially Duchamp's *Fountain* have been portrayed as the beginning of the end of art.[11] Similarly, I argue that the Spanish *movida* (as the institutionalized pop-art of the transition was labelled) and its Pop aesthetics could be classified historically as the beginning of the Spanish version of the end of art history.

Jorge Oteiza, the most renowned Basque aesthetician of his time, had already proclaimed the end of art as the result of its natural historical development. Art, according to his *Law of Changes*, would reach the moment when its message would be shallow and its only purpose decoration. According to Oteiza, that was the case of European art after the avant-garde movements. Oteiza argued that for art to be genuine it had to serve a sacramental purpose, which could be somehow related to Walter Benjamin's claim of the need of

---

9. Coupland, *Generation X*.

10. By non-historical I mean that the end of history as defined in the popular narrative was widely accepted by artists of the transitional period. By the same token, the mainstream artistic proposals of the *movida*, although on many occasions shocking and taunting in the Spain of the 1970s and 1980s, were apolitical in the sense that they did not question the illegitimacy of many powers directly inherited from the fascist dictatorship and the movement as a whole detached itself from traditional popular struggles.

11. See Danto, *The Transfiguration of the Commonplace*.

art to be linked to a ritual.[12] In that regard, what for Oteiza counts as genuine art could not be more detached to the institutionalized art of the transition. In 1963, Oteiza published his most controversial book, *Quousque tandem!* In it, the author proclaims the need to search for a cause worth living and dying for.[13] It was a sacrificial claim with many possible interpretations. In its later editions the book was dedicated to Txabi Etxebarrieta, the first member of ETA, the first *gudari* (Basque soldier), to give his life for the cause of the Basque Country after the Spanish Civil War. His death and that of José Pardines, the Guardia Civil who died as a consequence of his shooting, marked a tragic point of no return for ETA. From then on, ETA would be transformed from a subversive group to a terrorist organization and became a key political subject in Spanish politics.

Ever since childhood, Oteiza's apprehensive nature made him analyze his surroundings in a very particular way. For him, the world was an incredible aesthetic sight and the only way he could cope with it would be by competing with its creator.[14] Thus, this is art aimed at substituting God and creation in a need to replace conventional religious beliefs with sacramental art. In his *Quousque tandem...!* Oteiza finds the proof for his theory of sacramental art in the Basque cromlech. His avant-garde approach to the local archaeological remains and his plans to link that past with the most current artistic movements made him a pioneer in the aesthetic appraisal of Basque prehistory. Furthermore, Oteiza considered that the Basque Neolithic builder of the cromlech—a simple circle of stones reminiscent of Richard Long's Land Art—had a privileged aesthetic mindset that allowed him to interpret the importance of the void and its need for a limitation that would capture sacramental space.

Oteiza's *Quousque tandem...!* had a considerable influence on the young ETA members of the 1960s, although some of them[15] confessed to finding his theories rather obscure. In any case, he accomplished the goal of making the Basque tradition part of

12. Benjamin, *The Work of Art in the Era of Mechanical Reproduction*, iv.

13. Oteiza, *Quousque tande...!*, 20. Extracts from this work, translated into English, can be found in Oteiza, *Oteiza's Selected Writings*.

14. Oteiza's fight with God is a recurrent subject in many of his writings, and he would even coin a new term for this type of struggle: taken from bullfighting, instead of "*tauromaquia*" (the fight with the bull) he wrote about his "*teomaquias*" or fights with God. Examples of these can be found in Pelay Orozco's biography, *Oteiza, Su vida, su obra, su pensamiento, su palabra*; see Arana, *Oteiza y Unamuno*, 68.

15. Uriarte, *Mirando atrás*.

avant-garde movements. With that move, once and for all, Basque nationalism abandoned archetypical pastoral clichés as representative of modern Basques. Sacramental art, sacrifice for the cause, and a Unamunian agonic[16] art that understood creation as the struggle between opposing forces fuelled the young ETA generation in need of what in *Quousque tandem* Oteiza called, borrowing his words from Kierkegaard, *a reason to live and die for.*

Oteiza had already experimented with a series of prisms he called *maclas* (twinning crystals), taking the name from a specific type of natural crystal formed by the collision of two opposing geometrical minerals. Oteiza's twinning crystals would not grow together, but clash, and in their conflict they would create a tension, a force derived from the fusion of two simple elements. Their opposition would unveil a new reality in their relationship with their surrounding space and the gaps they had created in their fusion. The result would be a new object, just as the two elements of chemical reaction result in a compound with different properties than the original elements. That struggle of twin forces, which Oteiza also thought was the base of his experimental artistic process, brings to mind the *Fight With Cudgels* and its consequences, especially when Oteiza explicitly asserts the need for a cause to live and die for. According to Oteiza, creation is fuelled by an inner fight aimed at salvation and ready for sacrifice. ETA members such as Etxebarrieta, also a reader of Unamuno, understood that revolutionary action would have to follow a similar reasoning and opted for a literal fight and sacrifice, whereas Oteiza's struggle could also be interpreted as the personal urge to find meaning through artistic creation.

In another of his books,[17] Oteiza describes the different artistic cultures that have accomplished the goal of understanding the sacramental value of art in the history of mankind. He postulated three kinds of societies as protagonists of the history of art, successful in understanding the goal of art and reaching salvation through their creations. Oteiza termed these cultures the culture of "the man of

---

16. The etymology of agony is rooted in the Greek for combat and fight. Unamuno used its original meaning for what is considered to be the epilogue of his *magnum opus The Tragic Sense of Life* and bore the title *The Agony of Christianity.* Oteiza was very much impressed by this work and believed that the driving force of his art was a constant struggle against God. For more information about the concept of agony and its implications in Unamuno's philosophy and Oteiza's art, see Arana, *Oteiza y Unamuno, dos tragedias epigonales de la modernidad.*

17. Oteiza, *Ejercicios Espirituales en un túnel.* Extracts from this work, translated into English, can be found in Oteiza, *Oteiza's Selected Writings.*

the sky", the culture of monotheistic god, and the culture of hope. The "man of the sky" was the prehistoric man who, unable to find shelter and feeling abandoned to the mercy of nature, resorts to becoming one with it by using masks or paintings that transform his nature into that of the animal portrayed. Oteiza found examples of that art in the mountains of San Agustín, Colombia.

The second type of historically successful artist portrays God as a presence and not as symbolic representation; very much in the way Unamuno understood that the *Christ* of Velázquez[18] is not an image of the son of God, but his actual presence on earth.

The avant-garde artist, whom Oteiza calls the man of hope, was the modern man of the early twentieth century. This man believed in the transformative powers of mankind and the importance of art in the emancipation of the human race. The avant-garde movements and especially Russian constructivism would aim at controlling nature to provide mankind with a safe realm in which to develop fully and give birth to a new man.

Oteiza believed that all these cultures reached the fundamental truth of understanding the sacramental nature of art. All authentic artists were consequently heroes who granted salvation for their contemporaries. Unfortunately, the three types of men who had come together in the man of hope were assassinated by a new type of man, the North American man of consumerism who defended art as decoration, pastime, entertainment and consumption. In this regard, the Anglo-American influence that very much shaped the aesthetics of the Spanish transitional period has many traits in common with Oteiza's man of consumerism.

Oteiza had the chance to experience in person how his rationalist and cubic project for a museum and cultural center in Bilbao was condemned to oblivion with the development instead of a Guggenheim museum for the city. His final defeat was embodied by a franchised American gallery whose first two exhibits were dedicated to Armani clothes and chopper motorbikes. Oteiza would vehemently ask his friends[19] to kill the people in charge of the project. Against what he called *Euskodisney* (Basque Disneyland), for him the grotesque representation of consumerist culture and the remnants of decadent pop art, he would propose the truth of sacramental art. Along with ETA, Oteiza provided an alibi for the establishment not to consider any criticism outside the culture of consensus. All opponents of advances such as the developments undertaken for the ur-

18. Unamuno, *El Cristo de Velázquez.*

19. See Zulaika's testimony in Oteiza, *Oteiza´s Selected Writings*, 66.

ban renewal of Bilbao, all adversaries of cultural plans in the form of flamboyant museums that would return the ruinous postindustrial city in both geographical and historical terms, would be counteracted by the *reductio ad ETArum*. So Oteiza was conveniently dismissed by establishment politicians as extremist and was constantly depicted as such in mainstream newspapers. Oteiza recurrently overstepped the basic lines drawn during the transitional period and was seen as the party pooper of the most prosperous time in modern Spanish and Basque history. Yet now that the party is over, his figure comes back from death, as he had prophesized.[20] Bringing Oteiza to the discussion always meant going beyond what counted as artistically debatable. His art thus dwelled in the margins of institutionalized currents just as everything ETA proposed was contaminated by its violent means and was discarded as unattainable. This situation was somehow allegorically depicted by Oteiza, when he described the discovery of the meaning of the Basque cromlech as the delimitation of conceptual space beyond which nothing could be clearly said.[21]

The Plataforma Anti-Desahucios (Anti-eviction platform), a grassroots organization protesting against what it considers to be unjust evictions, was also recently dismissed with the *reductio ad ETArum* argument. The collapse of the housing bubble in Spain resulted in at least tens of thousands of families expelled from their homes[22] and obliged to keep on paying their mortgages, although they no longer own the property. Desperate victims of this obviously unfair deal protested in front of government representatives and left stickers on the front walls of their houses. In doing so, they were compared to Nazis and ETA terrorists.[23] For decades, ETA had laid the ground for marginalizing any dissent against the Culture of Transition. Today, ETA is on the verge of being dismantled. The arguments of those who oppose the system of the transition can

20. In his own words, "I take the name of what has just died. I return from Death. What we tried to bury grows here." See Oteiza, *Oteiza´s Selected Writings*, 244.

21. For his description and meaning of the Basque cromlech, see *Quousque tandem...!*

22. See Muñiz, "El número de desahuciados bate todos los records: 45. 559 en tres meses de 2012," *Público*, July 21, 2012.

23. For the original statement by the delegate of the Spanish government in Madrid, see www.rtve.es/noticias/20130325/cifuentes-vincula-plataforma-afectados-hipoteca-grupos-filoetarras/623823.shtml.

See also "El popular Iturgaiz arremetió contra Colau en el mismo Parlamento que ahora premia a la PAH," *El Periódico*, June 6, 2013.

no longer be disallowed, calling on the ghost of fratricidal killing. Today, according to polls, the protests of the Plataforma Anti Desahucios enjoy majority support in Spain.[24]

The economic situation in Spain shows the consequences of a construction bubble that not only affected private homes, but also involved unprecedented investments in overambitious projects all over the Iberian Peninsula. Indeed, it is not far-fetched to state that in Spain the inaugural era of incredible investments in flagship projects started with the Guggenheim Bilbao Museum. The Guggenheim Bilbao can be studied as a building that fits very well into that end-of-history or post-transitional Spanish culture that Oteiza would equate to the man of consumerism. It is by no means a coincidence that ETA, the ultimate anti-transitional subject, tried to disrupt the opening ceremony of the Guggenheim in 1997 and killed a policeman a few days before King Juan Carlos I of Spain inaugurated the museum. The symbolic content of the Guggenheim played against everything ETA represented: Basque nationalism against imperialism, socialism opposed to capitalism, and also revolutionary artistic sacrifice versus totalitarian artistic entertainment. The EAJ-PNV regional government ended up sharing the moment of a supposed unprecedented cultural success with the King of Spain. This makes complete sense within the Culture of Spanish Transition. Juan Carlos plays the role of the heroic figure in the narrative of the Spanish end of history, being the principal actor (according to the official narrative) in deactivating the attempted military coup on February 23, 1981. Moreover, from a traditionalist perspective, the defense and maintenance of what are usually called historical rights—they are included as such in the Spanish Constitution—are derived from the *fueros* or Basque charter laws, which were granted by the Spanish monarchs. It also makes complete sense that the king subscribes to the privilege Basques had to negotiate on their own with the director of the museum, Thomas Krens, without having to deal with the Spanish government. For a historical artistic account of the role of the king in the Basque Country, Francisco de Mendieta's *Jura de los Fueros de Vizcaya por Fernando V* is very representative of the ironic idea of freedom as being granted by an opposing and at the same time accepted power.

Also, during the transitional period and according to the terms of the 1979 statute of autonomy, the Basque government was given

---

24. See www.cadenaser.com/espana/articulo/59-ciudadanos-aprueban-escraches-mejor-instrumento-presion/csrcsrpor/20130415csrcsrnac_1/Tes.

the right to gather and spend its own taxes. The king's visit to the Basque Country, then, on the occasion of the Guggenheim Bilbao's inauguration, acknowledged the accommodation of the Basque government and its granted freedoms to the Culture of Transition. All in all, the main interest of the reformers of the old regime was to make Spain part of the globalized market and strengthen economic and military ties with the US and Europe. The Guggenheim museum epitomized the definitive opening up to global culture, and ended up with the era of European pressure on Spanish industries to establish a service sector economy and create a new bridge with New York City, the financial and cultural capital of the world. Again, the opening of the Guggenheim museum showed the compliance of the Basque government with the Spanish Culture of Transition.

On February 4, 1981, and a few days before he became the champion of democracy, King Juan Carlos visited the *Casa de Juntas de Gernika*, the seat of *foral* parliamentary authority in the Basque province of Bizkaia. The site was, and still is, full of symbolic content as the victim of catastrophic air raids and the motif for Picasso's universal representation. It is also the location of the oak tree that represents the old laws (*fueros*) and traditional *foral* institutions of the Basque Country. Under the oak tree, the King of Spain and the Basques would pay reciprocal respect to these customs. In 1981, Juan Carlos, the symbol of consensus and the Spanish end of history, had to face the radical chant of the culture of sacrifice in Gernika. Just as the king was ready to start his discourse inside the Casa de Juntas, (today's provincial parliament), left-wing Basque nationalists of Herri Batasuna (ETA's political wing) showed their disagreement with the visitor by singing the unofficial anthem of the Basque army during the Spanish Civil War.

Eusko gudariak gara	We are Basque warriors
Euskadi askatzeko	To free the Basque Country,
Geturik daukagu odola	our blood is here
Bere alde emateko	ready to be shed.

As the lyrics say, they claimed to be Basque warriors with the mission of liberating the Basque Country and were ready to shed their blood for the cause. In a strange and ironic twist, the former director of the Guggenheim Bilbao dreamed about Picasso's *Guernica* for his franchised branch in Bilbao. Taking *Guernica* to the Guggenheim would have meant that the very symbol of the most horrendous outcomes of the culture of sacrifice would be placed inside one of the most notorious monuments to art as part of the globalized free market, glamour, and entertainment.

Strictly speaking, and following José Gaos' definition of a work of art,[25] the Bilbao Guggenheim should amount to a historical work of art. Ultimately, it is a coherent and concise representation of the specificities of a given historical time. The Guggenheim can be defined as the archetype that represents a period in history in which art equated to any consumer good. At the same time the dubious cooperation between global economic powers and public local funding facilitated an era of untempered architectural and engineering developments.

The Guggenheim museum and the Bilbao urban renewal models are directly linked to later disastrous projects throughout Spain that tried to emulate the so-called Guggenheim effect. Among these quixotic projects were the City of Arts and Sciences in Valencia, the City of Culture in Santiago de Compostela, and the Airports of Castellón and Ciudad Real, interestingly enough named after Don Quixote. They all have in common the abundant use of public funding in opaque ways, supposedly to recover the economy and the image of a certain city and "place it on the map" in a sort of geographical pride that is customarily used to describe the success of the Bilbao Guggenheim.

And at this point we can ask ourselves: how was it that art and architecture became devoid of any social goal? What was the process that allowed for the forgetting about the motifs, functions, teachings, and enjoyment of art in favor of what is termed a Cinderella story in the *New York Times*?[26] How did consumerism art come to monopolize artistic creation?

Since Hegel there have been many prophets of the end of art: for example, Arthur Danto;[27] Susan Buck-Morss;[28] and, of course, Jorge Oteiza himself.[29] Their different accounts of the same story vary significantly, so I will provide just a rough version. Its beginnings can be placed in the first annual Exhibit of the Society of Independent Artists that took place in New York in 1917. There, Marcel Duchamp placed a urinal and presented it as art. This was a

25. See Gaos, *Historia de nuestra idea del mundo*. Here he states that a work of art should have historical relevance and depict the spirit of the age.

26. See Muschamp, "The Miracle in Bilbao."

27. Danto, "The End of Art," in *The Philosophical Disenfrenchisement of Art*.

28. Buck Morss would argue, along with Benjamin, that the end of art is not provoked by its commoditization, but rather by its technical reproduction. See Kester,"Aesthetics after the End of Art."

29. See "The End of Contemporary Art" in Oteiza, *Oteiza´s Selected Writings*, 259.

clear statement that any object could become a work of art if called so. Nobody in that early avant-garde would predict that in the future the ready-made object would be the first step toward consumer art. Of course, at the time, art also served to show status or as an investment, but nobody would dare to state—as Andy Warhol did decades later and taking this story to its conclusion—that making money was also a type of art.[30] That is, making money became an end in itself and art stopped being an end in itself to become instead a means for profit.

Years later, when he was already dedicated to what he considered an art of "non-communication" Oteiza cried: "Art is dead . . . I don't want to have anything to do with it!"[31] He claimed he had reached a final impasse in art and that from then on everything would be redundant. He embodied a compulsive artist devoted to his work, and at the same time suspicious of the world of art to the extent that he seldom sold his pieces. Only when he was already in his nineties and, according to some, in doubtful possession of his faculties, did Oteiza sell the copyright to some of his sculptures to the Marlborough Gallery.

In contrast to Oteiza, Andy Warhol's portraits of Mao and Marilyn Monroe, Campbell soup cans, and Brillo boxes were easily recognizable objects. Most of the public could instantly relate to those objects, whereas access to Oteiza's oeuvre required deeper scrutiny, even for the majority of Basques. The acceptance of Warhol's *Brillo Boxes* or his *Campbell Soup´s Cans* as art not only emptied the Pop art movement of all its previous meaning, it also meant the final transformation of a work of art into a consumption item. As a result of being easily recognizable for the masses and its goal of making money, art and marketing became indistinguishable at times. Such a turn in the history of art meant the final blow for art conceived as a resource to those areas inaccessible to the only use of reason or science and the victory of art as entertainment and decoration, and of course it meant the end of Oteiza's sacramental art. The Basque appendix to this narrative is the Guggenheim museum. Consumerist culture epitomized in the Bilbao Guggenheim museum's seductive contours came to monopolize artistic discourse in the Basque Country.

---

30. The actual quote goes: "Being good in business is the most fascinating kind of art (...) Making money is art, and working is art and good business is the best art." In Warhol, *The Philosophy of Andy Warhol (From A to B and Back Again)*, 87.

31. Oteiza on Youtube. At https://www.youtube.com/watch?v= TePFSD7n8Ss.

Oteiza made some very accurate remarks about this situation: in his aesthetic theories, genuine art had always been sacramental. Time, space, the relationship of mankind with God, death, love, and nature, with oneself, were the transcendental motifs artists would try to capture in order to be relieved of our original displacement in the world. The purpose was to found what Oteiza called habitable spaces. The history of art was, in his opinion, a heroic fight that tries to surpass the difficult relationship between man and his environment, the desperate attempt to find refuge in life. Unfortunately, consumerism had devoured art as a means of salvation. The man of consumerism had succeeded in making the important visual arts banal, accessible, and easily identifiable, a simple image that prevailed above its content and whose only objective was economic profit. Art had been killed in the hands of money.

In any case, that was not the only death of art. There have been others and even more dramatic still. Maybe the most renowned death was that marked by the suicide of the Russian artist Vladimir Maiakovski, which would in turn certify the demise of the Russian avant-garde and the rise of realistic Soviet propaganda. In the world of consumerism, art perished in the hands of marketing. In Soviet Russia the executioner was propaganda.

After the collapse of the Eastern Bloc, the only remaining culture was that of consumerism, in which everything can be subjected to the rules of the marketplace until the point that the value an object possesses is customarily economic. Art, Oteiza argued,[32] has been the same from Altamira to Richard Serra. One can conceive art beyond the marketplace, but this relationship is not reciprocal. That is to say that genuinely human beings resort to artistic expression, but its commercialization is a contingency. Oteiza showed us what is necessary in art (what he called sacramental) and its contingencies. The enjoyment of art is consubstantial with human nature, and its totalitarian commercialization prevents people from accessing it. In the battle to recover authentic art learning from past mistakes is mandatory. Struggle in the creative process, as Oteiza proposed, does not mean sacrificial death, and, in fact, a return to that culture would be disastrous. On the other hand, the value of art has to break the chains of the marketplace and recover its original worth as a special entity that transforms our relationships with the world and each other.

---

32. According to his *Law of Changes*, the purpose of art has been the same, from cave paintings through to contemporary art.

In the small milieu of Spain and in the still smaller one of the Basque Country, breaking the chains of silence accounts for breaking the conceptual structure of the Culture of Transition. A recovery of the hidden past, an in-depth study of the transitional period devoid of propaganda or foreign intervention, is key to revitalizing Spanish and Basque society. Regarding art, the hegemonic currents of today have been inherited from the transition and should also be questioned. An understanding of their contributions is also key, especially in their importance for triggering debates about gender and sexuality. And yet, today's political situation calls for a deeper engagement with crucial social and political issues, such as understanding the past and configuring new paradigms in art and politics.

In the Basque Country, the work of Maider López seems to aim at that urgency to reshape the idea of artistic space and human relationships. In her work *Polder Cup*, some soccer fields are drawn in the Dutch landscape. Soccer, a competitive game whose outcome provides winners and losers, heroes and villains, becomes a cooperative game in which participants have to overcome difficulties together and come to agreements.

On a field crossed by channels, the lines of the terrain are transformed from the depiction of the battleground into the enjoyable realm of play and cooperative discovery, a real post-historical arena. Conceptually, *Polder Cup* could be interpreted as a reconfiguration of the Oteizian sacramental space. It is not in need of a "cause to live and die for" and, moreover, it does not have to be profitable. What is more important, this type of space represents the value of social relationships and cooperation in providing existence with meaning. Maider López shows that art does not have to be sacramental, but it has to follow ritualistic purposes. *Polder Cup* is also play, but goes beyond totalitarian entertainment. It definitely proposes a first step for a way out of the impasse that art had reached. With contributions like those of Maider López and by revisiting the past with new eyes, art might be resurrecting.

Bibliography

Acebedo, Carlos, et. al. *CT o la Cultura de la Transición: Crítica a 35 años de cultura española*. Barcelona: Debolsillo, 2012.

Arana, Juan. *Oteiza y Unamuno: Dos tragedias epigonales de la modernidad*. Alzuza: Fundación Museo Jorge Oteiza, 2012.

Benjamin, Walter. *The Work of Art in the Era of Mechanical Reproduction*. Translated by J. A. Underwood. London: Penguin

Books, 2008.

Coupland, Douglas. *Generation X: Tales from an Accelerated Culture.* London: Abacus, 1992.

Danto, Arthur C. *The Transfiguration of the Commonplace: A Philosophy of Art.* Cambridge, MA: Harvard University Press, 1981.

Gaos, José. *Historia de nuestra idea del mundo.* Mexico City: Fondo de Cultura Económica, 1983.

Kester, Grant H. "Aesthetics after the End of Art: An Interview with Susan Buck-Morss." *Art Journal* 56, no. 1, (Spring 1997): 38–45.

Maxwell, Kenneth Robert. *The New Spain: From Isolation to Influence.* New York: Council of Foreign Relations Press, 1994.

Muschamp, Herbert. "The Miracle in Bilbao." *The New York Times Magazine*, September 7, 1997.

Oteiza, Jorge. *Ejercicios Espirituales en un túnel: En busca y encuentro de nuestra identidad perdida.* Alzuza: Fundación Jorge Oteiza, 2001.

———. *Oteiza's Selected Writings.* Edited by Joseba Zulaika, translated by Frederick Fornoff. Reno: Center for Basque Studies, 2003.

———. *Interpretación estética de la estaturaria megalítica americana: Carta a los artistas de América.* Sobre el arte nuevo en la postguerra. Edited by María Teresa Múñoz, Joaquín Lizasoain, and Antonio Rubio. Alzuza: Fundación Jorge Oteiza, 2007.

———. *Quousque tandem...! ensayo de interpretación estética del alma vasca.* Edited by Amador Vega and Jon Echeverría. Alzuza: Fundación Jorge Oteiza, 2007.

———. *Ley de los cambios.* Alzuza: Fernando Golvano Ed.; Fundación Jorge Oteiza, 2013.

Preston, Paul. *The Spanish Holocaust: Inquisition and Extermination in Twentieth Century Spain.* London: Harper Press, 2012.

———. *Juan Carlos: Steering Spain from Dictatorship to Democracy.* New York and London: W.W. Norton & Company, 2004.

Schopenhauer, Arthur. *Manuscript Remains in Four Volumes.* Edited by Arthur Hübscher. Translated by E.F.J. Payne. Volume 3. *Berlin Manuscripts (1818–1830).* Oxford, New York, and Munich: Berg, 1989.

Unamuno, Miguel. *Del sentimiento trágico de la vida en los hombres y en los pueblos.* Barcelona: Ediciones B, D.L., 1988.

———. *La agonía del cristianismo.* Madrid: Alianza Editorial, 1992.

———. *En torno al casticismo.* Madrid: Jean-Claude Rabaté, Cátedra, Letras hispánicas, 2005.

———. *El Cristo de Velázquez.* Madrid: Espasa-Calpe, 1957.

Uriarte, Teo. *Mirando atrás: De las filas de ETA a las lista del PSE.* Barcelona: Ediciones B., 2005.

Vilarós, Teresa M. *El mono del desencanto: Una crítica cultural de la transición española 1973–1993.* Madrid: Siglo XIX, 1998.

Warhol, Andy. *The Philosophy of Andy Warhol (From A to B and Back Again).* San Diego: Harcourt Brace Jovanovich, 1975.

Zulaika, Joseba, and William A. Douglass. *Terror and Taboo: The Follies, Fables and Faces of Terrorism.* New York and London: Routledge, 1996.

4

Art and Basque Artists: The Guggenheim Years

Adelina Moya Valgañón

For many people (including me), despite its widely recognized successes, the Guggenheim museum reveals one of the great paradoxes with regards to the way the Basque government[1] approaches culture: the incorporation of this internationally renowned museum, franchised from New York, into renewal plans for the city of Bilbao in a country that has reclaimed a considerable degree of autonomy from the Spanish state, the launching of this very expensive project, so dependent on the American institution, looked counter-productive—even like a gesture of cultural-colonial submission. Prestigious and renowned Basque artists (members of the Basque School of the 1960s) had reclaimed the identity and liberty of the Basque people during the previous decades, especially during the Franco dictatorship (1939–75). They had achieved a respect and appreciation for Basque art that still resonates today. In these circumstances, such an approach was surprising and even dispiriting. In my opinion, we may only understand it if we consider the relationship between politics and economics: and, more specifically, a particular point in postmodernity when art and culture went on to form such a substantial part of the economic system that they functioned on the margins of ideas like the meaning or necessity of art.

1. At that time the Basque government consisted of the Basque Nationalist Party (PNV) in coalition with the Basque Country's Socialist Party (PSOE-PSE).

This is why, in general terms, I will approach the Guggenheim Bilbao by reflecting on some of its art exhibitions and certain Basque artists. There is a sense in which these exhibitions could be seen as attempts to counter the perception that the Guggenheim was reluctant to exhibit them. One could say that the museum project that was used as a driving force for renovation and urban transformation had (and still has) something to do with the past art of the Basque Country in important ways.

Approaching the Guggenheim Bilbao Project from a Sociological Perspective

The idea of a Guggenheim museum in Bilbao was conceived in the late 1980s and was the result of a "convenient coincidence." The Guggenheim Foundation and Museum in New York had financial and management problems, and started a search for museums or contemporary art centers that could strengthen its patrimony (in the US as well as in Europe), extend its economic resources, patronage, and the recognition and value of its collections. At the same time, the government of the Basque Autonomous Community was eager to launch a project in its territory by attracting a consolidated institution that, due to its advanced modernity, cosmopolitanism, and symbolic (cultural and ideological) significance, could decisively contribute to generating a new image for the Basque Country, domestically and nationally. Ideally, the project would help attract people and resources, establish a positive image of the country and its entrepreneurial capacity, and overcome the region's profound industrial crisis as well as the negative image created by terrorist violence.[2]

The director of the Guggenheim Foundation was Thomas Krens and he had proposed a radical redefinition of this prestigious body's policy when it came to the acquisition of finances, the extension of artistic patrimony, and the strengthening of its image and presence in the world of art. This in turn resulted in a reorientation of acquisitions and the creation of a Guggenheim franchise.

The franchise would serve to enhance the presence and prestige of the Guggenheim brand insofar as it would gain more value by cir-

---

2. On the Guggenheim Bilbao, see Zulaika *Crónica de una Seducción*; Tellitu, Esteban, and Gonzalez Carrera, *El Milagro Guggenheim Bilbao*; Gonzalez de Durana, "Museo Guggenheim Bilbao"; Guasch and Zulaika, eds., *Learning from the Bilbao Guggenheim*; Various Authors, *Colección del Museo Guggenheim Bilbao*; Merino, *Guggenheim. Arquitectura y Arte*; and Van Bruggen, *Frank O. Gehry*.

culating its patrimony throughout a network of centers. At the same time, it allowed the Guggenheim Foundation to take new kinds of risks through the acquisition of art objects due to the "extensions of the franchise." This was conceptualized as a hierarchized structure with a central headquarters and a management model in which the owner of the brand and the art collection (namely, the Guggenheim Foundation) controlled the direction of the resources throughout the aforementioned network of centers.

All this happened in a globalized world (the Guggenheim network did not rule out establishing a new center anywhere in the world) in which a system of cities becomes a key structure in the dialectics of globalization-localization. Also, the prospect of such urban conurbations becoming key points in these networks was attractive for many cities as a means of promoting their historic and cultural heritage as well as their business interests.

By the 1980s, Bilbao had come to be defined by the decline of its iron and steel industries and the drastic downsizing of its great factories, with a concomitant increase in unemployment and decline of its infrastructures. This decline had major repercussions for Bilbao's historical models of financial capital and services. Specifically, it inevitably led to drastic changes in the primary sector, infrastructural changes along the river, and a recovery of the city's symbolic identity that had been visibly affected by the crisis.

The old industrial fabric that created an urban identity—the tough and powerful Bilbao and some of its life worlds (such as those of workers, the bourgeoisie and a quasi-aristocratic elite)—and that had once defined this singular Basque metropolis lost its capacity to collectively represent the population of the city.[3]

In its initial phase of development, the Guggenheim project was characterized by three features: First, as a political project, it aimed to change the city's image, to reactivate the tertiary economy, and to encourage urban renewal. The decision by the Basque government to accept (or "buy") the Guggenheim offer, unilaterally proposed by Thomas Krens, at all costs was made in a rather skewed manner. The project was also thwarted by secrecy, and a complete lack of participation on the part of the social actors involved in Basque art and culture. As a governmental decision, it was very economically-oriented and involved a select, limited number of actors. Second, as a museum project, it aimed to create a place—an exhibition

3. On cultural policy and urban renovation in the Basque Country see Arpal Poblador, "Cultura e desenvolvimento urbano"; Esteban, *Luces y sombras del titanio*; Holo, *Beyond the Prado*; and "Hiria eta kultura/Ciudad y cultura," special issue, *Inguruak* 9 (1994).

and evaluation center—within the franchised network proposed by Krens. It would participate in and sustain the circulation of products that were distributed from the central headquarters in New York. As such, the basic function of the museum would avoid any involvement in promoting or hosting any work originating in cultural and artistic movements of the Basque Country.

Third, as an architectural project, it had certain aesthetic aspirations and sought a specific location. It was strictly envisioned in a space that needed urban regeneration, and that would have spectacular effects with regard to the international standing and the symbolic representation of a new Bilbao in the Basque society of the immediate future. Juan Luis Laskurain, head of the government accountability office in the Basque Autonomous Community, and Thomas Krens sought to maximize international exposure for the first franchised Guggenheim museum. They agreed to commission Frank Gehry to design the museum.

The agreement was signed in New York in 1989 by the Basque government and the Guggenheim Foundation as a franchise: The Bilbao Guggenheim Foundation. As the Guggenheim project became public in the Basque Country the Basque art world responded by organizing a variety of events and shows. These ranged from a collective exhibition of moderately important "artists against the Guggenheim" in a Bilbao exhibition hall to the representation of the process of rupture and reconversion of the urban landscape and the irruption of the Guggenheim building in the works of Basque artists, painters, and photographers. Several ideologically-charged rallies and debates against the project also took place. Perhaps the most significant of these reactions—due in the main to the people involved (including, among others, Hans Haacke and Jesús Arpal) and what they did specifically—was a workshop entitled "interventions in the city," organized by Arteleku (the Basque contemporary art center) in the summer of 1995 and headed by Antoni Muntadas. The workshop required its participants to follow a route through Bilbao and along the river in order to document, first-hand, its theme, and incorporated a visit to the Guggenheim project office. The event took place within an international current of artistic actions on spaces and urban emblems that vividly represented the work of Muntadas.

This happened against a backdrop of major public and political debate about the Guggenheim project. Indeed, there was clear opposition to it on the part of left-wing Basque nationalist groups, as well as reservations on the part of the PSOE (the Spanish Socialist Party, at that time the coalition party in the Basque government).

There was even some discontent within the PNV (Basque Nationalist Party) itself, the ruling party in the Basque government. The media amplified the debate. Most of the issues centered on the economic cost of the project, with some people failing to see how the museum could be profitable and favoring investment in more traditional industrial development. There were also misgivings about an agency and art so disparaging of the idiosyncrasies of the Basque Country: the project was foreign to popular demands, and factored little in local cultural policy.

Moreover, an ETA attack occurred—the assassination of a police officer—during the preparation of the inauguration ceremony in 1997. The authorities had intended the ceremony to be an important and spectacular social event. The attack showed how the disastrous tradition of Basque violence could interfere with public debate in the Basque Country.

By then the project had been consolidated and realized. The imposing building was completed between 1993 and 1997. The media campaign, along with the evident transformations of the urban landscape (as exemplified by new transportation infrastructures designed by architectural and engineering companies and a new conference center in place of demolished shipyards very close to the museum) created an increasingly favorable public opinion of the new building. In short, the project resulted in the transformation of Bilbao's urban environment with the revitalization of certain economic sectors, especially the service sector and in particular catering.

Exhibition Strategies: The Tenth-Anniversary Celebration

From the outset, there was extensive media criticism about the scarce attention paid to, and even prejudice against, Basque art by the Bilbao Guggenheim project. One of the project's most radical detractors was Jorge Oteiza, whose continuous involvement in the development of Basque art was incompatible with the acceptance of a "Yankee" franchise. In his unusual and in this case violent manner, he declared to the media that if the project was not halted, it would have to be halted like Lemoniz.[4] It is a well-known fact that, some

4. See *Egin*. Translator's note: the Lemoniz Nuclear Power Plant was part of the Spanish nuclear program in the 1970s, and provoked great opposition. The separatist organization ETA planted bombs, which murdered several guards and workers, and kidnapped and killed the chief engineer of

years before, Oteiza had designed another project for a great "comparative and aesthetic Research Center" in Bilbao, which would be located in a transparent cube in the Alhóndiga, an old wine warehouse in the city center. It was an old dream of the famed Basque artist and did attract some support, most notably from the then mayor of the city, José María Gorordo, but it was ultimately rejected by the Bilbao City Council, resulting in Gorordo's resignation.

At the same time the sculptor Eduardo Chillida (like Oteiza, also a member of the Basque School and the most international of the Basque artists), who had never opposed the Guggenheim project, now felt neglected by the museum, which offered to exhibit one of his sculptures outside the building. Chillida declined the offer. He was also annoyed because the Guggenheim Foundation was not considering the acquisition of his recent work for the collection, claiming that the New York Guggenheim already possessed Chillida sculptures dating from the 1960s. This was how the franchise system operated; the Guggenheim Museum collection was considered to be the sum of the particular collections of each museum within the network.[5] These arguments apparently postponed Chillida's first formal exhibition at the Guggenheim Bilbao. In 1998 Cristina Iglesias, the noted Donostia-San Sebastián-based sculptor who had been trained in London, initiated the three great individual exhibitions that the Guggenheim Bilbao devoted to Basque artists. Finally, Eduardo Chillida's first exhibition for the Guggenheim, curated by Kosme Barañano, took place in 1999.

Oteiza passed away in 2003. Between 2004 and 2005, Margit Rowell and Txomin Badiola curated the exhibition, "Jorge Oteiza. Myth and Modernity," at the Bilbao Guggenheim. Later, the exhibition traveled to the New York Guggenheim museum. Chillida and Oteiza were, in a way, the two important Basque figures that the Guggenheim could not ignore. Apparently, prior to Oteiza's death, Richard Serra and Frank Gehry, two star artists of the American franchise, had a part in convincing him to exhibit in Bilbao.

After Chillida's death, in 2006 the Guggenheim Bilbao organized an exhibition in his honor, curated by Kosme Barañano. The event included the works of forty-three artists (including Eduardo Arroyo, Juan Genovés, Antonio López, Antoni Tàpies, Manolo Valdés, Pablo Palazuelo, Mimmo Paladino, Robert Rauschenberg,

---

the project between 1977 and 1981. As a result, the finalization of the plant was halted.

5. See Esteban and Carrera, "Eduardo Chillida, en desacuerdo con la exposición de su obra en el Guggenheim."

Anthony Caro, and Christo). Moreover, for the duration of this exhibition, Chillida's sculpture "Looking for the Light IV" was installed at the entrance to the museum, in a space usually reserved for Jeff Koons' "Puppy." This exhibition was exceptional in that it was supported by, and in effect entirely belonged to, one person: Antonio Iraculis, the CEO of the Urbaske Group, a construction firm in Bilbao involved in many of the new urban projects in the city.[6]

The Guggenheim also organized temporary shows made up of works from its collection. Sometimes these would combine the work of Basque artists with that of Spanish artists, as in the first collection titled "Basque and Spanish Contemporary Art" (1999), in which the work of Cristina Iglesias, Txomin Badiola, Juan Luis Moraza, Prudencio Irazabal, and Javier Pérez shared space with the work of Francesc Torres, Susana Solano, Mikel Barceló, and Juan Muñoz. On other occasions, such as in "Inhabited Architecture," the Guggenheim exhibited the work of Basque artists Pello Irazu and Cristina Iglesias together with that of international artists belonging to the collection: for example, Mona Hatoum, Doris Salcedo, and Lian Gillick. This is a typically "multinational" way of promoting local art.[7]

In 2000 Javier González de Durana, director of the Rekalde Hall (which functioned as an antechamber for the Guggenheim, and there was even a Rekalde II for young Basque artists), organized the first collective exhibition of Basque artists (or artists who were based in Euskadi). He selected people who were born in the 1960s: Mabi Revuelta, Javier Pérez, Francisco Ruiz de Infante, Gabriel Díaz, and Leopoldo Ferrán-Agustina Otero. These artists predominantly represented a poetic-literary current in line with the title of the show: "Tower Struck by Lightning: The Impossible as Goal." It was a selection sponsored by the Bilbao daily newspaper *El Correo Español - El Pueblo Vasco*, which visibly sought to distance itself from any reference to Basque art. According to González de Durana, this was the boldest possible exhibition among the orders

6. This sculpture was installed in the plaza between the twin towers making up the Isozaki Atea, designed by the architect Arata Isozaki. The work was sold at auction in London with other sculptures in the same exhibition by Iraculis. He organized the exhibition and acquired all the work. The company stated that it sold the collection so it could pay off its debts to the Provincial Government. See "4,8 millones por el *Chillida* de las Torres de Isozaki," *El Correo*, June 26, 2013.

7. For more information on the Guggenheim exhibitions, see www.guggenheim.es.

received from Thomas Krens. González de Durana also declared that the artists, although they were Basque, could have been from anywhere, thus setting out an obvious distance with respect to the idea of Basque art.[8] This was doubtless a matter of consensus: the rationale behind a show of young artists, as well as the introductions of both the *Lehendakari* (the president of the Basque government), Juan José Ibarretxe, and the general director of the Guggenheim Bilbao, Juan Ignacio Vidarte, avoided any mention of Basque artists. However, it was a completely different case for the 2007–2008 exhibition "Chacun à son goût" ("To each their own"), organized by the Guggenheim, that underscored the Basque dimension of the artists involved.

In any case, the "Tower Struck by Lightning" represented the first sign of the museum's receptiveness to young artists of the Basque Country. The artists, in turn, lent a spectacular and variable character to the exhibition with installations like the "Tower of Sound" by Javier Pérez. This was an elevated metal structure, a shelf-like support with many glass containers that, as they were shaken, produced a sound that accentuated a sensation of fragility. The exhibition also included "Aphrodite's Curls," a big bathtub filled with black feathers and slippers like the feet of a bird of prey, created by Mabi Revuelta. Each of the artists in the "Tower Struck by Lightning" produced various installations and works for specific spaces on the third floor of the museum, but the Guggenheim did not acquire any of the pieces. What was left from it was a thick catalogue dedicated to the idea of the Tower of Babel and the labyrinth.

The Bilbao Fine Arts Museum had a very different approach and position. From the outset of the Guggenheim museum project, it seemed to attempt to serve as a counterpoint to the foreign museum's leadership. In a major effort to reinvigorate its own position, the Fine Arts Museum organized a packed show featuring twenty-two Basque artists of at least two generations in December 2001. Its title was significant in that it incorporated the names of the three Basque Schools established in 1966: "Gaur, Emen, Orain" ("Today, Here, Now"). This was a foundational event that promoted a more extended and diverse selection of artists than its title suggests. The show started with artists who formed part of the New Basque Sculpture movement in the 1980s (Bados, Badiola, Morquillas, Marisa Pérez—Moraza), and was dominated by a number of art-

8. *El País*, February 1, 2000. See González Carrera, "El Guggenheim exhibe la obra plagada de sensaciones de seis artistas vascos," *El Correo*, February 1, 2000.

ists educated in the Bilbao Faculty of Fine Arts at the University of the Basque Country and Arteleku, a training center for artists in Gipuzkoa: Sergio Prego, Iñaki Garmendia, Itziar Okariz, Ana Laura Alaez, Asier Mendizabal, Ibon Aranberri, and Gema Intxausti, among many others. Moreover, interesting painters like Iñaki Sáez and photographers like Mikel Eskauriaza also participated. Nevertheless, there was a notable absence of other types of work, like the staged photography of Miguel Angel Gaueka or Eduardo Sourrouille. Ruiz de Infante participated again. The purpose of this exhibition, produced during Miguel Zugaza's time as director, was to give a reinvigorating impulse to this museum so representative of Bilbao; it also intended to reevaluate the here and now of Basque art in all its diversity. Without a doubt, something had to counter the politics of the Guggenheim. Precisely with a view to emphasizing the importance of this local museum, the works of Basque artists were displayed together with the outstanding works of its general collection, whether modern or historic.

In 2007 the Guggenheim Bilbao Museum organized two exhibitions of Basque art and artists in order to commemorate its tenth anniversary, which I will discuss shortly. It also organized an educational program titled "Laboratories: Glances around the Collection," which featured a work by the sculptor Koldobika Jauregi and another by J.M. Lazkano in the space intended for rehearsals (a space that is today connected to the museum exit). Then in 2012, the museum organized, in the same space, the project "Bilbao Guggenheim Wall. The project included five "emergent" artists, selected by means of a competition, who developed their projects on a wall of 20.6x5.9 meters (approximately 68x20 feet). The Guggenheim Bilbao Museum commemorated this fifteenth anniversary by setting up a jury comprised of representatives from the "official" art centers: the Dean of Fine Arts at the University of the Basque Country, the director of the Rekalde Hall, the director of Bilbaoarte (an important foundation promoting artistic creativity in the city), and the director of the exhibitions and activities at the Guggenheim Bilbao. The jury selected curators for the top three young artists in a competition sponsored by the museum. In November 2013, the Guggenheim announced the results. The jury had chosen Garmendia, Maneros, and Salaberria for a major artistic project entitled "Process and method: From archive to no-place."

Although Basque art was not a particular objective for the Guggenheim Bilbao, clearly the museum needed to legitimate itself by paying some attention to the subject, and this was most evident on the occasions of the museum's anniversaries.

I must discuss two exhibitions "of and on Basque art and artists" (according to its own publicity) that took place in 2007, the year in which the museum celebrated its tenth anniversary: "Unknowns" ("Incognitas"), a didactic exhibition on Basque art since the 1950s, and "To each their own" ("Chacun à son goût"), a show of Basque artists who considered themselves representatives of the late 1990s. Both exhibitions were presented as interrelated, although in reality "Unknowns" was put together in very little time and served to give theoretical coverage and a contextualizing introduction to "Chacun à son goût."

For "Unknowns (Cartographies of Contemporary Art in Euskadi)," a conceptual artist who had enjoyed a brilliant career, Juan Luis Moraza, produced a series of graphics on the world of art in the Basque Country. He structured it chronologically in three generations together with the emerging art of that moment. It constituted a model of succession (with each generation confronting the previous one), and highlighted the social and political transformations and the cultural centers associated with each generation. This sequence included changing identifications of the actors of art, of aesthetic trends, and the place that they occupied in the system. The exhibition became a cartographic study with a markedly sociological-anthropological orientation along the lines of a French model, presenting virtual diagrams and maps in careful detail. It also featured a model of a planetary system in which artists and other agents (promoters, critics, centers and activity groups, galleries, museums, and so on) were positioned in the different orbits. Its nucleus consisted of the key centers of art training emerging through time: from the Schools of Arts and Trades to the Faculty of Fine Arts and Arteleku, featuring the dates when they were founded. These diagrams formed a complex and effective image of the art world in the Basque Country. They also showed the impact of certain Basque groups and certain people in a geographically differentiated context in a given time, all linked to an international scene.

"The purpose of this show," the museum's presentation brochure states, "organized on the Tenth Anniversary of the Museum is to reflect the intensity and complexity of the relationships, interchanges and influences of the artistic context of the Basque Country without prescribing "the recognition of certain stylistic patterns that could serve for the recognition of an identity, of a differential artistic fact of the Basque Country."[9]

9. *Guggenheim Bilbao 10 Urte/años/years.*

In the plan-reliefs, which were quite exquisitely elaborated, the relevance of these achievements was represented like a landscape throughout the period: the generational sequence spanned from those born before 1945 (the avant-gardes of the Basque Country) to those born after 1976 (the young artists). This was accompanied by a very limited selection of works, most likely owing to a lack of time in preparing the exhibition. The result was a visual contribution that showed the reality of the landscape and system of Basque art; it was created on the basis of a hundred questionnaires answered by people who were active in this world (artists, critics, historians, and administrators). These generational reliefs also demonstrated an increasingly noteworthy number of female participants. And in greater detail, it was a graph that analyzed the precarious economic situation of most artists who sustained the art system in the Basque Country.

The exhibition had an unusual, groundbreaking way of representing the art of the Basque Country: in other words, it was "seen from the future" in a museum so dedicated to the appreciation of the spectacular force of works and the genius of the creative personalities of art. Considering the limitations of time and space with regard to the preparation of the exhibition, it was an exhaustive and at the same time imaginative form of presenting, for the first time, the art of the Basque Country in a global and systematic way in the Guggenheim Bilbao Museum. It also emphasized certain essential landmarks in the development of Basque art, like the figure and influence of Jorge Oteiza and Arteleku as an important site of artistic and cultural development. With a degree of critical logic, it could have become a series of explorations and exhibitions through changing the spatial-temporal scale of their diagrams and maps. It could have settled the issue of random shows of Basque artists that were being produced for the museum in recent years, of works that have become part of the collection, or the temporary and peripheral spaces given to young Basque artists so that they could organize a show of their work themselves. But, ultimately, the project was at root a response to more pragmatic issues, such as the Guggenheim evading criticism for its lack of engagement with Basque art.

"Unknowns" was held between July 6 and September 7, 2007. "Chacun à son goût" had been in preparation before "Unknowns" opened and took place between October 1 and February 1, 2008. "Chacun à son gout" occupied strategic places in the museum, from its antechamber to the third floor. It presented installations and interventions by twelve Basque artists who belonged to a generation that had been, in the words of the international curator Rosa

Martínez, "consolidated since the late 1990s." This was a time of subjectivities in which there was a major diversity of trends and individual options: "Taken from Diderot ('to each their own'), the title of the exhibition champions individual taste and freedom of choice. As a phenomenon relative to perception and time, taste may evolve according to social and individual preferences, and is influenced by class, gender, geopolitics, and aesthetic education."[10] One should note that among the twelve selected artists, five were women: Itziar Okariz, Ixone Sadaba, Elssie Ansareo, Abigail Lazkoz, and Maider López; together with Juan Pérez Aguirregoikoa, Segio Prego, Asier Mendizabal, Aitor Ortiz, Ibon Aranberri, Manu Arregui, and Clemente Bernard.

The title and the exhibition's orientation were designed to invoke the above-mentioned "Today, Here, Now," showing perhaps a greater diversity of projects and attention to the multiple orientations of photography, from photo-installation to documenting and staging. This time the works, the result of the museum exhibit in great part, went on to enrich the collection. The works doubled the heretofore insignificant number of women artists represented in the previous exhibition (only four). The total number of Basque artists featured in the collection increased from eleven to twenty-three when the purchase of the pieces was formalized in November 2008. These acquisitions later allowed the Guggenheim management to state that, "a third of the artists that constitute the collection of the museum are Basque." I would thus define these projects as legitimizing strategies, but strategies that are welcome if they are well managed.

This exhibition involved interventions in the architecture and distinct spaces of the museum; it asked for explanations and provoked questions about the political and aesthetic context. Some works reflected political positions, such as that of Ibon Aranberri, whose installation "Horizons" affected a certain demystification (or deconstruction) of the heroic era of Basque art. It consisted of zigzag rows of flags placed on the corridor of the third floor, which reproduced the logo of Chillida (five hundred printings in total). "Horizons" mixed printings that he had made for popular social movements (e.g. one that sought amnesty for political prisoners) with less idealistic ones, such as the commission Chillida undertook for a savings bank.[11] Political art was also represented in

---

10. www.guggenheim-bilbao.es/en/exhibitions/chacun-a-son-gout-2/.

11. See Various Authors, *Colección del museo Guggenheim Bilbao*. "Ibon Aranberri".

"Nom de Guerre," a small smoking jar located on a piece of concrete by Asier Mendizábal, which could not be exhibited because its flames required an extractor fan. In successive interpretations, the work developed into a very clear reference to street violence (*kale borroka*, a form of protest used by the left-wing Basque nationalist movement), according to Mendizábal himself. It was like a small censer whose fire signifies the extinguished life of the hero, to life interrupted, perhaps also to the very impossibility of the monument. The project "Irrintzi" by Itziar Okariz offers another example of political art. The work rendered the distinct spaces of the Guggenheim to resonate with the recording of an *irrintzi*, made by the artist himself. (The *irrintzi* is a shrill, piercing call closely associated with traditional Basque culture that may originally have been a Basque war cry.) The recording gave rise to criticism for being voiced by the artist in an inconvenient space, which could be perceived as "alien."

While Aranberri invoked Chillida, one of the most outstanding figures in Basque art, the work of Abigail Lazkoz, I think, implicitly pointed to Jorge Oteiza. The title of Oteiza's installation, called "130,000 of the latest trends," referred to Basque prehistory, on which he based his foundational text *Quousque Tandem* (1963) and the idea of a modern and ancestral Basque art. Lazkoz showed the bittersweet humor of Oteiza's elaborate black and white drawing in her work, inventing a cemetery (museum?) with clear local and universal references, and it was prepared for a specific hall. As in other pieces exhibited in very significant places, the painter Juan Pérez Agirregoikoa's "Project converted into installation" visualized, through elemental posters and banners, a "brutish" humor. It addressed mass society, which through maxims and "slogans" had altered the discourses of religion, politics, philosophy, and art, revealing their banalization. Many of his phrases were direct allusions to the museum: for example, "You have given ground to your desire" (following Lacan's well-known statement).

Juan Prego, Maider Lopez, and Aitor Ortiz, meanwhile, modified Gehry's much celebrated architecture with their interventions. Prego situated a mobile and opaque "Sequence of dihedrals" on the wall covering of the building, in both a dialogue with and opposition to its structure. Ortiz opened up a hole in the wall, which formed part of his photographic-architectural installation. The hole allowed viewers to appreciate a specific detail of the construction. He had been previously charged with the task of photographing the construction of the building. Lopez, an artist who was accustomed to remodeling and introducing alterations to all types of public spaces and architecture, transformed a hall in the museum into a space in the "Gehry style," as a form of homage to the architect.

"Irresistibly nice" by Manu Arregi consisted of two monitors facing each other that exhibited the disabled body of Vanessa Jiménez (the girl with glass bones) in a video recording. The image was placed in front of another infographic image, turning in a seated position on a stool, that showed the fine line that separates the virtual from the real in the society of spectacle. With some imagination, one might interpret this as a "Mona Lisa" of the mass media. Jiménez, with her seated posture and sweet smile, has been featured on television programs. The title of the installation comes from one of her phrases.

Clement Bernard, a press photographer who has won many awards for his critical-humanist vision, presented various series. They narrated, in images, distinct worlds of social reality, ranging from day laborers working during the wine harvest to the exhumation of tombs of executed Republicans from the Spanish Civil War. His series "Chronicles of the Basque Country (1987–2001)" provoked a violent reaction from Spain's Commission for the Victims of Terrorism, which, supported by the Popular Party (PP), attempted to get it removed from the exhibition. It was, however, unsuccessful in its demand. The museum came to its defense, and, with the artist's encouragement, an organization that protects the rights of reporters, "Reporters Without Frontiers," also intervened in its favor.

The artist Ixone Sádaba (who photographed her own performances) displayed the cryptic "Poetry of Disappearance," a self-referential work that implied a total interaction between photography and performance. The artist's naked body, lying on a bed, showed fragmented expressions of extreme situations that were recorded as her hand hit the camera trigger. While for Cindy Sherman the trigger moment was equivalent to the moment of adopting a fictional "I," for Sádaba it seemed to be the culminating moment of a tragic representation that develops through time.

The black and white photographer Elssie Ansareo presented a great frieze, "The dance of the Flaneuses," with numerous people from her world, her own self-portrait included. Her work has several references to the interrelation of painting and photography in history. It also shows a world of paradoxical or non-normative interpersonal relations.

As a project open to the distinct practices of contemporary art, and as an approach that aimed to address again the idea of Basque art as something diverse and plural, the artists were invited to express their critical modes of vision with regard to a place that at the same time they were legitimizing. In turn, their artistic careers gained new recognition, and a new momentum. Such is the mechanism of contemporary art: it is critical of the art system and yet, at the same time, it is in need of recognition in this world.

The political drive behind this project to feature Basque artists was nevertheless evident, and was clearly articulated in the catalog's introduction, written by the authorities in charge. After this exhibition, they compiled and published a catalog of the Guggenheim collection in 2009. In addition to showcasing a considerable collection, it was also clear that they had made an investment in purchasing work from all the participants in "Chacun à son gout." With the twelve new pieces, it was now effectively palpable that a third of the museum collection was by Basque artists.

Bibliography

Arpal Poblador, Jesús. "Cultura e desenvolvimento urbano: o caso do Pais Vasco." *Grial* 168 (2005): 42–49.

Colección del Museo Guggenheim Bilbao. Bilbao: Fundación Guggenheim Bilbao, 2009.

Esteban, Marisol. *Luces y sombras del titanio. El proceso de regeneración del Bilbao Metrpolitano*. Bilbao: UPV/EHU, 2000.

Gonzalez de Durana, Javier. "Museo Guggenheim Bilbao: ni cielo ni infierno, solo un instrumento." *Cuadernos de Alzate* 17 (1997): 231–39.

González Carrera, J.A. "El Guggenheim exhibe la obra plagada de sensaciones de seis artistas vascos," *El Correo*, February 1, 2000.

Guasch, Anna Mª and Joseba Zulaika, eds., *Learning from the Bilbao Guggenheim*. Reno: Center for Basque Studies, University of Nevada, 2005.

Guggenheim Bilbao 10 Urte/años/years.

"Hiria eta kultura/Ciudad y cultura." Special issue, *Inguruak* 9 (1994).

Holo, Selma. *Beyond the Prado: Museums and Identity in Democratic Spain*. Washington D.C.: Smithsonian Institution Press, 1999.

Merino, José Luis. *Guggenheim. Arquitectura y Arte*. Bilbao: Ayuntamiento de Bilbao et al., 2003.

Tellitu, Alberto, Iñaki Estaban, and J.A. González Carrera. *El Milagro Guggenheim Bilbao*. Bilbao: Diario El Correo, 1997.

Van Bruggen, Coosje. *Frank O. Gehry: Guggenheim Museum Bilbao.* Bilbao and New York: Guggenheim Museum Publications, 1997.

Zulaika, Joseba. *Crónica de una seducción: El Museo Guggenheim Bilbao.* Madrid: Nerea, 1997.

5

The Site for Controversy: The Case of New Basque Sculpture, from Roots to Rhizomes, in the 1980s

Txomin Badiola

Some years ago, I received a call from the Office of the President of the Basque Parliament. I was informed that the president, Izaskun Bilbao, wanted an appointment with me. A few days later we met at a hotel in Bilbao. The president came to the point immediately: the Basque Parliament had decided to build a Monument to the Victims of Terrorism in the entrance to its headquarters in Vitoria-Gasteiz, and wished to inquire about the possibility of my accepting the commission. She told me that the Basque Parliament had decided that the monument should be made by a sculptor of the 1980s generation. The parliament was in effect seeking to encourage a generational change by means of opening up the way, on the one hand, to sculptors different from those traditionally commissioned to create monuments in the Basque Country, and on the other, to projects not necessarily linked to old formal and iconographic repertoires and traditional materials.

I found the proposal not only surprising but also odd. The politician thought that what was needed was a "renewal" of names and forms associated with new monuments. What she was looking for was a new art-form to represent a pre-existent content, which was suggested in a naive and nonspecific way. But what she did not think about, something I tried to explain to her, was that new ways of understanding art-practice had turned the very notion of the monument into something extremely debatable, at least on the terms by which the commission was being made.[1] The confusion was somehow understandable because my name has always been associated with what was called "New Basque Sculpture" in the 1980s and, for want of a better critical reconsideration, is still regarded as a regenerative movement based on a preexistent tradition. However, that movement was, precisely, based on a way of working that questioned the very idea of content; instead, it made use of "bad form," which tries to expose the chains of signification in order to make content appear as such. Therefore, in my view, any approach to that commission would have to be made through deconstructing the content itself, in this case, the idea of a "Victim of Terrorism." Such a project could only be approached from a moral indifference that, no matter how respectful I wanted to be toward the pain of others, would probably add more pain, which for me made the monument unviable.

We artists have a dual responsibility as citizens: to society and to ourselves. However, on many occasions there are situations when it is difficult to combine both responsibilities. While understanding that this whole ethical/artistic/political dilemma could be a strictly personal problem,[2] I tried to warn the politician that if what she

---

1. The notion of a monument implies an artifact capable of translating into material form a subject matter for which there is sufficient consensus in the particular social context it is placed. Its role is to invoke the remembrance or celebration of certain values, fulfilling a public moralizing function. The characteristics of the monument tend to be antithetical to the function of art, as it is understood today in which a work of art is no longer a device in the service of a predetermined content. Moreover, the level of social consensus required to fulfill the aforementioned traditional function of the monument—when issues are involved that deeply affect social groups—is increasingly unattainable in increasingly diverse, conflictive, and relativistic societies. Only when there is an event of clearly overwhelming dimensions, such as in the case of the Holocaust, or when the event is almost instantaneous and therefore especially traumatic, such as in the case of the 9/11 or the 2004 bombings in the Atocha train station in Madrid, is a sufficient amount of consensus usually met.

2. There are notable examples of successful contemporary monuments such as the *Monument to the Victims of the Holocaust*, in Berlin, by Peter Eisenman. But, my approach to the commission would have been closer to the notion of "counter-monument," which makes a perverse use of the characteristics of the monument: it is usually ephemeral; it waives consensus and seeks discrepancy; it urges us to remember what no one wants to be reminded of. A good example of a counter-monument would be *Und ihr habte doch gesiegt* (1988) by Hans Haacke, for the Austrian city of Graz. This project made use of an existing seventeenth-century monu-

wanted was a real renewal, they should not expect Basque artists to simply update their objects. She would have to deal with all these new matters; unless, that is, she could find an artist willing to tackle the task with a plumber's professional asepsis, someone who could do "his/her thing" while bowing to the demands of the contracting part, and accepting without any problem the required title: "Homage to the Victims of Terrorism," as indeed eventually happened.

If I started my paper with this personal anecdote it is because I believe it highlights the difficulties (or, more precisely, "my" difficulties) in the relationship between art-practice (with the inevitable issues of artistic form) and politics (or politicians), particularly in a spatial context such as the Basque Country. It also speaks about the complexity of the very idea of "the political," especially when viewed from inside the arts: as something simply to ignore; as the mere expression of subject-matter (realism); as an effect in the social (activism); or as a strategy consisting of revealing the conditions of possibility and intelligibility of the political (deconstruction). In order to maintain the tone set from the beginning of this chapter, I will try to explain certain situations concerning the relationship between art and "the political," without withdrawing them from the context in which they arose. In this regard, I have opted to contemplate such situations from my own experience as a Basque artist belonging to a specific generation, and their impact on subsequent generations of Basque artists, in the hope that they will prove not categorical but, rather, symptomatic.

I began my artistic career in the late 1970s in Bilbao, in the hyper-politicized context resulting from the recent death of dictator Francisco Franco and the many political and social disputes that arose thereafter. Because of the incredible social activity at the time, with a proliferation of political parties — (as well as party dissolutions, takeovers, and mergers), the pragmatism of politicians seeking accommodation in the new status quo, the mannerisms of the

---

ment (a virgin on top of a tall column commemorating a victory over the Turks). Haacke evoked the transformation that the Nazis made of the same monument in 1938 to celebrate the invasion of Austria by Germany, but he included at its base a list of the victims of the invasion with the same slogan used by the Nazis: "And after all, you came out victorious." The project provoked much controversy, ultimately suffering a bomb attack that partially destroyed it. Another example would be Santiago Sierra's project for the Puhlheim-Stommeln synagogue. It consisted of transforming a synagogue into a gas chamber; something that was considered especially offensive to the Jewish community and it is difficult to figure out what the artist's goal was, beyond self-propaganda for the "controversial political artist" brand.

revolutionary and increasingly self-parodying Left, and the recrudescence of terrorism and counterterrorism, it was really difficult for an artist to politically position him or herself as such.

Moreover, there was no shortage of models in this context. In fact, the most important Basque artists of the moment represented very different approaches to the same problem. Jorge Oteiza embodied the artist who in 1959, after finishing his experimental process, had decided to abandon sculpture in order to pursue other activities with a greater impact on the social. In the early 1980s, after an ongoing series of failures in many initiatives of all kinds, Oteiza had become a peculiar figure, a sort of prophet who occasionally descended from the mountains to launch his admonitions on politicians and cultural agents alike, begging them for a political-cultural turnaround. Meanwhile, Eduardo Chillida and his international success as a sculptor represented the art celebrity, always willing to put his fame at the service of "good causes" such as making stickers for the antinuclear movement, donating etchings in benefit of the *ikastolas* (schools where the vehicular language is Basque), or collaborating with Basque institutions. The case of Agustín Ibarrola represented the politically committed artist, the artist victimized by Franco's regime because of his communist activism, the artist denouncing social injustice, labor exploitation, and political repression. Finally, Néstor Basterretxea represented the applied artist, very adept in his role as designer, architect, filmmaker, creator of propaganda posters, and sculptor giving body and image to Basque mythology in his *Cosmogonic Series*; someone who had once resisted the call of Basque nationalism but had nonetheless found his place within the newly established Basque institutional system (dominated by Basque nationalism).

All these artists and many others had met some years earlier, in 1966, in what became known as the Basque School Groups,[3] which brought together the most important artists in the country and which had a clear strategy: to occupy the Basque cultural space. For Oteiza and Ibarrola (although in different ways), this had little to do with art and much more with politics, that is, with the possibility of influencing society, emphasizing the propaganda and pressure within an integrating cultural project. However, the

3. After a conspiracy initiated by Oteiza, Basterretxea, and Ibarrola in 1966, four groups were created: Gaur, Emen, Orain, Danok, [Today, Here, Now, All], corresponding to each of the Basque provinces of Hegoalde [Southern Basque Country], including Navarre [Nafarroa in Basque, Navarra in Spanish].

project was frustrated partly because the respective groups in the provinces of Gipuzkoa (Guipúzcoa) and Araba (Álava) were (understandably) more focused on their own agenda to promote their art careers and not so interested in politics (which was what really gave meaning to the groups). As a result, after the groups broke up, both Ibarrola and Oteiza moved away, but still an idea of Basque art was consolidated with a certain pedigree of political resistance; that said, this same Basque art eventually found sponsorship and support in Basque banks such as Caja Laboral Popular and Caja Provincial de Gipuzkoa, and private foundations such as the Orbegozo Foundation linked to Mondragon cooperatives. It thus constituted a contemporary "Basque School," which found its symbolic and conceptual bearings in a vague interpretation of Oteiza's theories, but with a strong social component due to that particular political momentum. However, as an art-expression (a sort of abstract essentialist lyricism finding its ultimate justification in nature, and in mythical Basque culture), the Basque School was as far from Oteiza's works as it was from his aims of transforming society through political/aesthetical action. Meanwhile, Ibarrola, with his paintings on the working class—linked to themes of socialist realism but sifted through a range of abstract experimentations derived from the time he was involved in Equipo 57—did not fit into that essentialist aesthetic, nor was he entirely congenial with Oteiza, largely due to his status as a "man of the (Communist) Party."

Oteiza always criticized Ibarrola in this respect—he considered Ibarrola too obedient to the Party. Interestingly, Oteiza was nevertheless the artist spiritually closest to revolutionary attitudes in art. The matter of the survival of art—as a specialized practice, in a socialist society—or rather, its evolution toward applied art or education, was a question that was always on the table in the discussions of the Russian avant-garde, and it is an issue that Oteiza, in his own particular way, had taken from the figures associated with that movement. As a hard-core avant-garde artist—interested not only in changing art forms but also in transforming society—his ultimate goal could be nothing other than obtaining the political power that would allow him to effectively implement his social and aesthetic conclusions. Deep inside, Oteiza aspired to be the Stalin described by Boris Groys in his book *The Total Art of Stalinism*.[4] In the view of Groys, Stalin, by means of concentrating all political power, became the logical consequence of avant-garde postulates, and not merely, as systematically considered, its expunger. Stalin became the artist

4. Groys, *The Total Art of Stalinism*. .

of the "total art work" that was the Soviet Union. Oteiza, through his negative aesthetics, was to empty the mass of his sculptures to the point where the object would run out in his hands to address the ultimate elimination, that of the language itself, recreating himself in the process as the "new man," capable of acting directly on reality. Nevertheless, to prevent this process from being just a declaration or a matter of voluntarism, political power was needed.

Fortunately or unfortunately (I believe fortunately), Oteiza never attained the power to which he aspired, but not because he did not try. His book *Quousque Tandem ...!* (1963)[5] played a well-known ideological role in the formation of the incipient ETA.. Oteiza was a close friend of one of its leaders, Txabi Etxebarrieta. However, over the years, Oteiza quit such company, to the point of completely demonizing ETA and its supporters in the 1980s. With the arrival of democracy, Oteiza gave all his hopes to the creation of a Basque government. Thus, when Carlos Garaikoetxea was appointed *lehendakari* (President of the Basque Government), Oteiza imagined that his influence on political and cultural affairs would be assured. Nothing was further from reality; the last thing a newly established government would hear of was the connection between art and politics, and consequently Oteiza was ignored. This was his last and final frustration; significantly thereafter, Oteiza progressively put aside his political/cultural projects and focused more and more on poetry.

In the turbulent social and political situation between the mid-1970s and mid-1980s, the issues raised by the Basque School were increasingly ignored, if not outright discredited, by a new generation of artists. A first reaction consisted of a strategy of ironic detachment through the use of some of the *clichés* of Basque identity. I am referring to artists such as Vicente Ameztoy, Ramón Zurriarain, Andrés Nagel, Juan Carlos Eguileor, among others. In the inevitable dialogue—or contamination—at the time between art and politics, one could gradually perceive a flirtation between the language of art and that of violence, with some artists including specific images. This can be seen for instance with artists such as Juan Luis Goenaga, in his series *Encapuchados* (Hooded, 1977), or the images of torture from the series *Euskadi* by Xabier Morrás (1977), and in a more corrosive sense, the piece *Super Hero Euskaldunzarra* (1978) by the Roscubas brothers. This could not only be perceived in the iconography, but also in the structure of some performative actions. A good example of this are the actions performed by the EAE (Euskal Artisten Elkartea, the Basque Artists' Association), created in

5. Oteiza, *Quousque Tandem...!*.

Bilbao in 1983, of which I was also a part. Despite its short life of just a few years, this association conducted one of the most striking political/artistic acts of the time: *EAE. Action. The Museum,* which took place that same year.[6] It consisted of "kidnapping" a sculpture by Oteiza, *Homage to Malevich,* which was part of the permanent collection of the Museum of Fine Arts in Bilbao—and giving it back to its "rightful owner," the city of Bilbao, represented by its city council. Although a few claims about the cultural and political problems in the functioning of the museum were listed among the motivations that fueled this act, the truth is that it was a genuine art performance and its meaning is primarily to be found in the logic of the rules that made it possible. We were not only interested in the external goals but also in form; a form borrowed from the violent political acts that were affecting the Basque Country at the time. Assuming the role of an illegal act, for a while, EAE studied the museum's security conditions, created artist groups dedicated to specific missions, and tested and finally implemented a seamless operation that in the end allowed us to steal the sculpture within plain sight of the guards, take it out of the museum in a bag, and move it to the Bilbao City Hall, all of which was video-recorded.[7]

This mimicry with forms of violence (one might speculate whether it was a phenomenon related to the "aestheticization of the political" or rather of the "politicization of the aesthetic," according to Walter Benjamin's dichotomy) became increasingly insubstantial, as the violence was particularly acute in the Basque Country in

---

6. Another example of these performative acts was the "Storming of the Bilbao School of Fine Arts," conducted by Oteiza in 1979. Oteiza, with other people, took over the School of Fine Arts in Bilbao, demanding the immediate gathering in the courtyard of all teachers present at that time at the school. Oteiza asked for two witnesses from the students (I was one of them) and gave a speech full of threats (in a bullying style, which today would be considered unacceptable, but at that time we regarded as revolutionary) in which the teachers were urged to change the course of the curriculum and to establish a more direct link with Basque artists; otherwise they would have to face the consequences (implying some sort of violent action). The response was immediate, on November 8, two days after Oteiza's outbreak, the faculty sent a letter to the school's president's office stating a position aligned with that of Oteiza. The result was that the president accepted that Basque artists, even if they did not have academic qualifications to teach, would nonetheless be incorporated into the faculty of the School of Fine Arts.

7. The video *EAE. Acción el Museo* was edited in 2001, using the material recorded during the act and mixed with other materials taken from the media, all dating from 1983.

1984. That very year, Spain's governing Socialist Party (the PSOE) had intensified industrial rationalization. I remember vividly my own feelings as I crossed the Deusto bridge—the scene of daily confrontations between police and workers from the Euskalduna shipyard battling to save their jobs—every morning on my way to the Fine Arts School, contemplating the preparation of barricades, and returning early in the afternoon, passing with difficulty through those burning barricades and witnessing the clashes between the police and workers. This went on day after day. That same year, ETA killed a Socialist deputy, Enrique Casas, while the leader of the Basque nationalist left-wing political party Herri Batasuna and a practicing doctor, Santi Brouard, was shot dead at his surgery in Bilbao by the para-police GAL group. In these circumstances it is hardly surprising that most Basque artists at the time began to employ a "retreat to the barracks" mentality. In any other context it would seem interesting and even necessary to delve into the matter of violence in political art activism, but when produced in the heart of a real conflict and often with death as an outcome, one tended to separate poses from true attitudes.

In the mid-1980s, the art scene in Bilbao began to change as a result of one particular development. Some artists that had belonged to the EAE (Juan Luis Moraza, Maria Luisa Fernandez, Pello Irazu, and myself) along with a newcomer to Bilbao, Angel Bados, began a friendship and work relationship that would grow significantly in the years that followed. Out of this relationship came a sense of community of knowledge and experiences, quite different from classic artists' associations. Furthermore, all of us in this group had shared a common interest in minimalism, conceptual art, art as discourse, Joseph Beuys's social sculpture, and with such a background we were witnessing the cultural phenomenon of art-updating taking place in Spain at the time. As a consequence of this accelerated assimilation of artistic developments neglected in the decades of cultural isolation prior to the death of Franco, emerging trends—what was then understood as postmodern art—enjoyed an immediate and non-critical reception. This explains the profound impact of a first wave of the Italian Trans-Avant-Garde, German Neo-Expressionism, New American painting, British sculpture, and a second one of neo-pop-conceptualist postmodern attitudes linked to simulacra and appropriation.

From a theoretical point of view, we felt close to notions linking the idea of reality and that of linguistic mediation, in particular those issues related to the formal/logical analysis of language. From Saussure and Russian formalism, from Viktor Shklovsky and Roman Jakobson to Jan Mukarovsky's structuralism to Roland Barthes, Michel Foucault, Pierre Francastel, and Umberto Eco, such references led to a particular understanding of the art object and its social functions. One consequence we took out of all this was that the main commitment of the artist should not be toward what we were given in advance as reality, but rather toward the language "producing" reality; and therefore, what we made with the material artifact, and with its form, was more important than trying to control an effect on the social, which by definition is uncontrollable. While recognizing that for art to exist, it is essential that the artifact becomes an "aesthetic object," that is, an object anchored in the social, the effect does not depend on the proactive intentions aiming at such a situation, which are in any case vain, but on the proper handling of formal-material variables shaping the artifact itself.

During the first half of the 1980s, Expressionist positions prevailed in Spain, while thereafter that same decade, those oriented to "content" came to dominate. Consequently, the apparent formalism we defended unambiguously was, at best, irritating to Spanish art critics. In the first place, it referred back to formalizing moments of art practice against which the art of that moment was pronounced. Moreover, we were also trying nothing less than to reconsider formalism through exploiting, in a purely postmodern way, the figure of Oteiza (an artist considered as the epitome of formalism).

Any kind of a master-pupil relationship with Oteiza was suicidal. Basque and Spanish art is full of his disciples who in only a very few cases have exceeded mediocrity. Furthermore, Oteiza deftly handled a double standard: he was acquiescent and collaborative with those he considered mediocre, and terribly hard and daunting to those he respected. While he wrote ambiguous prologues for landscape painters or commercial sculptors, we were always dispatched with words like: "I still do not know why you are in art. Contemporary art is completed; what you call art is just entertainment, a popular art intended for the art market, real tasks are out; on education." For us, artists in their twenties who were not resigned to succumbing to such a lack of expectations, Oteiza's attitude made us stronger and, due to this, we had to recreate a different way of dealing with him; a way that had absolutely nothing to do with the Oedipal question and the so-often-invoked pressing need to kill the Father. It was rather something related to the "agonic," that is, confrontation as a form of self-creation, a struggle in which Oteiza—our own version of him—was used against Oteiza himself. When, years later, I read

Harold Bloom's *The Anxiety of Influence*,[8] I understood this better. In this work, Bloom, referring to poets—although I think it is also applicable to other artists—says that:

> poetic influence—when it involves two strong, authentic, poets—always proceeds by a misreading of the prior poet, an act of creative correction that is actually and necessarily, a misunderstanding. The history of the fruitful poetic influence, which is to say, the main tradition of Western poetry since the Renaissance, is a history of anxiety and a self-saving caricature, of distortion, of perverse, willful revisionism without which modern poetry as such could not exist.[9]

In fact, this strategy was not at all alien to Oteiza himself. In 1947, at the end of his Latin American tour, during which he had elaborated an aesthetic theory, and when he was about to resume his work as sculptor, he suffered the tremendous impact of Henry Moore's work. No doubt Oteiza was at that time a strong artist; an artist who had discovered another artist out of the blue—unfortunately (for him) a predecessor, even if just by a decade—with whom he shared too many things. The sculptor had to accept the tremendous blow produced by his work, but he also felt compelled to rebel against it. Oteiza inscribed not only Moore, but also Picasso, Alberto Sánchez, Mondrian, and Malevich, in a set of concerns corresponding to an intentional misreading of their work, at the end of which was Oteiza himself. This is not a genealogy of loans or influences, as these relationships are often interpreted, but rather a creative reinterpretation of their work that allowed him to define an experimental purpose—the annihilation of the statue and its conversion into pure energy—as something that, according to Oteiza, his predecessors had intuitively addressed, but only he, Oteiza, had carried out effectively.

It was clear that the relationship of our group with Oteiza was marked by a similar "agonic" strategy. In the first place, there was a need to introduce Oteiza into a tradition (both international and cosmopolitan) in which in fact he did not entirely belong. Somehow we tried to situate him "historically" beyond official history; we tried to operate from a specific standpoint: "as if" Oteiza were at the crucial place where we located him. But which place was this? Oteiza, an artist that no one knew internationally, was introduced by us, in this way, as a fundamental reference in the hinge between the

8. Bloom, *The Anxiety of Influence: A Theory of Poetry*.

9. Ibid., 30.

avant-garde of late-1940s and 1950s, and the new artistic behaviors of the 1960s and 1970s, between postwar formalisms and Art as Discourse, between the languages of form and those of politics, thereby establishing a link with the figure of Joseph Beuys. It is in this "misreading," introducing Oteiza in a semi-fictional historical situation,[10] wherein lies the origin of a practice to which we were fully committed. That practice later came to be called (by the media, not by us) New Basque Sculpture. There was, in the ideas associated with New Basque Sculpture, an implicit continuation of Oteiza's sculpture: making the sculpture that Oteiza did not make because he would not or could not do it. And make it from a perspective that was actually antithetical to Oteiza's own narration of it. We did not consider ourselves as disciples, nor even influenced by Oteiza; rather, our strategy consisted of going through the appropriation of some of his expressive modes (the opposition between instability and elements of stillness, for example) or of his best recognized images, like the "box", recreating Oteizian pieces but under new and bastard linguistic frames. These pieces exploited the counter-discourse of Oteiza's sculpture, that is, the vitalism shown in his handling of error, of exception, and the arbitrariness in his works as opposed to his presumed rigor. We also made our own return to some sources and references cited by Oteiza himself, such as, for example, Constructivism or Malevich, imagining parallel tracks of development through heteroclite stories.

Simultaneous to this process and much interwoven with it, intense work took place that culminated in 1988 in the first ever retrospective exhibition of Oteiza: *Oteiza. Propósito Experimental* (Oteiza: Experimental Proposition), which I curated. This exhibition came to be the climax of this process. It somehow established a canonical view on the sculptor's work resulting in fact from a process linked to the practice of the New Basque Sculpture. In such circumstances, Bloom's last revisionary ratio, "apophrades,"[11] comes into play: "The mighty dead return, but they return in our colors,

---

10. This fiction became somewhat factual, when, in 1983, Richard Serra first visited Bilbao and discovered, through me, the work of Oteiza. Thereafter, Serra expressed his admiration for Oteiza's work to the point of declaring himself, in a historic leap, heir to an artist whom he had known when the most important part of his career had been completed, and he was already an internationally recognized sculptor.

11. The six revisionary ratios are: *Clinamen* or "poetic misreading or misprision," *Tessera* or "completion and antithesis," *Kenosis* or "emptying out of the precursor," *Daemonization* or "counter-sublime," *Askesis* or "movement of self-purgation," and *Apophrades* or "the return of the dead."

and speaking in our voices, at least in part, at least in moments."[12] Our version of Oteiza, of his sculpture, prevailed over that of Oteiza's, who was too accustomed to representing himself to an extreme degree; so much so, indeed, that he felt the need to rebel against it. In the epilogue, which he himself wrote and which was included in the exhibition catalog, entitled *Postmodernism*, he says:

> I glimpsed in some cases something like hatred in the artist's work, for not having taking part in the creative adventure (of Modernism), but what I always recognize, and what explains postmodernism, is humor. Without humor, it would be offensive, so there will always be humor in the postmodern creator, for he/she knows that without copying, mixing, falsifying, destroying, and rebuilding . . . models of ancient and contemporary history, nothing can be done."[13]

Interestingly enough, this note is specifically aimed at our way of dealing with his work and in general at "postmodern" artists, but it should also be noted that, as a phenomenon, it is not too different to what he had to face in his "late modern" condition. His situation as an experimental artist in the epigones of historical avant-garde made him undertake, as a defense mechanism and in order to survive as an artist, a theory of "concluding," as if in the avant-garde there was an irresponsibly unfinished pending task he was willing to drive to a conclusion.

As Basque sculptors in the 1980s, we felt we embodied a triple "otherness" in the eyes of the general public. Firstly, by virtue of appearing Spanish in the international context; secondly, by the fact of appearing "too" Basque in the Spanish context; and finally, by not appearing "sufficiently" Basque enough in the Basque context (for the "Basque School" embodied Basqueness exclusively). This was not entirely new: since the 1960s and 1970s, there was a way of dealing with the "otherness" of Basque art by way of "autarky" that is, as self-sufficiency in cultural and artistic terms. In a second stage, during the 1980s, with New Basque Sculpture, we had an instrumental way of dealing with our own "otherness" by conquering a strategic non-site that was both excessive and insufficient, very Basque outside the Basque Country and not enough inside. I say it was a "non-site" because it was truly impossible for the general public to territorialize us — in the dual sense of subjecting us to a precise territory and also consuming us in a set of prefixed discursive

12. Bloom, *The Anxiety of Influence*, 141.
13. Oteiza, "Oteiza como epílogo," 270.

parameters. In the Basque Country, we were considered as "renegades" because we broke the silent pact of traditional autarky. Yet at the same time we embodied "Basqueness" from the external view, with destabilizing consequences that would come to fruition later in successive generations of Basque artists, who would have to deal with their identity in more complex terms (not only in terms of nation, but also in terms of gender, class, sexual preference, and so on).

The so-called New Basque Sculpture lasted just four years, between 1985 and 1988.[14] It was a necessarily transitional response at a time when everything was about to change; a solution for the artists, themselves part of the situation, who, after the experience, were better prepared to deal with new situations and realities. In fact, the real influence of this phenomenon did not occur at the time it took place, but instead during the following decade, the 1990s, through a social and pedagogical instrument called Arteleku. This institution, run by the Provincial Government of Gipuzkoa, was founded in Loiola, near Donostia-San Sebastian, in 1986. It was originally designed to offer workshops to artists in the traditional sense, providing them with equipment and technical assistance. However, very early on, Arteleku evolved organically, thanks to the contributions of the artists themselves as well as to the intelligent *laissez faire* policy of its director, Xanti Eraso, and it quickly became a reference point for the training of artists at a national and also international level. To make this development possible, the contribution of many artists and theorists (Basque, Spanish, and foreign) proved decisive, and significantly among them, those of us coming from New Basque Sculpture gave numerous seminars, courses, and workshops.[15]

Following the dispersion of our group, the deconstructive momentum (from Derrida and other authors), as well as a "textual" practice (via Barthes), which had been latent in previous works, assumed greater force—on each of us in different ways—as it opened us up to the incorporation of a wide variety of signs and ways of articulating, and also helped us focus more on issues regarding sub-

14. In 1988, at the time of its greatest professional success, the group dissolved. I went to live in London and then New York. Pello Irazu moved also to New York. Moraza went to Madrid, Maria Luisa Fernandez to Galicia, and Angel Bados stayed in Bilbao. The practice that identified us as a group disappeared.

15. Angel Bados gave two workshops, in 1989 and 1991; Juan Luis Moraza published several books and directed seminars in 1990, 1992, and 1993; Angel Bados and myself held two long-duration courses (lasting four and five months respectively), in 1994 and 1997, Maria Luisa Fernandez conducted one workshop in 1994, and Pello Irazu another in 1998.

jectivity, desire, and the critique of representation. In order to carry out such a project, it was important to approach certain texts by feminist theorists;[16] and indeed fundamental to explore the possibility of a more productive reading of Lacan's psychoanalysis.[17] In Lacan's work, besides an epistemological approach to understanding and interpreting reality, there is also an anthropological way of defining the human being beyond the clichés of humanism, which allows a renewed function for artistic activity through the use of these different levels of subjectivity in relation to images and structures. Besides, the question of desire was left open, in its capacity to structure and de-structure reality, and is treated by "rhizomatic" authors like Gilles Deleuze, George Guattari, and Jean-François Lyotard, as well as by a unique artist like Jean-Luc Godard.

I discussed all these matters at length with Angel Bados and many others over the months prior to our first course in Arteleku in 1994. We also defined our mode of operation that was characterized as "immersion." In addition to classes on theoretical issues and film screenings within a fixed schedule, both of us conducted separately two private conversations per day (one in the morning, one in the afternoon) with each of the participants, in a workflow beginning at 10 am and running through until 8 pm. Originally it was going to be a two-month course, but it had to be extended for two more months at the request of the participants. After completing the course, I wrote a text explaining the experience we had lived, entitled: *Arreglárselas sin el Padre* (Getting by without the Father).[18] Although everyone, considering the circumstances of the previous decade, immediately thought of Oteiza, my text had nothing to do with him. It really referred to the theoretical background of the course, which was supported mainly by films from the 1960s and 1970s; a period (exemplified by May 68, American Counterculture, the Underground movement, Situationism, and so forth) of

16. By Laura Mulvey, Julia Kristeva, Judith Butler, Luce Irigaray, and Elisabeth Groz, among others.

17. This reading was possible thanks to the application of Lacan's theory to the interpretation of popular culture made by authors like Slavov Zizek. Both Lacan and Julia Kristeva had been authors of reference for us, but always within the common framework of structuralism and post-structuralism. On this occasion, after their reinterpretation within the interdisciplinary context of cultural studies, their approaches appeared more linked to the everyday and to processes involved in the artistic activity and, therefore, more usable in this context.

18. "Aita gabe konpontzea /Arreglárselas sin el Padre / Getting by without the Father," in *Taller Ángel Bados-Txomin Badiola Tailerra*, 86–165.

annihilation of the Symbolic Father marked by the disrepute of the great ideological narratives. This was a situation after which we had to face up to a new reality, not only getting by without the Father, but also without the place 'he' left vacant. This has consequences in politics to the extent that it is becoming more and more difficult to identify sources of power, a power increasingly diluted both in the social fabric and even in the framework of subjectivity.

If the course at Arteleku was somewhat inspirational for a generation of artists, it was not only due to the novelty of its theoretical content, which the epochal sensitivity of the participants already embraced (issues related to subjectivity, feminism, sexual matters, deconstruction, among others). The important thing was that, as directors of the course, we offered them ways to deal with all these issues from an eminently practical point of view: from art itself; art not as a mere illustration of contents, but as a practice contemplating the unavoidable need of form; an inheritance whose originals lay, without question, in New Basque Sculpture. Following the artistic debate of the moment, in our view, it seemed necessary to subject the language of art to an ongoing critical review that could unravel the intricate maze of representation. But at the same time, this critique should entail an act of faith in art's own capabilities as technique, discarding the kind of "epistemological shame" traditionally associated with art practice, to the extent that art gets a sort of complex when confronted with other forms of knowledge (science, philosophy, psychology, sociology, anthropology, and so on). This act of faith could only be implemented by the artists themselves within an artistic community. Of course, communities, unlike associations, are not formed in an abstract manner; it is necessary for them to create the conditions in which they can naturally occur. In 1997, we imparted a second five-month course in Arteleku with similar characteristics and, as a result, the artistic community increased and was further intensified. Many of the most appreciated Basque artists today (including an art critic, a designer, and a dancer) attended these courses: Ana Laura Aláez (coming from a previous course given by Bados), Jon Mikel Euba, Itziar Okariz, Sergio Prego, Manu Muniateguiandikoetxea, Ibon Aranberri, Peio Aguirre, Gorka Eizagirre, Asier Mendizabal, Iñaki Garmendia, Xabier Salaberria, Abigail Lazkoz, Inazio Escudero, and Ion Munduate.

It is worth noting how this type of art grouping, whose main characteristic was precisely that of being a community, has established itself as distinctive of the general Basque art scene. In other parts of Spain, such as Catalonia for example, there are very powerful associations of artists, conceived to defend the interests of their members. However, in the Basque Country, either due to our cultural atavism to the inheritance of an alleged matriarchy, or to more mundane issues such as the effort some of us have put into it, reciprocal relationships between artists are closer to the idea of a "phratry" (brother/sisterhood). The current art community in the Basque Country tends to these archaic features. It is based on sharing work processes—whether technical, intellectual, or affective—and on getting involved in them, in some cases to incestuous levels, as demonstrated in the experience of the Proforma project.[19]

These matters make me reflect on the situation of young students attending the Fine Arts School today. I feel the pain of their demoralization: packed with technology but with no technique (here I mean "technique" as a consistent praxis, a way of dealing with intentions and results), having difficulty catching a glimpse of meaning in their own activity and therefore cynical in their behavior, leaning on the crutches of "the political" as mere content (whether social or anti-system movements, working class concerns, or personal issues such as gender awareness or sexual preferences). These are contents that function as surrogates for the meaning that they cannot find. In fact, the real problem is not so much about being unable to find meaning, but the reverse: finding quick meaning in the fashion of theses surrogates, something that usually proves to be frustrating in the long term.

I have always respected those people who, concerned with the "correct" shade of a color or the size of an element, can, through such an apparently inconsequential decision, call into question their own subjectivity and eventually transform it, while finding new ways of seeing and understanding. I think this attitude is as respectable from a political point of view as that of the so-called engaged artists. It would seem that such an approach could be naïve or even illegitimate, since the hegemony of counter-hegemony has established that it is unproductive from a social standpoint. I think the task of art must be separated from other responsibilities we undeniably have as citizens, and to be responsible to ourselves as artists, we have to get rid of complexes toward certain modes of sublimity. I

---

19. From January to June 2010, MUSAC (the Museum of Contemporary Art of Castille and León) hosted *Primer Proforma 2010. 30 exercises. 40 days. 8 hours per day,* an experiment in creating artistic projects and moving beyond conventional notions of exhibition and pedagogy. The artists Jon Mikel Euba, Sergio Prego, and myself locked ourselves up in our exhibitions at the museum for forty days, in order to develop together with fifteen volunteers a series of exercises to transform the works exhibited in front of the public.

strongly think that the fate of art will depend on that. Here I return to the beginning of this chapter, to my own dilemma regarding the commission for the Monument to the Victims of Terrorism—we have to choose and function either as artists or as citizens.

Many institutions dedicated to art and art education have forgotten that without love and respect for art—which does not imply evading any self-criticism no matter how fierce—neither art nor education is possible. Art institutions are very much obsessed with historicity, presenting art as an epiphenomenon of history and the artwork as a mere document whose value is only subject to ideological narrative. They forget that, although art is historical, as is any other human activity, it also goes against history. Art is imbued with a human will of transcendence that explains why works of the past, having lost their historical context, keep speaking to us in the language of today. Art and educational institutions seem designed to demoralize the young artist, while their mission should be the opposite; they should help artists to empower themselves in the specifics of their task. But, although any help is welcome, this is something one can only fully obtain from another artist. Jean Genet used to claim that there is no other moral authority but that of another artist's, and I totally agree with him. We artists must strengthen our ties and create our own institutions to regain control of our trade, both in terms of what concerns us as subjects in continuous transformation, revealing the conditions of the political, and in order to decide our proper mode of integration into the social fabric as citizens through the different political channels.

Bibliography

Groys, Boris. *The Total Art of Stalinism: Avant-Garde, Aesthetic Dictatorship, and Beyond.* Translated by Charles Rougle London: Verso, 1992.

Oteiza, Jorge. "Oteiza como epílogo: Utopia y fracaso del arte contemporáneo." In Propósito experimental. Madrid: N.P., 1988.

———. *Quosque tandem . . . ! ensayo de interpretación estética del alma vasca.* Donostia-San Sebastián: Editorial Auñamendi, 1963.

6

The Transmission of Values in Basque Art throughout the Twentieth Century

Ismael Manterola

In a recent lecture for the course entitled "The Transmission of Basque Cultural Activities" at the Faculty of Humanities and Educational Sciences at Mondragon University, I reflected on the passing of certain values in Basque art during the course of the twentieth century, which to some extent have filtered through into the twenty-first century. In this chapter, I analyze the question of this transmission of "Basque art," which, in the opinion of some scholars, was cut short in the last few years of the twentieth century (and specifically during the 1980s), thereby breaking a chain that had barely lasted one hundred years.

In my view, there are two culminating moments in the development and social integration of Basque art. The first was the attempt to modernize art in the Basque Country in the early twentieth century, in particular on the part of those artists who were members of the Basque Artists' Association. The second was the launch of the Basque School groups during the 1960s in a context that, under the dictatorship of General Francisco Franco, was hostile to modernity and freedom.

More recently, artistic activity in the Basque Country has become integrated into international trends, with the result that some of the defining characteristics of the two culminating moments just identified no longer apply with the same force. Nonetheless, as I will argue, this heritage has not been abandoned entirely.

The First Concept of Modernity

Modern art emerged in the Basque Country around 1876, coinciding with the abolition of the *fueros* (a body of consuetudinary law that guaranteed a high level of decision-making authority for the Basque Country) and the implementation of the Restoration Monarchy in Spain. A defining moment in this shift was the decision by two artists who had assimilated modernity in different forms of expression elsewhere to establish themselves in the Basque Country: Dario de Regoyos in Donostia-San Sebastián in 1884 and Adolfo Guiard in Bilbao in 1886. Regoyos had belonged to the thriving artists' colony in Brussels, whose members belonged to the *L'Essor* (Progress) and *Les XX* (The twenty) groups. Guiard, meanwhile, had left Bilbao for Paris to continue his studies, rejecting a more conventional and academic education in Rome, as was often recommended at the time to young artists.

Both were relatively young when they returned more or less permanently to the Basque Country. They introduced new forms and ideas of modernity to a Basque society that had not previously shown signs of being an important source of artistic production, but which was in full economic and social progress. The avenues opened up by Regoyos and Guiard became more firmly established with the next generation of artists such as Ignacio Zuloaga, Manual Losada, and Francisco Iturrino, all of whom clearly opted for Parisian modernity. The result was the emergence around 1910 of a generation of younger artists who would form a group that aimed to create a certain type of art responding to a new social context. Many were members of the Basque Artists' Association, founded in 1911, and whose membership ranged from architects to designers, painters, and sculptors. Spanning different generations, in addition to Regoyos and Guiard, the association included younger artists born in the last decade of the nineteenth century such as Aurelio Arteta and Gustavo Maeztu. Overall, there is evidence of shared intentions and a major desire to influence Basque society.

This loosely organized project[1] can be referred to as Basque *Novecentismo*. It marked a desire to create an independent, specific art for the twentieth century, rooted in a sense of place and modern social and economic reality.[2] As members of the Basque Artists' Association, the most active among them (Aurelio Arteta, Alberto

1. It was perhaps less organized than the Catalan *Noucentisme* cultural movement, but not lacking in common interests and similar ideological and aesthetic programs.

2. Moya, *Orígenes de la vanguardia artística en el País Vasco*, 14.

Arruda, Antonio Guezala, and Gustavo Maeztu) aimed to bring together all the artists who had committed to Post-Impressionist Parisian modernity (many of them spent the early years of the twentieth century in Paris, usually after having been awarded grants by Provincial Council of Bizkaia). They shared a strong anti-academic consciousness while being aware of a particular tradition of Spanish classical art as a source of renewing academic art in its own right, an element that differentiated their concept of modernity from the avant-garde concepts emerging in Paris at this time.

Added to all the above, a strong link to the notion of place[3] would lead them to set about creating a style of painting that honors the traditions and themes of the Basque Country. Far from nineteenth-century Basque *costumbrismo* (the literary or pictorial interpretation of local everyday life) in which local issues became anecdotes and a mere excuse to represent the picturesque variety of certain exotic locations, the artists attempted to portray the fundamental values of the Basque countryside and coastline as an alternative to the standardization and materialism of the new capitalist economic system that was being established in the cities, particularly in Bilbao.

The artists' identification with place is clearly expressed in the writings of the period, which highlight the need for every artist to respond to the place where he or she lives, making it clear that an artist cannot carry out an aesthetic project without responding to his or her roots.[4] This sense of belonging was shared with other early twentieth-century Novecentista movements such as the Catalan *Noucentisme,* which insisted on the need for culture to have a strong social outreach unconstrained by nineteenth-century attitudes of art for art's sake. Art in the previous century was noted for its aesthetic autonomy. In contrast, the new century called for art

---

3. Another difference between avant-gardism and more conservative elements of modernity was its internationalism and the attention paid to location. For example, while commenting on an exhibition by Gustavo de Maeztu in London in 1920, P. G. Konody said: "Maeztu is one of the most modern artists in his country. He has victoriously withstood the trend emanating from Paris, which tends toward the internationalization of art . . . It is apparent that this artist firmly resists everything related to a modern ephemeral whim, and shows reverence for tradition."

4. "Art seen outside the place where it was created, appears to lose some of its aesthetic energy: offspring from a particular landscape and historical breeding, undoubtedly specifies the framework for the landscape and breeding to spontaneously declare their secret". Juan de la Encina, *La trama del Arte Vasco* (Facsimile edition, Fine Arts Museum, Bilbao, 1998).

that was participatory, passing on values that supported (primarily urban) coexistence and that was expressed in a modern language that was comprehensible (in this respect, too, in opposition to the avant-gardists) and that encouraged mutual recognition through symbolic images or images that were easily inserted into the social imaginary.[5]

This social consciousness can be seen in the importance given during the early part of the twentieth century to public artworks. In urban environments, artists from this period attempted to promote public projects such as frescos in places accessible to the majority of the population, applying art techniques classified as artisan architecture and organizing public exhibitions to make art accessible to as many sections of society as possible. They also pushed for the creation of cultural infrastructure that would ensure public outreach such as museums, concert halls, and theatres—ultimately platforms for disseminating modern art in order to raise awareness and integrate cultural activity in the city, far removed from the elitism of nineteenth-century century bourgeois culture.

The 1930s: Unsuccessful Avant-Gardism

During the 1930s, a new political climate and a new generation, accompanied by the slow assimilation of the European avant-garde in Spain (particularly surrealism), opened up new avenues of opportunity for Basque artists. The crisis that hit Bilbao during the 1920s prompted the art scene to move to Donostia-San Sebastián, where groups of artists emerged as a driving force behind exhibitions and other activities to disseminate not only current Basque art but also the most avant-garde European developments and trends represented by young artists responding to competitions for emerging artists promoted by the Provincial Council of Gipuzkoa (Guipúzcoa).

The younger artists started employing bolder concepts and producing artwork influenced by surrealism, as seen in the work of Juan Cabanas Erauskin, Carlos Ribera, and Nicolás Lekuona. The latter exhibited his work along with Jorge Oteiza and Narkis Balenziaga, forming an active trio not only in the area of plastic arts, but also as instigators of artistic activities and theorists of ideas that would resurface later in the 1940s and 1950s.

In contrast with the generation of the Basque Artists' Association, which promoted a conservative concept of modernity that did

5. Manterola, *Hermes y los pintores vascos de su tiempo.*

not break with tradition, Oteiza and Lekuona marked a first step toward the creation of an avant-garde movement in the Basque Country. Oteiza sought to promote a Basque cultural renaissance, based not so much on the tradition of Spanish art of the previous centuries, but rather on a reputed Basque aesthetic substrate with prehistoric or ancestral roots. In this sense, Oteiza went to the very heart of some of the main European avant-garde trends that proposed avant-gardism as the end to an open cycle in prehistory that had been closed by western classical art.

The departure of Oteiza and Balenziaga for the Americas in 1935 and the outbreak of the Spanish Civil War the following year cut short any chance of avant-garde art flourishing in the Basque Country. Following the victory of Franco's troops and his subsequent dictatorship (1939–1975), the implementation of a standard national, Catholic, and academic aesthetic by the new Franco state confined any interesting artistic accomplishment to the side of the victors, notably avant-garde artists related to the Falange, the official party of state.

A Second Opportunity for Avant-Gardism: The 1960s

Impracticable though it was during the post-civil war years to strive toward something comparable to the achievements of the early part of the century, Oteiza played a seminal role on his return to Spain in instigating attitudes that, in turn, gave new impetus to careers and tendencies that had been cut short by the war. He was not alone in his desire to promote a return to the normality of modern art by means of linking up with the prewar art scene, getting up-and-coming young artists to be more involved and restoring contact with links abroad. Experiments such as those carried out by the Studio Gallery in Bilbao bear witness to a broader desire (weak compared to the official art, but essential for what was to come later) to shake up the downtrodden cultural landscape of the postwar period that had left the Basque Country materially and culturally impoverished.

An unusual and highly important project in the decade immediately after the Spanish Civil War, both because of the risk involved in its undertaking and because of its unusual setting in a twentieth-century context, was the construction and decoration of the Basilica of Arantzazu, near Oñati in Gipuzkoa, in the 1950s. Bringing many artists together to work on a symbolic project from the perspective of Basque culture, it was a source of confrontation and controversy among both conservative and liberal social sectors. And the ferment to which it gave rise led eventually to the creation of the Basque School Movement in the 1960s.

The Basque School groups became known in the public arena when their manifesto was published in April-May 1966 in Donostia-San Sebastián. Once again, here we see an attempt to set up a modern art project for the Basque Country as a whole that was avant-garde in nature and with similarities to the project previously promoted by the Basque Artists' Association, but also with obvious differences. One of these was the level of organization involved in the Basque School Movement, which involved drafting a manifesto and a program designed to modernize the Basque art scene from an avant-garde perspective. Another difference was the presence of a single figure who acted as project leader and driving force behind the scheme: Oteiza.

While the Basque Artists' Association brought together artists from different trends using one single selection criteria, namely an identification with modernity based on Impressionism, the Basque School Movement called for a commitment to turn-of-the-century avant-garde movements. However, the Emen (Here) group from Bizkaia did not, in principle, have any clear selection criteria and therefore in theory artists who followed completely different trends in the plastic arts could come together, from the young with more ground-breaking ideologies to artists from previous generations with artwork linked to a reformist trend of Spanish pre-civil war figurative art.

There was, however, some common ground between these two projects, that of the early twentieth century and that of the 1960s: namely, an awareness of the need for artists to join together to make a difference in the environment in which they lived by engaging that very society. In both cases, the artists involved commented publicly on the shortcomings that existed in modern art at significant junctures for the Basque economy. The lack of proportionality between economic and cultural development in the early twentieth century was mirrored in the 1960s when a second wave of industrial growth shook traditional Basque society.

The 1960s movement involved organizing groups of artists by historical territories (chiefly Araba, Bizkaia, Gipuzkoa) with a view to creating a kind of federation of groups, which would ultimately become the Basque School Movement. These organizations were intended to serve as a social stimulus for modern art by promoting it and creating a safety net for the solo artist struggling to break into a conservative social environment hostile to modern artwork and uninformed about the most modern trends. Another feature common to both movements was their advocacy of social involvement on the part of artists.

One of the most interesting initiatives in the private sector, promoted by some members of the Gaur (Today) group, was the creation of the Barandiarán Gallery under the heading "Composite Art Exhibition Producer." Other 1960s initiatives aimed at widening the scope of art and making it more readily available to the Basque public included setting up public exhibitions outside the conventional and official settings for art, such as organizing exhibitions in cultural centers or *pelota* (handball) courts[6] in rural communities that would otherwise not have access to galleries and exhibition halls traditionally located in cities.

In pursuit of the idea of the artist being able to have direct contact with the public, the manner in which art was displayed was not to be limited to a mere exhibition of works of art in a place where the public came to look at them, but rather the artists would provide an explanation about the work to help the public understand the art on display. In this regard, the approach of the Estampa Popular (Popular print) groups, who preferred to exhibit in places where it was assured the public would engage with their art and where they could present their work directly to viewers and potential buyers, was crucial, because many members of the Bizkaia (Vizcaya) group were also members of the Basque School Emen.[7]

From a more popular perspective, musicians, painters, sculptors, architects, and writers created groups and occasional shows in which they were all involved: for example, as in the case of the cultural collective *Ez dok Amairu*, which included singers, writers, and artists.[8] Other interdisciplinary projects included the *Argia* dance group, the *Jarrai* theater company, and—perhaps the most interesting popular initiative of all—the filming of *Ama Lur* (Mother Earth), a documentary film directed by Fernando Larruquert and Nestor Basterretxea and funded through public donations.[9]

Finally, a third feature that the Basque School Movement groups had in common with Basque *Novecentismo* was their com-

---

6. In the absence of cultural infrastructure in villages across the Basque Country, Basque pelota courts became venues that hosted almost all cultural activities such as concerts, plays, and even exhibitions.

7. The preference of these artists to express themselves through the medium of engraving gets to the very heart of notions associated with popularization, anti-elitism, and the widespread dissemination of art, because this form is easy to reproduce and can be sold at affordable prices.

8. Remigio Mendiburu designed the group's logo.

9. The film raised some four thousand anonymous donations.

mitment to transferring knowledge. Both groups demonstrated a tremendous interest in art education. In theory, the ultimate goal of the Basque School group was to set up a Basque University in Pamplona-Iruñea by way of concluding the project that would have visited all Basque provincial capitals: in Oteiza's words, "it is our intention at the Basque School that Basque artists should establish our university and make Pamplona our cultural capital of the Basque Country."[10] Ultimately this project was never realized, but Oteiza and some of his collaborators (especially the artist Agustin Ibarrola) pushed forward their idea of creating an educational system to spread their ideas. These led, among other things, to the creation of the Deba School of Art in 1969. But the most interesting educational experiments were directed at children, viewed as the future custodians of art, and especially by the artists Jose Antonio Sistiaga and Esther Ferrer.

The assimilation of certain stylistic signatures that were created, in particular by Eduardo Chillida, became an indication of a certain kind of "Basque style" that, though difficult to define, has become unmistakable when it comes to Basque graphic art and sculpture from the 1960s onward. Even without a clear understanding of what some of the graphic art produced during those years was based on, a quick visual inspection identifies them as Basque.[11]

From the Grand Finale of the 1970s to the New Basque Sculpture of the 1980s

The early 1970s witnessed a further change in the development of artistic expression in the Basque Country. "Grand Finale of Experimental Artistic Practice," the title of an exhibition on the 1972 Pamplona-Iruñea Encounters that was held at the Reina Sofía Museum in Madrid in 2009–2010, clearly reflects this. Associative tendencies, though they continued, were weakened by increasing artistic individualism and a propensity to fragmentation and confrontation that had been the hallmark of previous years. Additionally, the particularly conflictive political situation in the Basque Country, despite Spain's return to democracy, posed other challenges for art. Trends in the 1980s pointed to a crisis surrounding the issue of identity that had hitherto been a pressing topic in art. A weakening in group affiliation may also have contributed to a progressive iso-

---

10. Oteiza, "Notes to the Third Edition," *Quosque Tandem...!* .

11. The work of Ibon Aranberri entitled *Horizons* (2001–2007) and the work by Asier Mendizabal entitled *Hard Edge* (2011) emphasize this.

lation of artists in relation to demands for social commitment, in contrast to the integration achieved in previous years.

Such trends coincided with a more generalized convergence of Basque and Spanish art with international art movements. Spain was branching out into an international context in an environment of apparent political, social, and cultural normalization that paved the way for a shift from a socially or politically committed art to an art that was more interested in the aesthetic aspects and art itself. The creation of a Faculty of Fine Arts within the University of the Basque Country and a cultural policy specific to the autonomous Basque region in the 1980s did little to counter trends that had already begun to appear in the second half of the 1970s.

In such a context, it is difficult to talk about continuance or transmission of values. Aside from a few exceptions, the artistic activity of the 1980s was largely based on assumptions opposed to the values of the 1960s and the early 1900s. For example, individualism became generally more attractive than collectivism; internationalism and cosmopolitanism[12] enjoyed more appeal than an art responding to identity problems; and autonomous art values were held in higher esteem than those associated with social engagement.

Despite these trends, nonetheless, a number of young artists did not lose sight of what the preceding generation of artists offered them, continuing (in particular on a theoretical level) to try and produce art that was both integrated internationally and also specifically Basque. As a group of artists associated with the Faculty of Fine Arts at the University of the Basque Country and subsequently classified as New Basque Sculpture, they pursued the constructivist rigor of the sculptor Oteiza and his aesthetic and social commitment, while at the same time abandoning the production of objects to focus on theory and an interest in the aesthetic education of society.

While the New Basque Sculpture artists ignored the Basque identity-based problems of the Basque School Groups in favor of asserting their international and cosmopolitan vocation, they still showed a particular interest in creating and promoting art in the Basque Country. They were still concerned that the place where they came from or where they worked should have an artistic life on a par with the rest of the world.

In an effort to build partnerships, some artists associated with the New Basque Sculpture, along with others who were not part of this movement, created an association called Euskal Artisten

12. Perhaps it would be more accurate to speak in terms of an emphasis on different identities, such as racial or sexual identities.

Elkartea (The Basque Artists' Association) in 1983. Some of its members have since served as a bridge between Oteiza's ideas and the new generations. In particular, Angel Bados, Txomin Badiola, and Juan Luis Moraza conducted theoretical and practical work that asserted the need to find a solid foundation for art. Using Oteiza's formalism as a basis, they also referred to international trends such as minimalism to introduce problems related to conceptual art as well as some postmodern theoretical trends and Lacanian psychoanalytic theories. All this resulted in artworks that integrated very neat, formal structures with materials and forms that echoed Oteiza's work, along with materials linked to more experimental trends, supporting complex conceptual content specific to the international debate.

In the late 1990s and early 2000s, some members of the New Basque Sculpture movement were acknowledged for setting the standard for young artists as a result of their work in the University of the Basque Country's Faculty of Fine Arts;[13] and also in the contemporary art center Arteleku,[14] where Txomin Badiola and Angel Bados taught two courses during the summers of 1995 and 1997. These courses served as a platform for these two sculptors to convey their ideas and practices to the younger generations, producing interesting results as we have seen in the careers of some of the artists who attended the courses, such as Ibon Aranberri, Asier Mendizabal, and Iñaki Garmendia. These are members of a younger generation that has, in varying degrees, inherited certain values that have been at the fore in the art world since the beginning of the twentieth century. These include concern for the role of the artist in society, the balance between the local and the international, and the artist's commitment to the place where he or she works. In creating and dismantling myths, in their commitment to public art and to the balance between being an individual and being a member of a group, as well as in their interest in formal experimentation as a basis for a solid conceptual discourse and awareness, they ultimately form a link in the chain that binds a strong artistic tradition together and that can now be passed on to future generations.

---

13. Angel Bados was Professor of Sculpture in the Faculty of Fine Arts at the University of the Basque Country during the 1990s and 2000s until his retirement in 2008.

14. An Art Center founded in Loiola, a neighborhood of Donostia-San Sebastián, by the Provincial Council of Gipuzkoa in 1986.

Bibliography

Manterola, Ismael. *Hermes y los pintores vascos de su tiempo*. Bilbao: Diputación foral de Bizkaia, 2006.

Moya, Adelina. *Origenes de la vanguardia artística en el País Vasco: Nicolas Leku Ona y su tiempo*. Madrid: Electa, 1994

Oteiza, Jorge. "Notes to the Third Edition," *Quosque Tandem...! ensayo de interpretación estética del alma vasca* Third edition. Donostia-San Sebastián: Hordago, 1975.

Encina, Juan de la, *La trama del Arte Vasco*. Facsimile edition. Bilbao: Fine Arts Museum, 1998.

7

The Politics of Art in the Rural Inland of the French Basque Country: The Case of the Cultural Association Haize Berri

Zoe Bray

This chapter looks at Haize Berri, a cultural association active in the rural French Basque Country from the 1980s to 2009, as a means to reflect on the different understandings of art and culture and their political implications in the particular political context of this region. Haize Berri, whose name means 'New Wind' in Euskara (the Basque language), had the ambition of bringing culture and art to the rural interior of the French Basque Country. It was innovative in offering the area's population a rich array of artistic and social initiatives. Thanks to the participation of some prominent figures in the art world of the Basque Country, Haize Berri was at the heart of a cultural renaissance in the region and came to be known well beyond its locality.

However, both despite and because of these successes, Haize Berri was also the focus of local political controversy. The founders of Haize Berri had a Basque cultural agenda and saw themselves as a grass-roots organization, acting autonomously and independently of French state institutions. As such, it somewhat disturbed the local

* I wish to thank all interviewees cited in this article. I am grateful to Prof. Sandra Ott, Nicholas Bray, Josette Dacosta, and Dr. Christian Thauer for reviews of earlier versions of this text. Research for this article was made possible thanks to the funding from the Center for Basque Studies's quasi endowment fund and a grant from Eusko Ikaskuntza Iparralde, during 2012 and 2013. An early version of this paper was published with *BOGA: Basque Studies Consortium Journal* (Vol. 1, Issue 2, 2014) as "Bringing 'New Wind' to the Rural Interior of the French Basque Country: The Association 'Haize Berri' and the Politics of Culture."

political establishment and became a source of disputes relating to local identity politics and culture. The case of Haize Berri serves as a lens through which to explore the politics of culture and the role of art in drawing the boundaries of collective identity, particularly in the context of the Basque Country, marked by conflict over different definitions of national and regional identity and belonging.

Nationalism is not only a political but also a social and cultural project.[1] Competing concepts of nationalism and, correspondingly, different notions of identity create an environment in which anything may have political significance. This is no exception with art. Special significance may be conferred on artistic production as an element of national identity. Since identity is a contested and ever-evolving concept, different social and political factions in a politically contested region appreciate different artworks and artists in different ways.[2] This is also very much the case for Basque identity. While the importance given to art for Basque identity has been explored by some scholars,[3] researchers have not focused much on how the different understandings of local, regional, and national identity in the Basque Country clash when it comes to relating with art. Furthermore, the particular case of the French Basque Country is notably understudied, in quite a different context to the Spanish side, which tends to be the main focus of researchers when studying the Basque Country (as is the case of the three sources cited in note 2).

This chapter begins with a brief introduction to the cultural and political boundaries of nationalism in the Basque Country, and explains the particularities of the French side. I then introduce Haize Berri, describing some of its activities in the context of local social and political dynamics. Then the chapter draws some conclusions about the specific importance that Haize Berri gave to 'culture' and 'art', and on the role of art and culture in the context of identity politics in the Basque Country.

The Social and Political Context of Haize Berri

Over the course of the twentieth century, the combination of French centralizing policies and rural economic decline led to decreasing use of Euskara in the French Basque Country, henceforth referred

1. Billig, *Banal Nationalism*. I make this same argument in "Basque Nationalism at a Political Crossroad" and *Living Boundaries*.

2. Gell, *Art and Agency*; Van Laar and Diepeveen, *Active Sights*.

3. MacClancy, *Contesting Art*; Guasch, *Arte e ideologia en el Pais Vasco*; Arribas, *Cuarenta años de arte Vasco*.

to as the Pays Basque. People increasingly favored French over Euskara as the expression of the more prestigious French identity.[4] Modernity was associated with the French-speaking elite, while Euskara was largely confined to the rural and traditional world and the private sphere. Until the 1970s, there was little concept of Basque modernity as a context within which the Basque language and a Basque identity could compete with French. Basque themes could be exploited as folklore but were deprived of political meaning.

Until the 1980s, mobilization in the Pays Basque was absorbed in the localistic form of politics known in France as the *notables*, based on the local implantation of political brokers and clientelistic networks.[5] The notables included representatives of the church and the state, in the form of the priest, the municipal secretary, the schoolteacher, and elected officials. Their role in these traditional networks was to mediate between the political center of power, in this case the seat of national government in Paris, and the locality of their power base, by bringing back a share of central resources.[6] Administrative politics cut across historic and cultural boundaries: the Pays Basque forms part of a culturally diverse *département*, the Pyrénées Atlantiques (Atlantic Pyrenees), which in turn is part of a larger and equally culturally arbitrary region, Aquitaine. In contrast with the predominantly industrial economy of the Spanish Basque Country, Euskadi, the Pays Basque has been more dependent on tourism and agriculture. A lack of educational infrastructures, combined with a relative paucity of job opportunities, has meant that a significant proportion of young people have had to leave the Pays Basque to study or find employment.

Modern Basque nationalism only emerged as a social and political force in the Pays Basque in the 1960s.[7] Much of its inspiration came from the Spanish side of the border, fuelled by the Basque militants who had fled Franco's Spain and taken refuge on the French side.[8] The influence of these Spanish Basque dissidents on the political climate in the French Basque Country was limited, as they were often treated with suspicion by the majority of the local population who considered them negatively as Spanish, foreign, and Communists.[9] Some young people nonetheless began to reflect

4. Oronos, *Le mouvement culturel Basque. 1951–2001.*

5. Bidart, *Société, politique, culture en Pays Basque.*

6. Jaureguiberry, *Questions nationale et mouvements sociaux en Pays Basque.*

7. Jacob, *Hills of Conflict.*

8. Peio and Jon Etcheverry-Ainchart, *Le mouvement Enbata.*

9. Izquierdo, *Le Pays Basque en France.*

on their situation as part of a culturally and linguistically distinct area marginalized from the rest of France, and to see the French government as deliberately keeping the Pays Basque in a state of "third worldishness."[10]

The first organized group of modern Basque nationalists in the Pays Basque was created in 1960 under the name of Enbata.[11] A few years later, following a model launched in the Spanish Basque Country over a decade earlier, a few parents wishing to give their children a Basque-language education opened an independent school, known in Basque as *ikastola*, and formed an association, *Seaska* (meaning 'cradle'), to provide funding and administrative support for it and help create more *ikastolak*.[12] In 1975, a group of Basque nationalist youths also set up Iparretarrak,[13] a militant organization modeled on the violent Basque separatist organization ETA (Euzkadi ta Askatasuna, Basque Country and Freedom), active in Spain since the 1960s. Iparretarrak claimed responsibility for a series of attacks on French government offices and tourist trade initiatives. Their militant actions culminated in the early 1980s with a series of dramatic events involving the death of militants and police officials, as well as a few people mistaken as targets.[14] Tensions were increased by the actions of the secret Spanish paramilitary organization GAL,[15] which engaged in shootings and assassinations of ETA activists hiding on French soil.

At the same time, French governmental policies regarding the peripheral regions of the French state were changing under the presidency of François Mitterrand who had promised decentralization.[16] Actions were initiated to allow regional councils to exercise some degree of budgetary autonomy, in particular in the areas of local development and culture.[17] However, this process of decentralization in the distribution of power followed formal channels that, in the Pays Basque, remained in the hands of the established elite.[18]

---

10. Collins, *The Basques*, 121.

11. It was originally called Embata. See also Izquierdo, *Le Pays Basque en France*, 123.

12. The suffix 'k' marks the plural in Basque.

13. Iparretarrak means 'Those of the North' in Basque.

14. Bidegain, *Iparretarrak*.

15. GAL stands for Grupos Antiterroristas de Liberación, which is Spanish for Antiterrorist Liberation Groups. It was active during the 1980s, operating on the French side of the border thanks to the connivance of the French authorities. Several members of Spain's then Socialist government were later proven to have had links with this organization.

16. Wangermée and Gournay, *La politique culturelle de la France*.

17. "Cultural Policy in France."

18. Bidart, *Société, politique, culture en Pays Basque*.

As a result, French Basque nationalists mobilized against the perceived internal colonialism of the French state in the Pays Basque. They did so by promoting grassroots economic development. At village level, younger people with a budding Basque consciousness began organizing alternative networks, coordinating activities promoting Basque nationalism, and engaging in contacts with the Spanish Basque Country.[19] They experimented with different styles of music, singing in Basque, and launching concerts and festivals. Breaking away from older militants seen as too old-fashioned, who were more concerned with the preservation of Basque culture and language in terms of immutable traditions, they called instead for a focus on urban problems and the current challenges faced by young people. They also adopted a strategy of noncooperation with state military authorities that was thriving on the Spanish side of the frontier—*insumisoa,* the refusal by young men to fulfill national conscription requirements.[20]

Until the 1990s, the local population was broadly divided between the minority involved in these various initiatives, often self-identified as *abertzaleak,* meaning Basque patriots in Euskara, and the majority, who believed all this was mere trouble-making, and who favored a continued political and social order closely linked with the French institutional establishment. While this conservative majority entertained a notion of Basque identity that was fixed and unquestionable—one is Basque simply because one's ancestors are Basque—the *abertzaleak* minority urged a more active approach to identity: one is Basque because one wants to be, irrespective of origins. For this group, the important thing is to speak Euskara and to identify with a Basque national project.[21] In this atmosphere, political engagement and personal expressions of identity were often interlinked. Xavier Gizard, who provided legal and institutional advice to set up Haize Berri, recalled: "If you were at all in favor of developing Basque culture, or some kind of autonomous grassroots initiative, you were immediately tagged as *Enbatiste*, sometimes even as a terrorist."[22] *Abertzaleak* could be found involved in a wide range of Basque cultural initiatives, as Gabi Aguerre, for many years a member of the Haize Berri executive, recalled. "It was pretty much always the same people—those who had their children in the *ikastolak* were also teaching Basque, or were in some alternative local development cooperative, or in the local self-funded radios, or one of the grassroots political

19. Jacob, *Hills of Conflict*.

20. Ahedo Gurrutxaga, *The Transformation of National Identity in the Basque Country of France, 1789–2006*.

21. Bray, *Living Boundaries*.

22. Xavier Gizard, telephone interview, July 3, 2012.

movements."[23] Many of these initiatives drew inspiration or support from similar activities on the Spanish side of the Basque Country, and because of this, were negatively seen by the conservative population as a foreign influence, Spanish and pro-ETA.[24] Given that the violence of ETA was the main protagonist of the (negative) international news on Basque nationalism, this population tended to associate local *abertzale* activities as mere trouble-making.[25]

If Haize Berri was also relegated by a large sector of public opinion to this negative camp, it was due to the involvement of its main founders in *abertzale* activities. Eñaut Larralde, the first president of Haize Berri, was a famous singer in the Basque Country, often performing alongside *Ez Dok Amairu,* a collective of singers and musicians who explored new musical expressions in Euskara in the Spanish Basque Country during the years of Franco's dictatorship and thus represented a Basque cultural reaffirmation with nationalist goals. Among other grassroots initiatives, Larralde had helped support the first *ikastola* in the area, marking a clear breach with the local custom of sending one's children to either a local French state school, or a school run by a Catholic religious organization. A self-identified *abertzale*, he was also suspected of sheltering individuals linked to ETA during the 1980s.[26]

Daniel Arbeletche, a co-founder of Haize Berri and a subsequent president, was also an *ikastola* parent and an active participant in other grassroots initiatives in Euskara, as were most of the members of the executive board of Haize Berri. He owned (and still does) a bar and hotel in Izura (Ostabat), and broke with local convention by having the name of his establishment written in Basque rather than the usual French. Later, José Perez, who was hired by Haize Berri to run its operations, was one of the first young men to benefit from the official status of conscientious objector by working for an association or social institution as an alternative to doing military service. He was a punk rock fan from the suburbs of the city of Baiona (Bayonne), who had been brought up speaking French but had learnt Euskara as a condition of his employment. As such,

---

23. Gabi Aguerre, telephone interview, July 3, 2012.

24. Telephone interviews with Gabi Aguerre and Xavier Gizard, plus four other villagers (names withheld upon request). July 2012.

25. Ibid. "Metteurs de bombes" (French for 'people who put bombs') was a common derogatory term used by local critics of *abertzales*, which I also often heard used during the 1990s.

26. This information was gathered from talking with various local inhabitants. The suspicion was later confirmed to be true. I choose here to retain the anonymity of these sources.

he cut a peculiar figure in the rural environment of Izura. Through such challenges to local conservative social and political norms, Haize Berri, right from its early days, was tainted as political.

Haize Berri

The birth of Haize Berri as part of a general grassroots movement in favor of Basque identity coincided in the early 1980s with a shift in French institutional policies to support limited local development initiatives.[27] After long negotiations, Basque activists had succeeded in 1984 in setting up a cultural center for the Pays Basque, the Centre Culturel du Pays Basque (CCPB). This had the institutional role of advising on Basque cultural policy-making and redeploying state and regional funds to the area. Under a special institutional contract, the Contrat de Pays, funds were to be redistributed locally for cultural projects. Municipal councils and local associations were expected to work together to spend this money. In Lower Navarre (one of the three provinces that make up the Pays Basque), a group of individuals joined together to found Haize Berri as the cultural center for the area. In the neighboring provinces of Zuberoa (Soule) and Lapurdi (Labourd), other associations, respectively named Uhaitzea and Eihartzia, were set up to serve as their cultural centers. Haize Berri stood out among them, though, for the strong desire of its founders to work autonomously of institutions and to make the promotion of art one of its main objectives.

After much negotiation with local officials, the cultural center was finally launched in the village of Izura in 1983. Neighboring bigger municipalities had vied to have the cultural center in their own locality, attracted by its prospects as a source of funding, and had proposed other associations to set it up that were not connected with the *abertzale* movement. Haize Berri finally won the day thanks to a handful of local influential political arbitrators who were sympathetic to the *abertzale* cause, particularly from the CCPB.

While Haize Berri enjoyed institutional support under the umbrella of the Contrat de Pays, however, its beginning was not smooth. The mayor of Izura at the time is reported to have stated that he could not see the use of a cultural center in his village.[28] Indeed the idea of investing money and energy in 'culture' and 'art' was incom-

27. Itçaina, "Appartenances linguistiques, identités collectives et pratiques culturelles en Pays Basque," 79–80; Oronos, *Le mouvement culturel Basque*.

28. Interviews with local inhabitants. Names withheld.

prehensible to many of the villagers for whom such things were quite foreign to their daily rural lives. Beyond their work, they were accustomed to social relations and leisure activities revolving around the church and religious festivities, and the annual village fiestas, whose organization was traditionally delegated to the local youth.

On the day of the inauguration, the president of the CCPB, Ramuntxo Camblong, hailed Haize Berri as "a veritable decentralized antenna of Basque culture."[29] However, the relationship between Haize Berri and the CCPB was fated to remain tense, as the CCPB, although favorable to the *abertzale* movement, tended to back more centralized and mainstream Basque cultural activities.[30] By contrast, Haize Berri wished to retain autonomy of action, away from centralized control, and to support more local and grassroots cultural programs.[31] Indeed, such center-periphery tensions are characteristic of the way culture is defined and promoted in France.[32] The tension between CCPB and Haize Berri is also a good illustration of the kind of conflict that often emerges when one branch of the alternative movement begins to work with the blessing of the establishment, in this case, the CCPB with French institutions.

It is equally in this French context that it helps to understand how Haize Berri had an impact on the local, generally conservative population, and how this population reacted to it. Most of the inhabitants were used to politics being managed by more or less by the same people, the various aforementioned notables, that is, those with the most formal education and connections beyond the locality.[33] The municipal counselors of Izura therefore did not welcome Haize Berri in their midst, associating its supporters with *abertzales* and Enbata.[34]

29. Quoted in "*Haize Berri* ouvre ses portes," *Sud Ouest*, March 1, 1983.

30. Interviews with Pantxoa Etchegoin, current director of the Basque Cultural Institute (the BCI is the successor organization to the CCPB), and Daniel Landart, former president of the BCI, both on July 1, 2013 at Chateau Lota, seat of BCI, Uztaritze (Ustaritz). Interview with Txomin Heguy, also former president of the BCI, July 3, 2013, at Bar des Pyrenees, Baiona. Interview with Daniel Arbeletxe, December 28, 2012, at Bar Ametza, Izura. Interview with Marie-Jeanne Mercapide, former coordinator of Haize Berri, June 27, 2013, at her home, Armañakenea, Izura.

31. See for example, *Résumé de la réunion du group de réflexion sur l'avenir d'Haize Berri (Gogoeta Taldea)*, November 24, 2000. *Résumé de la réunion du Conseil d'Administration d'Haize Berri*, June 6, 1997.

32. Wangermée and Gournay, *La politique culturelle de la France*.

33. Ott, *The Circle of Mountains*; Jaureguiberry, *Questions nationale et mouvements sociaux en Pays Basque*; Bidart, *Société, politique, culture en Pays Basque*.

34. Conversations with villagers (names withheld for upon request),

From the outset, the board of Haize Berri sought to ensure its autonomy with respect to its programming. This meant having just 50 percent of its budget covered by institutional funding. Its main financial partner was the CCPB, which either granted the funds or helped it obtain funds elsewhere, especially from programs linked to the French Ministry of Culture or to the European Union. The other half of its budget came from donations, income from ticket sales of its shows and concerts, rental of its facilities and technical material, and from membership fees. Haize Berri also sometimes obtained funding for a specific project in collaboration with municipalities in Navarre or Euskadi, as well as from the Basque government.

As the name 'New Wind' suggests, the founders of Haize Berri sought to bring new life to the area. In the words of its pioneers, they wished to bring about a so-called "Basque cultural renaissance"[35] and "to promote and develop Basque culture."[36] They framed their motivation in terms of the "preservation and renaissance of our millenary culture" and the conviction that "our identity is a boon in global competition."[37] For them, "The whole area would benefit from the abundance of activities generated by the cultural center."[38] And promoting their work in Euskara was repeatedly stated as a priority.[39]

Haize Berri embarked on its mission with a rich list of activities. It launched numerous creative projects, including concerts, theatrical productions, workshops, and art exhibitions. It made a point of trying to engage with the local population and get them to participate in its activities and contribute new ideas. Haize Berri also framed its raison d'être in the fact that Izura is at the crossroads of three pilgrimage routes leading to the famed tomb of Saint James in the Spanish city of Santiago de Compostela.[40] The paths merge in Izura and continue on, through the town of Donibane Garazi (Saint-Jean-Pied-de-Port), into Spain and Navarre and on to Santiago de Compostela in Galicia. From its beginnings, Haize Berri launched a series of activities celebrating Izura's particular historical profile,

---

July, 2012.

35. Eñaut Larralde, quoted in "*Haize Berri* ouvre ses portes," *Sud Ouest*, March 1, 1983.

36. Haize Berri pamphlet: "Notre Proposition: Participez à notre Entreprise de Renaissance!" Date not given, but estimated to be 1995.

37. Ibid.

38. Ibid.

39. Haize Berri document: *Haize Berri Kultur Etxea. Centre culturel des cantons d'Amikuze et Iholdy. Avant Projet 2005*, July 22, 2004.

40. Ibid.

emphasizing the village's historical heritage as a crossroads of cultures and exchanges. The association regularly invited other communities located on the pilgrimage routes to exhibit artwork or to present dance and musical performances in Izura.

Haize Berri also organized seminars on current social and political topics that questioned locally established modes of thought and social relations and reflected on new ways and philosophies of life and work. Guest speakers included representatives of the local workers' syndicate Euskal Herriko Laborarien Elkartea, members of Basque activist youth movements, and spokespersons of alternative farming methods and sustainable development. Contemporary dance and gym lessons were also offered to the general public, causing a sensation especially among the older male inhabitants as many for the first time saw women in tight Lycra pants with their legs up in the air.[41]

In the 1980s, Haize Berri also housed a local Basque-language radio station, at a time when this project was still in its infancy and the idea of Basque media, as opposed to the French mainstream, was still controversial. It also organized sessions of traditional Basque improvised singing in rhyming verse, *bertsularitza*, in a non-traditional fashion: Haize Berri introduced a radical change to this custom of Basque improvised singing by bringing in cartoon artists who illustrated live the verses as they were sung on the spot. Haize Berri also organized an annual exhibition of humorous illustrations, *Marrazkiri,* around a theme of current affairs, which would often have political undertones. Another ambitious initiative was the organization of Kantu Xapelketa, a Basque singing competition which especially mobilized *ikastola* children and their parents (given they were the ones most sensitive to such an initiative involving promoting the Basque language) across the Pays Basque. These were all pioneering activities in the emergence of a now fully established Basque national cultural scene.

Haize Berri also sought to work with local traditional village youth groups in charge of organizing the annual festivities in their villages. As Haize Berri's permanent member of staff in the early 1990s, José Perez helped launch a rock competition titled *Iparrock* to encourage local rock bands to compose music in Euskara. With this, Izura became a major rendezvous for concerts in the new Basque punk rock scene. Revelers came from far and wide across the Basque Country, including from the Spanish side. When they

41. Recollections based on interviews with former participants of these classes, July 2012, Izura.

descended upon Izura, the motley group indulged in alcohol and drugs and loud music and left the village in considerable disarray. Their behavior, appearance, and attitude made an impression on Izura's citizens, which was not exactly positive.[42] Thus, in general, Haize Berri's dynamism disturbed as much as it intrigued.

Basque Art

Haize Berri became most famous across the Basque Country, however, for its work with fine art. This is quite significant in that fine art, generally meaning drawing, painting, and sculpture, then played a very minor role as a medium of cultural expression in the Pays Basque. Traditional Basque culture has tended to revolve around singing and dancing, the practice of fine art being a more upper class activity. For this reason too, it has developed only slowly and recently. On the whole, cultural activities in the Pays Basque have focused their energies more on the development and promotion of music, dance, and theatre.[43] This is in contrast to the significant art scene existing on the Spanish side of the Basque Country, especially since the 1960s, when the Basque avant-garde art movement developed as a Basque renaissance during the oppressive years of General Franco's dictatorship. When the regions of Euskadi and Navarre obtained autonomy with Spain's return to democracy, they were able to mobilize funds and infrastructure to develop and promote the arts as part of local culture. In the meantime, the Pays Basque remained a largely rural and peripheral part of France.

In contrast to the Spanish Basque Country, fine artists in the Pays Basque have tended to be isolated figures, self-taught, working

42. Recollections of a variety of local inhabitants, July and August 2012 and July 2013, Izura. As a child during this time, the early 1990s also remember local villagers, days after the festivities, expressing outrage at the dirty state in which their village had been left. I also remember these topics being great sources of gossip.

43. Interviews with Pantxoa Etchegoin, current president of the Basque Cultural Institute, and Daniel Landart, former president of the BCI, both July 1, 2013 at Chateau Lota, seat of BCI, Uztaritze. Interview with Txomin Heguy, also former president of the BCI, July 3, 2013, at Bar des Pyrenees, Baiona. Interview with Daniel Arbeletxe, December 28, 2012, at Bar Ametza, Izura. Interview with Marie-Jeanne Mercapide, former director of Haize Berri, June 27, 2013, at her home, Armañakenea, Izura. Interview with Piarres Erdozaintzi, June 22, 2012, at his home, Donaixti (Saint Juste Ibarre). Interview with Arño Uhalde, member of board of Haize Berri, June 25, 2012, at his home, Donaixti.

in the privacy of their homes and keeping their artwork secondary to their prime professional occupation. Those who sought to professionalize themselves as artists have tended to leave home for more urban parts of France with more opportunities. Over the course of the twentieth century, the Pays Basque offered few institutional infrastructure and professional outlets to train and promote oneself as an artist. Baiona, the main city in the Pays Basque located on the coast, only has a small *Ecole d'Art,* whose mission, since the 1950s, is to prepare students with the necessary basics to apply to university art faculties in other parts of France. The Pays Basque does not have a university of its own, but only a small so-called pluridisciplinary faculty in Baiona, a branch of the University of Pau, which is located approximately 100 miles away outside the Pays Basque. Only in very recent years have there been more significant public activities relating to fine arts. The *Ecole d'Art* in Baiona has, since 2008, been complemented by the existence of another more advanced art school in Biarritz, the école supérieure d*'art des Rocailles.* Some artists' communities and exhibition spaces have existed for a few years longer, but tended to remain restricted to the urban coastal area. It was only in 2011 that a prize for contemporary art in the Pays Basque was created, called the GazteArtea, based unusually, in the main inland town of Donibane Garazi, launched by a small group of outsiders.

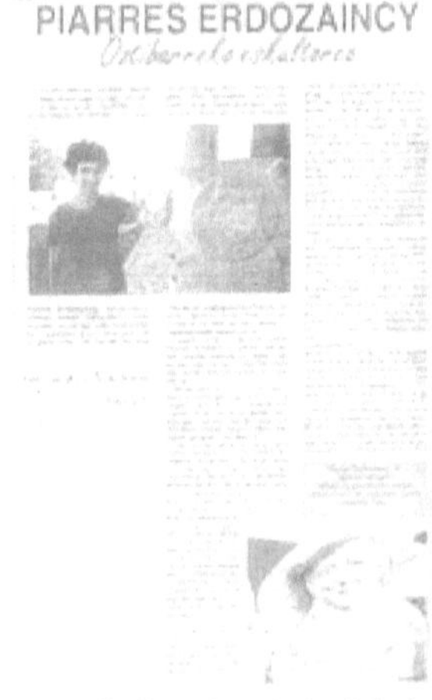

PIARRES ERDOZAINCY

Figure 9.1. The artist Piarres Erdozaintzi. Article in Herria, *August 9, 2001.*

The founders of Haize Berri became interested in fine art principally because of the passion of one of its members, Piarres Erdozaintzi (see figure 9.1), a local farmer who also practiced as a sculptor whenever he found the time. He had learned to sculpt thanks to a local carpenter and had taught himself about art essentially through reading. As Haize Berri sought to "be the showcase of creativity in the Pays Basque"[44] and promote new innovative forms of self and Basque expression, Erdozaintzi's idea of working with fine arts was well taken. The original aim was "to make the local population more sensitive to art, especially to contemporary art, as an important part of culture."[45]

The association began hosting annual summer exhibitions as from 1989, thereby becoming the first exhibitor of fine art in the rural interior of the Pays Basque.[46] At the start, the exhibitions displayed the work of approximately twenty local artists during the month of August. After a few years, as part of Haize Berri's ambition to reach a broader audience and to become more professional,[47] the organizers invited a wider variety of artists and of more established quality and renown. At the same time, they continued to believe in the importance of working with local artists, with the desire to "give the opportunity to local and beginner artists to exhibit and work with more established ones."[48]

In this vein, Izura-based artist Josette Dacosta, whose art is featured on the cover of the book, was invited to exhibit her paintings of Basque houses during the summer of 1996. According to Beñat Oteiza, the then coordinator of Haize Berri, this was the first time that an exhibition by Haize Berri attracted so many of the village's inhabitants; they came regularly during opening hours and also to the inauguration and closing festivities. They came, according to Dacosta and Oteiza,[49] because they knew the artist and because many of her paintings portrayed their houses. This familiar exhibition was then a helpful way to tap into a local population that was otherwise unaccustomed to appreciating art.

Toward the late 1990s, as part of their desire to improve their professional profile and play a significant role on the Basque cultural scene, Haize Berri's organizers decided to ask regionally known art historian and curator Jean-François Larralde to advise them in organizing exhibitions. Larralde was a university professor in Bilbao

---

44. "Nous voulons être la vitrine de la créativité en Pays basque," Minutes of Haize Berri administrative council meeting, July 10, 1997.

45. Interview with Beñat Oteiza, former employee of Haize Berri, July 6, 2012, Baiona.

46. Ibid.

47. Interviews with Daniel Arbeletche, June 24, 2012, and Piarres Erdozaintzi, July 3, 2012, both in Izura. See also "D'Oteiza à Erdozaintzi," *Sud Ouest*, June 14, 2001.

48. "Nous voulons être la vitrine de la créativité en Pays basque," Minutes of Haize Berri administrative council meeting July 10, 1997.

49. Ibid. Interview with Josette Dacosta, July 18, 2013, at her home, Peikonia, Izura.

and at the time chief curator of the museum of Getaria (Guéthary), a nearby seaside town in the Pays Basque. Among other shows, Larralde had exhibited the works of Spanish Basque artists and had close contact with some of the most established of these, including Jorge Oteiza and Agustin Ibarrola, original proponents of the Basque avant-garde art movement. It was reportedly[50] Eñaut Larralde, then president of Haize Berri, who had first suggested the importance of making contact with Spanish Basque artists. As an *abertzale*, he was motivated by the importance of collaborating with cultural actors on the Spanish side of the Basque Country where the art scene was much more vibrant and also clearly linked to Basque nationalism.

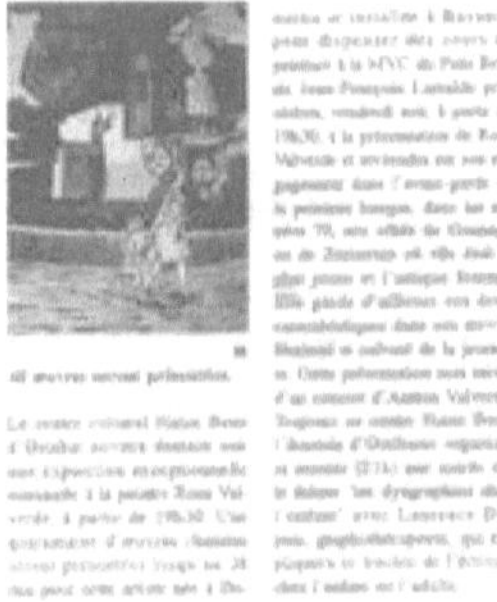

Haize Berri s'ouvre à Rosa Valverde

Figure 9.2. "Haize Berri welcomes the artist Rosa Valverde", in Le Journal du Pays Basque-Euskal Herriko Kazeta, *April 27 2006.*

So, during the late 1990s and in early 2000, Jean-François Larralde served as artistic director for Haize Berri's annual art events. He did this for free, he said, out of solidarity to Haize Berri, which he saw "was doing an admirable job in organizing so many cultural initiatives on a voluntary basis" and out of fellow "abertzale"[51] feeling. With his help, Haize Berri hosted a series of exhibitions showcasing the work of some of the key figures of the modern Basque avant-garde movement: Jorge Oteiza, Nestor Basterretxea, José Antonio Sistiaga, and José Luis Zumeta. Over the years, Jean-François Larralde helped invite other established Basque artists including Juan Luis Goenaga, Christiane Giraud, Christine Etch-

50. Interviews with Daniel Arbeletche (as above), Piarres Erdozaintzi (as above), and Gabi Aguerre, July 1, 2012, Izura.

51. Interview with Jean-François Larralde, July 16, 2012, Donibane Lohitzune (Saint-Jean-de-Luz).

evers, Zigor, Javier and Rosa Valverde (see figure 9.2), Koldobika Jauregui, Iñaki Olazabal, Xabier Morras, José Mari Lazkano, and José Mari Anda.

The annual artistic events of Haize Berri consisted of an artist in residence, a collective exhibition, and a special feature exhibition, which all took place over the summer months. The idea of an artist in residence came after some incidents during the collective exhibitions when several artworks had upset some of the villagers. On one occasion, an artist had constructed a sculpture made of body parts, which she had exhibited in a field at the bottom of the village (figure 9.4). She had inadvertently placed her work close to a household that had two physically handicapped children. Within a few days, the sculpture was destroyed, allegedly by the family.[52] On another occasion, the artists' collective Uztaro, from the nearby province of Zuberoa (also known as Xiberoa), had set up a series of metal and wooden sculptures in a field and hung underwear there. Offended by this intimate clothing, the farmer had removed the underwear. More positively, during another exhibition, an artist had created a big spherical sculpture out of barbed wire. This impressed the local farmers who, in this case, could appreciate the hard work involved in having to deal with such a difficult material with which they had direct experience of their own. The organizers of Haize Berri realized then the importance of presenting art in a way that the local public could identify with, and which could help them understand how an artist works.[53] In this vein, Haize Berri began, in 1998, to invite an artist every year to work in situ during the summer.

The first of these resident artists was Christiane Giraud, a non-Basque-speaking sculptor based in Baiona (see figure 9.3). She spent approximately two months in Izura, working in the open air on a large stone from a nearby quarry. She conceived her sculpture as a landmark, carved with fictitious names of pilgrims who would have walked on the path to Santiago de Compostela, and on either side she chiseled in the name of the village, Izura in Basque, and Ostabat in French. Giraud recalls positively her experience of working on this project.[54] Regularly, local farmers on their way back and forth to the fields with their cattle or sheep would stop and watch her at work and talk with her. At the end of the summer, Giraud's sculpture was

52. Interviews with various villagers, July 2012.

53. "On veut aussi que les gens se rendent compte du travail réalisé par les artistes," Beñat Oteiza in *Sud Ouest*, June 14, 2001.

54. Interview with Christiane Giraud at her home in Uztaritze, July 2012.

inaugurated with a gathering over drinks and food, and Haize Berri noticed many more of the villagers attended.

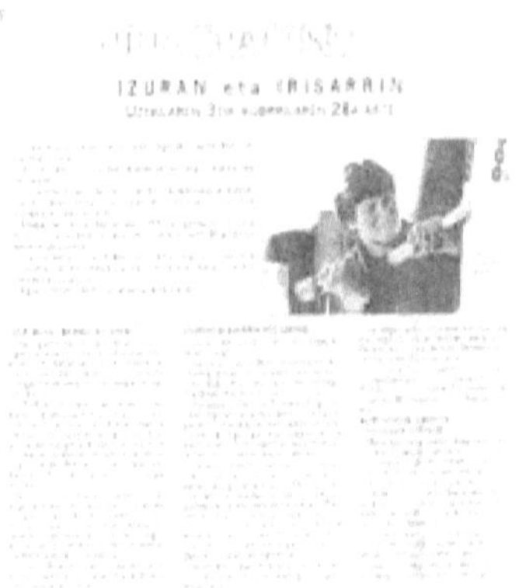
IZURAN eta IRISARRIN

Figure 9.3. The artist Christian Giraud working in Izura. Article in Herria, *July 23 1998.*

The artist in residence program continued the following year with another local sculptor, Guanes Etchegaray, and two years later with Piarres Erdozaintzi, both also recommended by Jean-François Larralde. Larralde explained his recommendations purely on the basis of quality of work by these local and little-known artists: "They were from the area, were available and willing to work in situ, and could communicate with the surrounding population."[55] But, despite the inclusive qualities and positive results of the project, Haize Berri continued to find it difficult to win over local officials and obtain funds. The last artist in residence was in 2003, with the partnership of a gallery recently opened in the nearby town of Donibane Garazi. On this occasion, the resident artist was Spanish Basque sculptor Iñaki Olazabal. Olazabal worked with large sheets of zinc, which he molded together with firing material. He worked outside, close to the main village square, and attracted the curiosity of passersby. He would often finish his day with a visit to the village café run by Daniel Arbeletche. Olazabal did not speak French, but was able to communicate with locals in Basque, despite his different accent and vocabulary. Through his sociability, Olazabal was able to connect somewhat with the villagers, in spite of their differences in appearance and politics—he resembled more the revelers who attended punk rock concerts than the farmers of Izura. He also had an ETA militant background, which he did not speak about but which some villagers suspected.[56]

55. Interview with Jean-François Larralde, July 15, 2012, at his home in Donibane Lohitzune.

56. Conversations with local inhabitants (names withheld upon re-

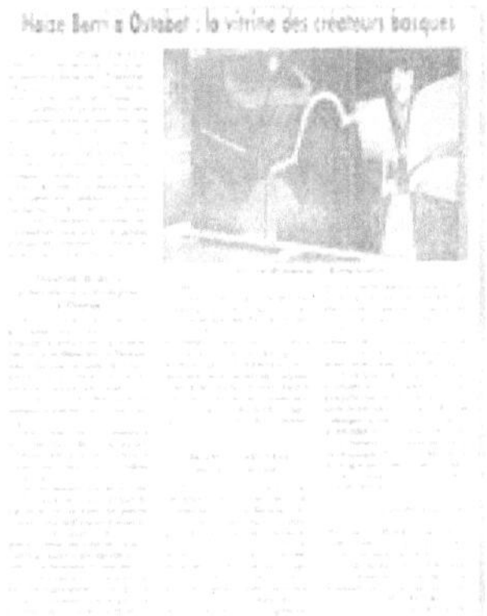

Haize Berri à Ostabat : la vitrine des créateurs basques

Figure 9.4. "Haize Berri in Ostabat: showcasing Basque creatives" in La Semaine du Pays Basque, *July 16-22 1999.*

After Olazabal, the artist in residence program stalled again for lack of funds. The other artistic projects, on the other hand, were able to continue, as they were less costly, relying on the goodwill of artists to cover their own expenses. *Uda Erakusketa*, which means 'summer exhibition' in Basque, became the main feature of Haize Berri's art projects. The exhibition drew upon the original idea of inviting artists to create a work in the open air, in the streets or fields of the village, over the course of July and August. Getting the artists to interact with their environment created some interesting synergies, often challenging the villagers' perception of their surroundings. For instance, Juan Luis Goenaga, a well-known artist in Euskadi, created an artwork in the tradition of land art, arranging stones in a field, which, seen from afar, suggested a human figure. On another occasion, French artist Michel Duboscq created large cartoon figures, which he hung on the façade of an abandoned farm at the bottom of the village (figure 9.4). Meanwhile, Josette Dacosta painted gigantic handmade canvases evoking the colors and spirit of old farm walls, suspended between two buildings to float in the breeze. Every year, Haize Berri proposed a theme for the artist that was sufficiently open to different interpretations, such as "light," "music," "the city," and "movement."

Many of the artists returned year after year. Juan Luis Goenaga, for example, was willing to drive the two hours from his home in Euskadi to take part, motivated by his love of the rural countryside, the opportunity to work in the Pays Basque, and out of a budding friendship with the organizers of *Haize Berri*.[57] He did not speak

quest), and with Olazabal over the course of several meetings in the summers of 2011, 2012, and 2013.

57. Interview with Juan Luis Goenaga, July 16, 2012, Donostia-San

French but was able to communicate with Haize Berri members and villagers in Basque. Both for him and other artists from the Spanish side, including Iñaki Olazabal, a Basque cultural or nationalist affinity with the French side was also a clear motivation to come.[58]

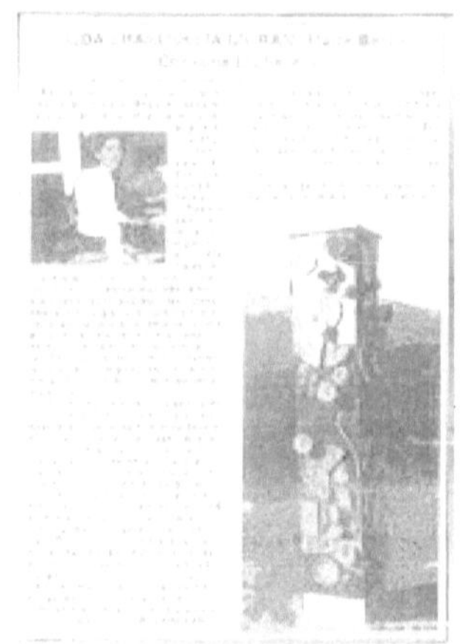

Figure 9.5. The artist Christine Etchevers working in Izura. Article in Herria, *August 3 2000.*

The first of the summer special feature exhibitions launched under the direction of Jean-François Larralde, in 1998, involved a partnership with the nearby village of Irisarri (Irissarry) to showcase the work of José Luis Zumeta, a member of the historical Spanish Basque avant-garde movement of the 1960s. Two years later, another member of this avant-garde, Nestor Basterretxea, exhibited his famous sculptures *Serie Cosmogónica Vasca,* which explore different themes of traditional Basque mythology in abstract form through wood and metal. His work shared the exhibition hall with younger and less established French Basque artist Christine Etchevers who, using the medium of paint, cardboard, and collage, also worked on the basis of traditional Basque themes and artefacts, with abstract bright colors (figure 9.5). The so-called leader of the historical Basque avant-garde, the sculptor Jorge Oteiza, who was a close friend and collaborator of Basterretxea, was also present at the inauguration. The following year, it was Oteiza's turn to exhibit, this time having the whole exhibition room to himself as one of the most widely recognized and celebrated pioneers of Basque modern art.[59]

These three important shows were well covered by the local

Sebastián.

58. Interviews with Goenaga and Olazabal respectively, July 21 and 23, 2012.

59. Jorge Oteiza passed away a year and a half later.

media and succeeded in increasing the number of visitors to Haize Berri's exhibitions. Haize Berri's reputation as an unusual contemporary art center was growing in the region. In 2002, again with the help of Jean-Francois Larralde, the summer exhibition featured the sculptures of Jesus Echevarria, another member of the older generation of celebrated Spanish Basque avant-garde artists. There again, such a feature exhibition succeeded in bringing an audience from further afield, especially from the urbanized coastal part of the Basque Country, a population that would not usually come to what they consider an isolated and insignificant part of the region. Haize Berri was now clearly on the Basque cultural map.

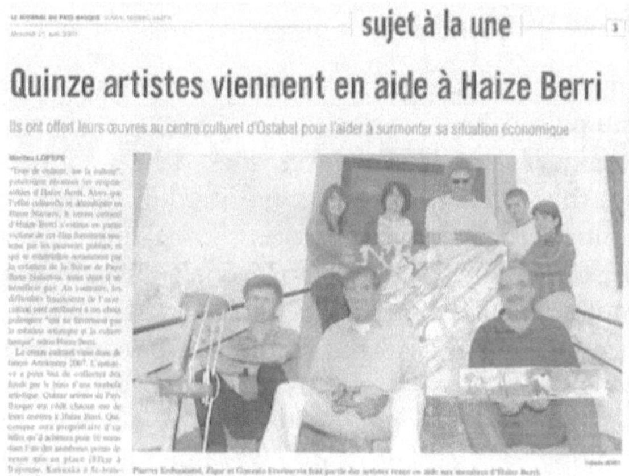

sujet à la une

Quinze artistes viennent en aide à Haize Berri

Ils ont offert leurs œuvres au centre culturel d'Ostabat pour l'aider à surmonter sa situation économique

Figure 9.6. "Fifteen artists come to help Haize Berri", in Le Journal du Pays Basque-Euskal Herriko Kazeta, *April 25 2007.*

In the years that followed, the exhibitions always mixed artists who were more established, especially from the Spanish side of the Basque Country, such as Jose Antonio Sistiaga, Juan Luis Goenaga, Rosa and Javier Valverde, Koldobika Jauregui, Xabier Morras, Jesus Mari Lazkano, and Antton Mendizabal, with younger or lesser-known artists, more often than not from the French side. Some also made their debut with Haize Berri, such as Aitziber Akerreta and myself. Haize Berri had become an important reference with which Basque artists wished to be associated. This was demonstrated when a number of artists contributed works to raise funds for Haize Berri in 2006 (figure 9.6). Spanish Basque sculptor Zigor, a former ETA member now married and settled in Biarritz, explained his reason for doing so as follows: "What is done here [at Haize Berri] is not done anywhere else. Its work is indispensable for going forward with creativity in the Pays Basque."[60]

60. Quoted in "Haize Berri organise une tombola pour miser sur la culture basque," *Le Journal du Pays Basque*, April 25, 2007, at www.lejpb.

This success notwithstanding, Haize Berri remained locally controversial and regionally a financial failure. Local inhabitants did not become more involved with Haize Berri over the years. Politicians gave it little support and regional institutions continued to give only limited and intermittent funding to its projects. Much of Haize Berri's success was due to the personalities, charisma, and energy of some of its key members. As these started getting older or tired, and the younger generation was engaged elsewhere, the project lost its impetus. Beset by growing financial and internal difficulties, Haize Berri eventually held the last of its activities in 2009.

The Politics of Culture

The explanation for the controversies around Haize Berri can be found in the political and sociocultural context in which it was active. The organizers of Haize Berri worked in a context that was rural, where the population had little initiation to cultural matters beyond traditional folkloric expressions. Local customs were being lost, and Euskara had given way to French through mass media, public schooling, and the general economic and political structure. The local population was on the whole conservative and set in its ways. Haize Berri, by contrast, was associated with a new Basque political and cultural movement, which, particularly during the 1980s and 1990s, was a focus of much conflict in the region, especially due to the violent activities of ETA and Iparretarrak.

Haize Berri came in with a vision and a project to promote "Basque culture."[61] While its organizers claimed not to be political, they did see culture as part of politics, and in the context of the region, they were indeed political. Whilst Haize Berri did win over some people, especially thanks to the charisma of specific members and participants, it continued to be viewed by many local people as a separate group with an agenda. In its project to develop and promote "Basque culture," its founders worked with a diversity of expressions, including artists who did not necessarily identify themselves as Basque. Yet they still worked within specific parameters: they talked about Basque culture in a way that was perceived as overbearing and imposing by a local population who either already felt Basque in their own local way or did not wish to be associated with a Basque identity. Unwittingly, Haize Berri imposed a set of boundaries that directly affected the local population, whose feel-

---

com/idatzia/20070425/art201846.php.

61. This term is repeatedly mentioned in Haize Berri documents throughout the years of its existence.

ing of being disturbed and imposed upon was accentuated by Haize Berri's organization of cultural activities and showcasing of art from the Spanish Basque world, presenting it as Basque.

Since the mid-2000s, the Basque nationalist discourse has been normalized to the extent that it is no longer the source of strong identity conflict in the region. Numerous local inhabitants who would not have done so only a few years ago now readily say they are Basque and are part of "the Basque nation." During Haize Berri's existence, Izura's municipal council was dominated by generally conservative forces. Today, by contrast, Izura has a younger, dynamic mayor, Daniel Olçomendi, who is well educated and with both social and political ambitions, and who identifies himself as *abertzale*.[62] He grew up on a farm and speaks Euskara fluently, having taken lessons to refresh his knowledge of the language he spoke as a child. He has also taken a leading role as a member of the left-wing Basque nationalist coalition that serves as the local opposition to the established mainstream parties of both the left and right. None of this upsets local people in the way that it would have only a few years ago. This, I venture to say, has much to do with not only the personal charisma Olçomendi enjoys among the other local members of his generation, many of whom have joined him on the municipal council, but also the fact that Basque nationalism is now generally normalized in the Pays Basque. Basque nationalism, or the idea of the existence of a Basque nation, is no longer a disputed fact as it was only a few years back.[63] Basque nationalist parties of varying ideologies have succeeded in making Basque national identity an established idea and reality. This is embraced by a younger generation that has grown up with the more active and widespread presence of Basque nationalism, and so is also more accepted by the older generations. With the normalization of Basque nationalism comes the normalization of a notion of a Basque culture and art.

Bibliography

Ahedo Gurrutxaga, Igor. *The Transformation of National Identity*

---

62. "Entretien avec Daniel Olcomendy/Maire d'Ostabat-Asme: 'Les habitants de ce territoire doivent prendre leur destin en mains,'" *Le Journal du Pays Basque*, March 2, 2013.

63. An example of this is the title of a conference held by the abertzale organizers of the Manu Robles Arangiz Foundation in Bayonne in February 2006 "Le Pays Basque: une nation à part entière?" (French for 'The Pays Basque: a nation of its own?'). There are many examples of such questionings and debates on 'who are we?'

in the Basque Country of France, 1789–2006. Translated by Cameron J. Watson. Reno: Center for Basque Studies, 2008.

Arribas, Maria-Jose. *Cuarenta años de arte Vasco, 1937–1977: Historia y documentos*. Donostia-San Sebastián: Erein, 1979.

Bidart, Pierre. *Société, politique, culture en Pays Basque*. Baiona: Atlantica, 1986.

Bidegain, Eneko. *Iparretarrak histoire d'une organisation politique armée*. Baiona: Gatuzain, 2010.

Billig, Michael. *Banal Nationalism*. London and Thousand Oaks, CA: Sage Publications, 1995.

Bray, Zoe. "Basque Nationalism at a Political Crossroad." *World Politics Review* (May 9, 2012).

———. *Living Boundaries: Frontiers and Identity in the Basque Country*. Reno: Center for Basque Studies, 2011.

Collins, Roger. *The Basques*. London: Blackwell, 1990.

Etcheverry-Ainchart, Peio, and Jon Etcheverry-Ainchart. *Le mouvement Enbata*. Baiona: Elkar, 2013.

Gell, Alfred. *Art and Agency: An Anthropological Theory*. Oxford: Clarendon Press, 1998.

Guasch, Ana Maria. *Arte E Ideologia En El Pais Vasco: 1940–1980*. Madrid: Akal, 1985.

Itçaina, Xavier. "Appartenances linguistiques, identités collectives et pratiques culturelles en Pays Basque." *Cultures & Conflits* 3, nos. 79–80 (2010): 19–36.

Izquierdo, Jean-Marie. *Le Pays Basque en France*. Paris: L'Harmattan, 2001.

Jacob, James E. *Hills of Conflict: Basque Nationalism in France*. Reno: University of Nevada Press, 1994.

Jaureguiberry, Francis. *Questions nationale et mouvements sociaux en Pays Basque*. Paris: Ecoles des Hautes Etudes en Sciences Sociales, 1983.

MacClancy, Jeremy. *Contesting Art: Art, Politics and Identity in the Modern World*. Oxford: Berg, 1997.

Oronos, Michel. *Le mouvement culturel Basque. 1951–2001*. Baiona: Elkar, 2002.

Ott, Sandra. *The Circle of Mountains: A Basque Shepherding Community*. Reno: University of Nevada Press, 1993.

Van Laar, Timothy, and Leonard Diepeveen. *Active Sights: Art as Social Interaction*. Mountain View, CA: Mayfield Publishing Company, 1998.

Wangermée, Robert, and Bernard Gournay. *La politique culturelle de la France*. Strasbourg: La Documentation française. Council of Europe, Council for Cultural Co-operation, 1988.

Part 2

Artistic Political Engagement

8

An alle Künstler!: The Politics of Place in Max Pechstein's Images of Palau

Brett M. Van Hoesen

Germany's post–World War I era was a ripe context for politicized artistic communities such as the November Group and the Arbeitsrat für Künst (Workers' Council of Artists), who critically evaluated the role of the artist in larger society (figure 8.1). The postwar years, in particular, prompted artists to engage in overtly political practices generating posters, print series, manifestos, journals, and alternative exhibitions as a means to disseminate critique concerning a range of social injustices. While many artists rejected traditional media during this time, others such as the German Expressionist Max Pechstein specifically chose to engage with seemingly apolitical subject matter, continuing to paint and sculpt while simultaneously creating caustic political commentaries in print. As a result, it has often been assumed that Pechstein's paintings and sculptures are devoid of political content. This chapter counters that claim by charting the intersection of these creative zones. Collectively these works situate *place* as an arena in which to debate the immorality of war, paradoxes of modernity and European colonialism, and the ideal of universalism.

Primitivism and Politics

Early twentieth-century European artists' engagement with cultures, material objects, landscapes, and architecture from outside of Europe has long functioned under the rubric, *Primitivism*.[1] An over worn construct of European modernism, this umbrella term prohibits a more pointed examination of the underlying politics inherent to what I would like to call the *artist-traveler paradigm*. This chapter seeks to move beyond the problematics and pitfalls of Primitivism to situate the travels, writings, and visual work of the German artist Max Pechstein within the ideological framework of *Weimar postcolonialism*. Beginning in 1906, Pechstein was an affiliate of the Dresden-based expressionist group, *Die Brücke* (The Bridge) and later served as a founding member of the postwar revolutionary artists' communities in Berlin, the *Novembergruppe* (The November Group) and the *Arbeitsrat für Kunst* (Workers' Council for Art). Commissioned by the Berlin-based Fritz Gurlitt Gallery to visually record his experiences in the South Seas, Pechstein traveled in 1914 to the islands of Palau, then a German colony. Due to the outbreak of World War I, however, his stay on the islands was dramatically cut short. Soon after his arrival, Pechstein was interned as a prisoner of war by the Japanese and returned to Germany only several months later. The writings and drawings that the artist composed during his short excursion became his obsession beginning in 1917, after he served in the German army. Attempting to resurrect his Palau experiences, Pechstein used written excerpts and sketches from his *tagebuch* (journal) to build a body of paintings nostalgic for a nonexistent time and place. This commitment to visually restoring the era of German colonialism, which came to an official end in 1919 with the Treaty of Versailles, was consistent with Pechstein's political devotion to the German Social Democratic Party (Sozialdemokratische Partei Deutschlands, SPD). Following the war, the SPD significantly shifted its position concerning the German colonies and became a major proponent of Weimar neocolonialism. Seen in this context, Pechstein's body of work that dates from 1917 through the early 1920s assumes a subtle political character. While the Weimar-era politics intrinsic to redefining the legacy of Germany's colonial history was likely lost on gallery-goers and collectors who frequented Pechstein's exhibitions at the Gurlitt Gallery, his works nevertheless reinforced a pointed political position. His paintings and later print series regurgitated and aggrandized aspects of his travel writing, supplying the artistic avant-garde of Berlin with colonial nar-

1. The research for this essay was funded by the generous support of a Scholar in Residence Fellowship from the Robert Gore Rifkind Center for German Expressionist Studies at the Los Angeles County Museum of Art. I want to sincerely thank Tim Benson, Chris Vigiletti, and the staff at the Rifkind for their time and assistance.

ratives characteristic of a bygone era. In this chapter, I will illustrate the way in which Pechstein's seemingly paradigmatic engagement with the people, vegetation, architecture, and material culture of Palau actually referenced a political stance specific to the Weimar era of the 1920s (1919–1933). While Pechstein's travels, writings, and visual productions might be labeled as predictable examples of European Primitivism, this simplistic circumscription ignores the complex political structures embedded in his work that are intrinsic to Weimar-period postcolonial discourses.

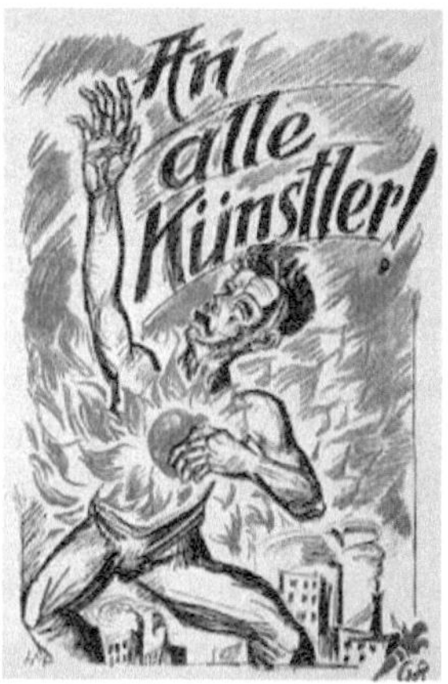

Figure 8.1. Max Pechstein, An Alle Künstler! *(To All Artists!), 1919. © 2015 Artists Rights Society (ARS), New York / Pechstein Hamburg / Toekendorf / VG Bild-Kunst, Bonn*

The Artist-Traveler Paradigm and Weimar Postcolonialism

Pechstein's travels abroad and his reportage of these excursions have been examined within the context of German imperialism, dating from the late nineteenth century through the start of World War I.[2] While this framework serves as an accurate means to evaluate Pechstein's commitment to the tenets of Expressionist movements such as Die Brücke, it fails to accommodate the fact that a majority of his Palau works were not begun until 1917, many dating into the early 1920s, well after Pechstein's disassociation with Die Brücke and the end to Germany's status as a colonial power. Giv-

2. For essays devoted to the colonial (but not the *postcolonial*) discourses embedded in Pechstein's Palau works see: Lloyd, "A South Seas Odyssey": Max Pechstein's Visionary Ideals," in *German Expressionism* and Lülf, "Die Suche nach dem Ursprünglichen." For a recent exception to this approach see Soika, "Max Pechstein," 71–83.

en this unusual dynamic, I would like to analyze Pechstein's Palau works from a different vantage point, one that is rooted in an early nineteenth-century European phenomenon—the *artist-traveler paradigm* as well as a postwar construct intrinsic to the Weimar era, *Weimar postcolonialism*. Before examining the specifics of Pechstein's travels and responses to Palau, the ideas behind these two concepts, the *artist-traveler paradigm* and *Weimar postcolonialism* warrant some explanation.

Artists have long accompanied travel excursions to record pictorial interpretations of lands, people, objects, buildings, customs, and atmospheric conditions that exceed the boundaries of written accounts. Despite this established tradition, the artist-traveler paradigm that most impacted early twentieth-century painters such as Pechstein has its roots in France beginning a century earlier. In 1832, the French Romantic painter Eugène Delacroix traveled to Morocco and Algeria with a delegation sponsored by the Count of Mornay, who was the special envoy to the Sultan of Morocco. French colonial rule in North Africa expectedly articulated the details of Delacroix's six-month-long trip, determining where he traveled and with whom he met.[3] While Delacroix's actual experiences in Algeria and Morocco colored his interpretations of the Muslim world, his impressions of the Orient as an *imagined space* was somewhat predetermined by his admiration for the work of Napoleonic painters like Antoine-Jean Gros who traveled decades prior to Egypt and Syria. These preconceived ideas belonging to a time and place far-removed from his actual destination dominated Delacroix's work. Consequently, the drawings and paintings that resulted from his 1832 expedition relied heavily upon tropes of the Orient, playing to European audiences' expectations for subjects such as the harem. This dialectic intrinsic to the artist-traveler paradigm became a prevailing pictorial formula—an ongoing tension between preformed ideas of a culture and authentic experiences.

Other French nineteenth-century painters helped to reinforce this phenomenon. Paul Gauguin began his engagement with the so-called "Other" in 1885 in Bretagne (Brittany), a region in western France known for its Celtic heritage. Gauguin, who was born in Peru and left his career as a stockbroker in Paris to become a painter, imagined the Breton people, their customs, churches, farms, and villages such as Pont-Aven to be emblems of an untouched *paradise*, particularly in contrast to urban life. "I love Brittany," he wrote. "I

---

3. For details concerning Delacroix's trip to North Africa see: Grimaldo Grigsby, "Orients and Colonies."

find something savage, primitive here. When my clogs echo on this granite earth, I hear the dull, muffled, powerful note that I am seeking in painting."[4] In reality, by the time Gauguin visited Bretagne, towns like Pont-Aven were well developed artists' communities, inundated with tourists. While aspects of authentic Breton dress and customs remained, a certain extent of the culture Gauguin witnessed was manufactured for tourist spectacle.[5] Beginning in 1891, Gauguin traveled to Tahiti where he stayed until 1893. After a return to France, he settled in 1895 on the island of Dominique in the Marquesas Islands, where he died in 1903. His time in Tahiti and the Marquesas resulted in canvases that conflated photographs of woodcarvings from Java (modern-day Indonesia), sculptures from ancient Egypt, cloisonné jewelry techniques from the Middle Ages, and standard French academic genres such as the reclining nude. While he imbued his canvases with authentic experiences, Gauguin's interpretations of Tahitian culture were mediated through a roster of visual resources that had little to do with his actual experiences in the South Pacific. Following Gauguin's death in 1903, there were a host of large-scale posthumous exhibitions, which focused upon his works from Tahiti. As a result, his oeuvre as well as his diary—*Noa Noa*, published in 1919—served as inspiration for a number of younger German painters who also traveled to the South Seas, including Pechstein and fellow expressionist artist Emil Nolde.

This tendency to conjure preconceived notions of a travel destination is certainly not unique to an artist-traveler paradigm of the nineteenth century, yet the influence of Delacroix and Gauguin on younger generations reinforced particular patterns of engagement and reportage. The fact that these individuals were traveling to lands under European colonial occupation also helped to ensure commonalities between their works. Coupled with indebtedness to a French artist-traveler tradition, German artists were also inspired by a rich heritage of German explorers, whom they attempted to emulate. The most prominent was Alexander von Humboldt, who among other things helped to establish the field of botanical geography. His extensive travels to Latin America and his prolific written chronicles of these expeditions established a paradigm of its own that later infiltrated the colonial era. The trope of the German explor-

---

4. Gauguin in a letter to his wife from Malingue, ed., *Paul Gauguin—Letters to His Wife and Friends*, p#.

5. For discussion of Gauguin's stay in Bretagne and the inherent contradictions between his renditions of the region versus the reality of the times, see sections of Perry, "Primitivism and the *Modern*," 3–27.

er also proliferated Weimar postcolonial discourses despite the fact that Germany no longer had colonial properties. The popular press, including venues such as *Berliner Illustrirte Zeitung* (*BIZ*), *Münchner Illustrierte Presse* (*MIP*), *Der Querschnitt*, and others played to a public thirst for fictive and non-fictive tales of Germans, other Europeans, and Americans exploring territories in Africa, the South Seas, Asia, and parts of South and North America. Although these types of stories, many of which featured photographs or photomontages, played to nostalgia for Germany's colonial past, they also functioned as a means to re-author Germany's postcolonial present. The economically unstable postwar years also helped to foster a renewed interest in Germany's former colonies and subsequently prompted a movement to revise Paragraph 119 of the Treaty of Versailles, which precluded Germany from functioning as a colonial power. In the early months of 1920, officials at the Reichstag virtually unified over the colonial question as only the German Communist Party (Deutsche Kommunistische Partei, KPD) and a majority of the members of the German Independent Social Democratic Party (Unabhängige Sozialdemokratische Partei Deutschlands, USPD) rejected the call to arms to re-obtain colonial properties. These neocolonialist aims radiated well beyond the political sphere, corresponding with, if not prompting, a whole range of pro-colonial stances. Historian Mary E. Townsend, traveling through Germany during the 1920s, noted the growing strength of the "contemporary colonial movement," which "told Germans more about their former colonies than they ever knew when those lands were German soil."[6] Townsend reported on the increasing membership of the *Deutsche Kolonialgesellschaft* (DKG, German Colonial Society) and its support for a range of affiliated societies including the *Kolonialkriegerdank* (Colonial Veterans' Society) and the *Frauenverein vom Rotem Kreutz für Deutsche über See* (Women's Branch of the Overseas Red Cross). Pro-colonial periodicals such as the *Koloniale Rundschau* and *Der Kolonial-Deutsche* helped to sustain the impression that colonial issues were viable topics during the 1920s. University programs such as the *Kolonialinstitut* at the University of Hamburg, paired with a plethora of scientific and pseudoscientific publications devoted to geographical and cultural studies of former colonial lands, also contributed to the postcolonial era. Additionally, popular venues such as city-sponsored colonial weeks, featuring Völkerschauen (human zoos), exhibitions replete with live actors, mannequins, masks, weapons, stuffed

6. Townsend, "The Contemporary Colonial Movement in Germany," 65.

animals, and so on, further reinforced the mythology of Germany's continued expansion, despite its postwar relegation to a highly circumscribed domestic sphere. Importantly, it is this climate, and the multi-faceted character of Weimar postcolonialism, which set the stage for the travels and work of Max Pechstein.[7]

German Colonial Interests in Palau and Pechstein's Trip

Palau is located in western Micronesia, roughly 500 miles east of the Philippines and 2000 miles from Tokyo. An archipelago renowned for its geographic diversity and natural wonders, today eight of the islands are inhabited.[8] While limited and in some cases inadvertent European experiences with Palau date to the early eighteenth century, the first extensive German knowledge of the territory began in roughly 1789 when a British report, entitled *An Account of the Pelew-Islands*, was translated into German and published by a Hamburg press.[9] The account told the tale of an East India Company ship, the *Antelope*, under the command of Captain Henry Wilson, which was shipwrecked in 1783 off the coast of Palau. Embracing the concept of the "noble savage," the chronicler of Captain Wilson's tale, George Keate, noted the unusual cooperativeness of the island inhabitants, who built a new boat within three months, enabling the British company to resume their journey toward Macao.[10] During Captain Wilson's stay, he befriended the King of Pa-

7. For additional discussion of *Weimar Postcolonialism* see my essays in the following publications: "Weimar Revisions of Germany's Colonial Past"; "Postcolonial Cosmopolitanism"; and "Weimar Postcolonialism and the Rhineland Controversy."

8. According to the *Deutsches Kolonial-Lexicon*, published in 1920, Palau was believed to consist of seven larger inhabited islands with as many as twenty smaller uninhabited islands. See Schnee, ed., *Deutsches Kolonial-Lexicon*, vol. 3 (P–Z), 3. In terms of its more contemporary history, Palau gained independence from the United States as part of the UN Trust Territory in October of 1994. The current population of the collective islands is 20,796. See https://www.cia.gov/library/publications/the-world-factbook/geos/ps.html.

9. See English-language excerpt from George Keate's *An Account of the Pelew Islands* (London, 1788) in *Strangers in the South Seas*, ed. Lansdown, 99–104.

10. According to Lansdown, Keate corresponded with Voltaire and subscribed to the philosophical treatises of the Enlightenment. See *Strangers in the South Seas*, 99.

lau, whom he called "Abba Thule." The king convinced the captain to take one of his sons, Lee Boo, with him to England, although the son died of smallpox just six months later. Despite his sudden death he was celebrated in England as a royal from the South Pacific; a highly popular biography of the prince was published in tandem with the tale of the shipwreck.[11] This positive reception to Lee Boo was attributed in part to Wilson's experience of the extreme good will of the Palauan people.

> The conduct of these people towards the English was, from the first to the last uniformly courteous and attentive, accompanied with a politeness that surprised those on whom it was bestowed. At all times they seemed so cautious of intruding, that on many occasions they sacrificed their natural curiosity to that respect, which natural good manners appeared to them to exact. Their liberality to the English at their departure, when individuals poured in all the best they had to give, and that of articles too of which they had far from plenty themselves, strongly demonstrated that these testimonies of friendship were the effusion of hearts that glowed with the flame of philanthropy.[12]

The pleasant tenor of these interactions made Palau an attractive destination for German businessmen a century later. While Palau officially became a German colonial territory in 1899 under the auspices of Adolf von Hansemann, German commercial contact with the area began at least two decades earlier when, in 1874, the Rhinelander businessman Eduard Hernsheim established trading agents at Malakal.[13] From 1885, Germany occupied some of the islands in the region and by 1899 acquired the territory from Spain following the Spanish-American War. Purchased in conjunction with the Caroline and Mariana Islands, the cost for the three prop-

---

11. According to Lloyd, Keate's account, which included the "interesting and affecting history of Prince Lee Boo," was published in at least twenty editions between 1789 and 1850. See "A South Seas Odyssey," 201.

12. Keate, in Lansdown, *Strangers in the South Seas*, 99. There is no direct evidence to suggest that Pechstein read Keate's account of Palau, yet his preformed optimistic attitude toward the islands likely came from publications that were indeed informed by these early encounter tales.

13. Firth, "German Firms in the Pacific Islands, 1857–1914," 5–6. Hernsheim also established trading agents on the Duke of York Islands in the Bismarck Archipelago in October 1875 as well as similar establishments just a year later in the Marshall Islands.

erties totaled roughly twenty-five million pesetas.[14] The main island of Babeltaob housed the German colonial administration. Not as commercially developed as other South Sea Islands, Palau's commerce was based upon a small range of items. These included the mineral phosphate, present in lesser quantities than initially expected, and copra, which is dried coconut milk that is later processed into oil and often used for cosmetics and other skin products. Additionally, pearl farming as well as coffee and cocoa plantations provided commercial interest in the islands. In terms of the economic gains associated with Palau, the colonial administration grouped it with other Pacific Island territories such as the Caroline, Marianne, and Marshall Islands, which collectively generated a modest export business.[15] Ultimately, Germany's colonial occupation of Palau was short-lived as by the start of World War I, Japan invaded the territories, officially assuming control just five years later in 1919 in compliance with the Treaty of Versailles.

Pechstein's fascination for Palau was prompted by visits as early as 1906 to the Dresden Völkerkunde Museum, in which he viewed two carved wooden beams from men's clubhouses. Carl Gottfried Semper, a German ethnologist and zoologist, brought these objects back from Palau after he spent ten months there in 1862 following a shipwreck. After 1881, the beams were on display at the museum in Dresden.[16] The roughness of the wood carving technique, the abbreviated human forms, and the simplified pictorial space inspired Pechstein's desire to see these types of objects in actual use. Pechstein's trip to Palau was originally planned as a two-year excursion. The artist received funds for his travel from the art dealer Wolfgang Gurlitt, the eventual owner of the Fritz Gurlitt Gallery in Berlin.[17] The funds were provided with the stipulation that Gurlitt receive exclusive exhibition rights for the works upon Pechstein's return to Germany. This might sound like an extravagant investment, but at the time Pechstein was a well-established commodity. By 1911, his works were selling for roughly 1,000 and 2,000 marks each.[18] The six-week-long journey to the archipelago began in April of 1914.

14. Gründer, *Geschichte der deutschen Kolonien*, 94–95.

15. Townsend, *The Rise and Fall of Germany's Colonial Empire, 1884–1918*, 266.

16. Lülf, "Die Suche nach dem Ursprünglichen," 79.

17. Wolfgang Gurlitt (1888–1965) was the son of the art dealer Fritz Gurlitt after whom the gallery was named.

18. Lloyd, "A South Seas Odyssey," 200. She notes that these prices appeared in the third and fourth Berlin Secession exhibition catalogues from 1911–12.

Pechstein accompanied his wife, Lotte Kaprolat, and traveled first by train through Switzerland to Genoa and then via a ship bound for the Indian Ocean, with eventual arrival in Micronesia passing through several locals including Nepal, Ceylon (Sri Lanka), India, China, and the Philippines. From Manila the Pechsteins traveled by Japanese boat to Palau, not before enduring a dramatic derailment as a result of a typhoon. They reached the main island of Palau in May of 1914.

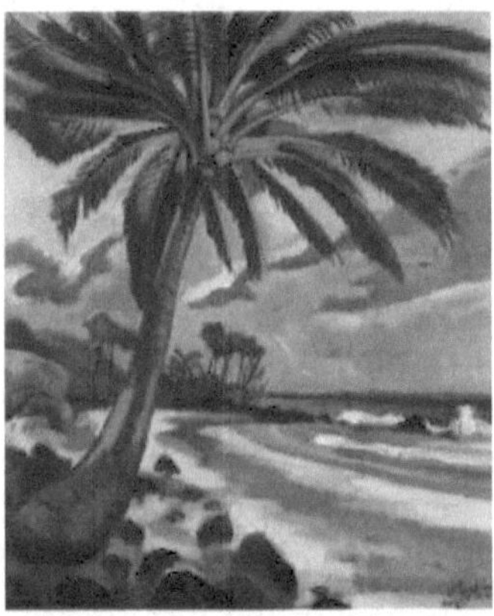

Figure 8.2. Max Pechstein, Monsunstimmung in Palau, *1914. © 2015 Artists Rights Society (ARS), New York / Pechstein Hamburg / Toekendorf / VG Bild-Kunst, Bonn*

For the next six months, Pechstein recorded his impressions through written accounts in his *tagebuch* (diary), roughly forty-one drawings (later known as his *Palau-Zeichnungen*), and a number of paintings. While these works reinforced the idea that Palau was an island paradise exempt from European conventions, a *natural world* disconnected from the troubles of modern urban life, there were challenges to this idealized conception. Starting with his arrival in Angaur, the southernmost island of the archipelago, Pechstein noted the prominent presence of the German South Seas Association, a component of the colonial administration. Recounted in several pages in *Erinnerungen* (Recollections) a journal he penned in 1945–46, Pechstein lamented and even scoffed at the invasion of the island by Europeans. Critical of their methods, Pechstein derisively described these individuals as occupiers of well-furnished houses who oversee native laborers and guest workers, many of whom were on two-year-long contracts to work the mines extracting phosphorus. Only one village on the island, Pechstein noted, remained a "peaceful oasis in this world of money-hungry European business activity."[19] In contrast

19. From Pechstein, *Erinnerungen*, 60.

to this description, as Pechstein migrated to less inhabited islands, he claimed to have finally discovered the world of his dreams. In a journal entry from his Palau *tagebuch* of 1914, he recounts the idyllic traits of the land: "Incomparably fertile growth extended everywhere, plants never before seen, palms and breaded fruits rose up, bamboos and sugar beet."[20] This fascination for the vegetation of the islands was also captured in early paintings he produced upon his arrival. Paintings such as *Monsunstimmung in Palau*, 1914 (figure 8.2), one of the few paintings to survive from his 1914 stay, showcases the lushness of the coastline and the impressive striations of palm fronds of one large tree that juts over the sea. Seen in juxtaposition to the impending drama of the monsoon reflected in the color tones and patterns of the sky and ocean, Pechstein's idyllic world sees nature as a romanticized, uncontrollable force, not far removed from the German Romantics' landscape paintings dating a century earlier. Despite this prescribed, romanticized notion of island culture, Pechstein's characterization indicates a sincere wonder and surprise for the sights, sounds, and smells he encountered firsthand. This type of attention is comparable to accounts found in colonial records of the islands, sources such as the *Deutsches Kolonial-Lexikon*, a hefty three-volume, nearly 3000-page encyclopedia edited by Heinrich Schnee in 1920, which devoted considerable attention to the "Planzenwelt" of Palau. [21] From a detailed description of the vegetation lining the coast to accounts of the lush bushes and trees of the inner-island territories, the entry in Schnee's *Lexikon* notes the wide range of flowers, fruits, and plants indigenous to the archipelago. Both Schnee's entries and Pechstein's renderings also devoted considerable attention to the people, the *Bevölkerung*, of Palau. With particular focus on their skin tones, physique, perceived level of intelligence, social interactions, and daily activities, it is clear that more than any other aspect of the colonies, the inhabitants of these locales preoccupied German visitors.

> The Palauans are thin, indeed a strong, seemingly homogenous breed of people. Of the inhabitants of the Caroline Islands, the Palau islanders are the lightest skinned. Their skin color ranges from a rosy flesh tone to a yellowish-brown. The women are considerably lighter than the men. Their hair is brown-black and for the most part wavy. . . . They are very intelligent individuals, who are clean, happy to work and willing; they embody a relatively high level of culture.[22]

20. Ibid., 77.
21. Schnee, ed. *Deutsches Kolonial-Lexikon*, vol. 3 (P–Z).
22. Ibid. 4.

Pechstein's renditions of the Palauans dovetails with Schnee's ethnographic accounts provided above. All of Pechstein's paintings (those completed during and after his stay) feature lean individuals with goldish-brownish hued skin and dark, wavy hair. Pechstein's attentiveness to the appearance of the islanders was likely in part inspired by the emphasis on figure studies in the work of earlier French artist-travelers such as Gauguin or Henri Matisse. A number of Pechstein's sketches from 1914 almost directly reference the *lens of Gauguin*, featuring couples or clusters of figures, often women engaged in conversation or common activity. Some of these compositions incorporate Gauguin's fantasy realms—combining figure studies from life with citations of female types from Egyptian paintings or Javanese sculptures. This technique was even more pronounced in Pechstein's paintings from 1917 on. Other drawings from the *Palau-Zeichnungen* appear to be more impromptu renderings of scenes Pechstein witnessed on the islands—ranging from fishing expeditions to the gathering or harvesting of foodstuffs.

With the outbreak of World War I, Pechstein's stay was abruptly cut short. In November, just months after his arrival, Pechstein and his wife were captured by Japanese soldiers in November and imprisoned at Nagasaki. Pechstein was not released from the Japanese prison until early 1915. He left Nagasaki for Shanghai and then Manila. Due to the war, he was forced to travel back to Europe via the United States, stopping first in San Francisco and then New York. Thanks to the intervention of officials at the American consul, some of Pechstein's paintings and drawings from Palau, those that survived the Japanese invasion, were returned to Germany in April of 1915. Pechstein's return home, however, was not quite so expedient. As a German citizen in the midst of wartime, his status in the United States was quite delicate. Waiting in New York until August of 1915, Pechstein boarded a ship bound for the Netherlands. Working as a ship's mechanic and sleeping in servants' quarters, his status on the journey home was considerably different than the status he enjoyed in route to Micronesia. Crossing the Atlantic in the late summer of 1915, stopping in London and then at ports in the Netherlands, Pechstein eventually returned to Germany on September 12, 1915, marking the official cessation of his Palau excursion. Soon after his return home, Pechstein was drafted into the German army, in which he served until 1917. It was not until his discharge in that year that he revisited his sketches, extant portions of his *tagebuch*, and the few surviving paintings that he created in Palau.

Pechstein's Postwar Nostalgia for Palau and the Politics of Place

Throughout the late teens into the early 1920s, Pechstein re-engaged with his South Seas experiences, fostering a longing for a land, people, climate, and way of life that was no longer physically accessible to Germans. This was a recuperative period for Pechstein, who spent much of his time repainting from memory canvases he had created in Palau, but which had not survived the war. Additional *new* works were created with the aid of extant writings and sketches. Beginning in late 1917 through 1918, Pechstein exhibited a series of his Palau-inspired paintings at the Fritz Gurlitt Gallery, prompting one to wonder if Berlin audiences were in any way sympathetic to Pechstein's nostalgia for the former German colony. Pechstein's political affiliations at this time were with the SPD, which by the early 1920s had dramatically reversed its previous condemnation of German colonial enterprises. Whether Pechstein's works were pointed pro-colonial statements or merely sentimental reconnections of a prewar era is difficult to say. What is clear is that Pechstein devoted several years to pictorially restaging his Palau excursion at

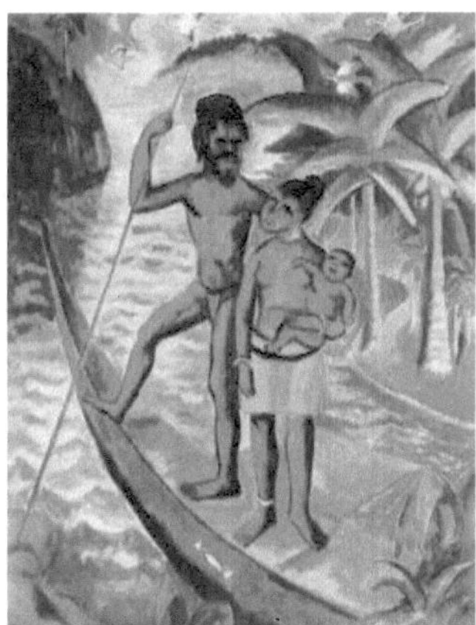

Figure 8.3. Max Pechstein, Palau Triptych *left panel, from 1917. © 2015 Artists Rights Society (ARS), New York / Pechstein Hamburg / Toekendorf / VG Bild-Kunst, Bonn*

a time when Germany no longer had colonial territories. As a result, his works operated within a zone of considerable flexibility as there were few contemporaneous reports relating to Palau that might counter his subjective depictions. It is not surprising that a number of his works incorporated the tactics of Gauguin, conflating fictive and in some cases outdated details with a roster of European genres.

Perhaps the best example of this technique can be seen in Pechstein's largest work, the *Palau Triptych* from 1917 (figure 8.3). The tri-part painting features three stylized vignettes—a family portrait on the left, a boating pair on the right, and a central panel combining gendered activities such as men fishing and women processing foodstuffs. In the background of the central scene are two men's clubhouses—the very structures that inspired the artist's initial visits to the Dresden Museum. By the time that Pechstein visited Palau in 1914, these structures were no longer in use. They remained in villages as fixtures of the past—a symbol of dramatic changes within Palauan culture, ripe emblems of Pechstein's desire to invent an *authentic* Palau.

The body of Pechstein's works that are affiliated with his Palau trip including paintings, drawings, prints, and sculptures, all too numerous to cover here, collectively function within the complicated conceptual terrain of Weimar postcolonialism. In an odd twist of fate, Pechstein's longing for Palau resurged again after World War II. His apartment and studio were bombed destroying a number of his Palau works. As an attempt to recapture the details of his trip, taken over thirty years earlier, he authored a post–World War II diary entitled *Erinnerungen* (Recollections), which was exclusively devoted to the Palau-Reise. The autobiographical account relied heavily upon a 1922 biography of Pechstein written by Max Osborn. Despite the odd medley of sources used to write these "recollections," their publication in the mid-1940s helped to foster a renewed interest in Pechstein's *Palau-Zeichnungen*, which featured in an unprecedented show at the Galerie Henning in Halle in 1947.

Images of the South Seas and the "Entartete Kunst" Exhibition

Pechstein's fascination with Palau stretched through many decades of his life: from his early interest in the carved wooden beams of men's club houses exhibited at the Völkerkunde Museum in Dresden in 1906 to the pages of *Erinnerungen* written during the mid-1940s. While Pechstein's South Seas experiences dominated his work from the late teens to the early 1920s, the reality is that Palau never completely left his system. From the mid-1920s through the 1930s, Pechstein returned to painting sun-drenched coastal landscapes replete with palm trees and shorelines dotted with the boats of fishing communities. While these works reflect trips that he made to northern Italy and southern France, they are nostalgic for a simpler life removed from the urban dynamism of Weimar Berlin; they recall the Pechstein's days in Palau as well as the postwar years he spent in his studio reliving the excursion. In the absence of German colonies, France and Italy served as surrogate, exotic locales, despite the fact that they were still within the boundaries of Europe. Rendered in vibrant colors, exploiting the presence of palms trees, these sites served as a stand-in for the vistas and tropical plants of the South Seas. Interestingly enough, despite this longing for Palau, Pechstein never again traveled beyond the boundaries of Europe. Berlin remained his home base until his death (in 1955).[23]

In 1933, Pechstein, like hundreds of other modern artists became the target of the National Socialists. He was dismissed from his professorship at the Prussian Academy of Fine Arts (later renamed the Akademie der Künste (AdK)) and was forbidden to exhibit his works in Germany, even though the previous year he was awarded a prestigious state prize. The situation only worsened as in 1937, three hundred and twenty-six of Pechstein's works were removed from German art museums, of which six paintings and nine graphic works were included in the so-called *Entartete Kunst* (Degenerate Art) exhibition. The Nazi Party sponsored the show, which featured works by all of Pechstein's Die Brücke colleagues as well as over a hundred famous modernist painters, printmakers, and sculptors from Germany and other parts of Europe, and it toured Germany and Austria for four years. Nearly three million people saw the exhibit, which consisted of six hundred and fifty works arranged in chaotic fashion accompanied by caustic critiques in the form of text panels and wall graffiti.[24] Of the fifteen works of Pechstein's on display, at least two depicted scenes from Palau. They included the left panel of the *Palau triptych* from 1917 (featuring a couple with their young child) and a lithograph from the *Palau Portfolio* dating to 1918. In spite of Hitler's aspirations to re-obtain former colonial properties, Pechstein's Palau works were not viewed sympathetically. Instead of being read as glorified remembrances of Germany's colonial past, these works were interpreted as signs of German weakness, particularly perceived as indicators of modernist

23. In the mid-1930s, Pechstein did receive offers to teach in Turkey and in Mexico. The National Socialists refused him a travel visa; the trips were never made.

24. For a full account of the *Entartete Kunst* exhibition, the display tactics used in the show, and the artists included, see Stephanie Barron's catalogue, *"Degenerate Art": The Fate of the Avant-Garde in Nazi Germany*, which accompanied the Los Angeles County Museum of Art's 1991 show of the same title.

corruption or degeneration through the glorification of the aesthetics, lifestyle, and philosophies of members of a non-Aryan race.

Pechstein was not the only expressionist persecuted for such renditions. Emil Nolde was also targeted for works he created during and after his trip to German New Guinea in 1913. Nolde and his wife joined a scientific expedition to the South Seas, which journeyed first across land covering Russia, Siberia, and China before reaching Japan and the islands of the South Seas. While Nolde was a short-lived member of Die Brücke, he mirrored the members' use of non-representational color, bold paint application, and interest in legends and artifacts from Africa, New Guinea, as well as South and North America. Nolde's trip to the South Seas reinforced his commitment to material objects from New Guinea. Upon his return he wrote a letter in 1914 to the Berlin Colonial Office, revealing his disdain for the infiltration of "civilized powers" on "tribal cultures." This dynamic Nolde reported was putting the authentic quality and aesthetic worth of native art at risk.[25] He further called upon German ethnographic museums to collect these works before they became a lost art. This mentality was used against Nolde as grounds for the inclusion of thirty-seven of his paintings and prints in the *Entartete Kunst* exhibition as well as the removal of over one thousand of his works in 1937 from German art museums.[26] Despite the fact that he had been a member of the North Schleswig branch of the National Socialist (NS) party since 1920, his paintings and prints were perceived to be degenerate. Nolde pleaded with Nazi officials and recommitted his belief in the superiority of Nordic peoples; but these attempts were futile.[27] Interestingly enough, none of Nolde's South Seas works were featured in the exhibit.

Like Nolde, Pechstein also attempted to resurrect his reputation; his grounds, however, were considerably different. In 1937, upon his removal from his academic position, Pechstein appealed to the NS by confirming his commitment to German nationalism. He recounted not only his past military service during World War I, but also played up the military duties and political affiliations of his sons. One son was a member of the *Sturmabteilung*, a storm trooper, while another son had been a participant in the *Hitler Jugend* (Hitler

25. Shapiro, *Painters and Politics*, 99.

26. Barron, *"Degenerate Art,"* 319. The exact total of works removed was 1,052.

27. For additional information on Nolde and his relationship to the Nazi party, see Berman, "German Primitivism/Primitive Germany: The Case of Emil Nolde," , 112–22. Also see Jill Lloyd,"Emil Nolde and the Paradox of Primitivism," in *German Expressionism*, 161–88.

Youth).[28] Despite these claims, Pechstein's earlier political engagement with the SPD and the perceived nature of his work precluded him from any exceptions. Other unsuccessful attempts to redeem his reputation included his willingness to aggrandize the German colonial administration. In a 1933 letter concerning the earliest Nazi attacks of his work, Pechstein wrote to his colleague Arthur Kampf. In his letter he characterized his Palau drawings and paintings as "an expression of pure, ideal attitude to the old German colonial power."[29] Given that Pechstein was actually quite critical of the colonial administration during his 1914 trip, his statement seems to betray his original reactions for the sake of avoiding further criticism and persecution.

While Pechstein received considerable attention from the teens through the early 1930s on the part of collectors, museums, and critics, following the war and beyond his fame was comparably less than his Die Brücke colleagues such as Ernst Ludwig Kirchner, Erich Heckel, Karl Schmidt-Rottluff, Otto Mueller, and Nolde. Dietmar Elger notes that while three monographs were written on Pechstein from 1916 to 1922, this level of attention was not mirrored during the late 1950s through the 1960s when several academic volumes were published on artists affiliated with Die Brücke and German Expressionism, in general.[30] While Elger's assessment does not account for the English translation of Pechstein's *Erinnerungen*, which was published in 1960, he is right to note that additional milestones seemed to have come and gone without much attention to the artist. Elger writes, "Even the centenary of his birth in 1981 passed relatively unnoticed and without any retrospective exhibitions, which are normally organized with great enthusiasm on such occasions. When the Royal Academy of Arts held its retrospective called *German Art in the Twentieth Century* in 1985, Pechstein was the only Brücke artist whose works were missing."[31] This was certainly not the case at the 2005 exhibition marking the one hundred year anniversary of the founding of Die Brücke, hosted by the Neue Nationalgalerie in Berlin. Pechstein, like his expressionist colleagues, was extremely well represented in the show. This said, one aspect of the exhibit intimated a similar type of neglect or

28. Barron, *"Degenerate Art,"* 328.

29. Lloyd, "A South Seas Odyssey," 211. Original citation from Erich Frommhold, "Zwischen Widerstand und Anspannung: Kunst in Deutschland 1933-1945," in *Stil und Gesellschaft*, ed. Friedrich Möbius (Dresden: VEB Verlag der Kunst, 1984), 262.

30. Elger, *Expressionism*, 79.

31. Ibid. 82.

overshadowing of Pechstein characteristic of Elger's analysis. Of the seventeen galleries that comprised the large-scale exhibition, one in particular, gallery 9 was devoted to "Travels to the South Seas." Based upon the title, one might presume that this space would be equally devoted to Nolde and Pechstein. Curiously enough, while Pechstein was referenced and a small selection of his works dating to 1914 were included in the room, Nolde's presence dramatically dominated the space. In fact, if one did not carefully examine all of the works in this gallery, one might have left thinking that Nolde had been the only one of the expressionists to travel to the South Seas. This privileging of Nolde's renditions of New Guinea over Pechstein's visions and revisions of Palau might be attributed simply to curatorial decisions owing to the accessibility and quality of the Pechstein's extant works. However, the fact that only one of his *Palua-Zeichnungen* versus several of Nolde's New Guinea sketches were included in the show does warrant some skepticism about the way in which these two artists and their respective trips to German colonial territories has been historicized. While Nolde's excursion has been the subject of an extensive catalogue and numerous essays on the subject, Pechstein's Palau-Reise remains a somewhat obscure topic, treated extensively by only a handful of scholars. What exactly this is due to is not entirely clear. However, it might relate to the fact that there is little literature devoted to Germany's colonial history in Palau. In contrast, there is significantly more scholarship devoted to the German presence in New Guinea. Furthermore, Pechstein's engagement with the island culture of Palau is considerably more complicated than Nolde's story. Pechstein's work bears the mark of several different chronological engagements with the details of his South Seas trip. In this sense, one might suggest that Nolde's body of work from 1914 provides a more accurate reading of his experiences and mindset as he encountered the people and geography of New Guinea. Additionally, Pechstein's case, unlike that of Nolde's, has been historicized as acritical of German colonial practices.[32] What I have attempted to suggest in this chapter is that Pechstein's work cannot be so easily relegated to this apolitical realm. Without question, his work reinforces the inherent pitfalls of the artist-traveler paradigm. His writings, paintings, drawings, prints, and sculpture created after World War I attempt to restage the archipelago and its inhabitants as symbols of an ideal world, a

---

32. The main argument for this distinction between the two artists resides in the work of Jill Lloyd. See her "Emil Nolde's Critique of Colonialism," 212–34.

paradise accessible as a result of German colonial rule. Pechstein's Palau-inspired oeuvre provides an intriguing indication of the complex intersection of colonial and postcolonial discourses intrinsic to the Weimar era.

Bibliography

Barron, Stephanie. *"Degenerate Art": The Fate of the Avant-Garde in Nazi Germany*. Catalogue accompanying show at the Los Angeles County Museum of Art, 1991.

Berman, Russell A. "German Primitivism/Primitive Germany: The Case of Emil Nolde." In *Cultural Studies of Modern Germany: History, Representation, and Nationhood*. Madison: The University of Wisconsin Press, 1993.

Dieterich, Gerd. *Max Pechstein—Das Ferne Paradies: Gemälde, Zeichnungen, Druckgraphik*. Exhibition Catalogue. Ostfildern-Ruit: Gerd Hatje Verlag in association with the Städtischen Kunstmuseum Spendhuas Reutlingen, 1995.

Elger, Dietmar. *Expressionism: A Revolution in German Art*. Translated by Hugh Beyer. Edited and produced by Ingo F. Walther. Cologne and New York: Taschen, 1998.

Firth, Stewart G. "German Firms in the Pacific Islands, 1857–1914." In *Germany in the Pacific and Far East, 1870–1914*, edited by John A. Moses and Paul M. Kennedy. St. Lucia, Queensland: University of Queensland Press, 1977.

Flam, Jack and Miriam Deutch, eds. *Primitivism and Twentieth Century Art: A Documentary History*. Berkeley, Los Angeles and London: University of California Press, 2003.

Grimaldo Grigsby, Darcy. "Orients and Colonies: Delacroix's Algerian Harem." In *The Cambridge Companion to Delacroix*, edited by Beth S. Wright. London: Cambridge University Press, 2001.

Gründer, Horst. *Geschichte der deutschen Kolonien*. Paderborn: Ferdinand Schöningh, 2004.

Hiller, Susan, ed. *The Myth of Primitivism: Perspectives on Art*. London and New York: Routledge, 1991.

Keown, Michelle. *Pacific Islands Writing: The Postcolonial Literatures of Aotearoa/New Zealand and Oceania*. Oxford: Oxford University Press, 2007.

Lansdown, Richard, ed. *Strangers in the South Seas: The Idea of the Pacific in Western Thought*. Honolulu: University of Hawai'i Press, 2006.

Lloyd, Jill. *German Expressionism: Primitivism and Modernity*. New Haven and London: Yale University Press, 1991.

Lülf, Barbara. "Die Such nach dem Ursprünglischen: Max Pechstein und Palau." In *Max Pechstein: Sein malerisches Werk*, edited by Magdalena M. Moeller. Munich: Hirmer Verlag, 1996.

Malingue, Maurice, ed. *Paul Gauguin—Letters to His Wife and Friends*. Translated by Henry J. Stenning. Boston: MFA Publications, 2003.

Moeller, Magdalena M., ed. *Max Pechstein: Sein malerisches Werk*. Munich: Hirmer Verlag, 1996.

Osborn, Max. *Max Pechstein*. Berlin: Propyläen Verlag, 1922.

Pechstein, Max. *Erinnerungen*. Edited by L. Reidemeister. Wiesbaden: Limes Verlag, 1960.

Perry, Gill. "Primitivism and the *Modern*." In *Primitivism, Cubism, Abstraction: The Early Twentieth Century*, edited by, ed. Charles Harrison, Francis Frascina, and Gill Perry. New Haven: Yale University Press in association with the Open University, 1993.

Schnee, Heinrich, ed., *Deutsches Kolonial-Lexicon*. Volume 3 (P–Z). Leipzig: Quelle & Meyer Verlag, 1920.

Shapiro, Theda. *Painters and Politics: The European Avant-Garde and Society, 1900–1925*. New York and Amsterdam: Elsevier, 1976.

Soika, Aya, "Max Pechstein: Ein Südsee-Insulaner in Berlin." In *Die Brücke in der Südsee—Exotik der Farbe*, edited by Ralph Melcher. Ostfildern-Ruit: Hatje Cantz Verlag in association with the Saarlandmuseum Saarbrücken, 2005.

Townsend, Mary E. "The Contemporary Colonial Movement in Germany." *Political Science Quarterly* 43, no. 1 (March 1928): 64–75.

———. *The Rise and Fall of Germany's Colonial Empire, 1884–1918*. New York: Macmillan, 1930.

Van Hoesen, Brett M. "Weimar Revisions of Germany's Colonial Past: The Photomontages of Hannah Höch and László Moholy-Nagy." In *German Colonialism, Visual Culture and Modern Memory*, edited by Volker Langbehn. London and New York: Routledge, 2009.

———. "Postcolonial Cosmopolitanism: Constructing the Weimar New Woman out of a Colonial Imaginary." In *The International New Woman: Representations in Photography and Film, 1890s–1930s*, edited by Elizabeth Otto and Vanessa Rocco. Ann Arbor: The University of Michigan Press, 2010.

———. "Weimar Postcolonialism and the Rhineland Controversy." In *German Cultures of Colonialism: Race, Nation and Globalization, 1884–1945*, edited by Geoff Eley and Bradley D. Naranch. Durham, NC: Duke University Press, 2014.

9

Vive l'Art Révolution: Gérard Fromanger and the Revolutionary Discourse in Painting

Catherine Dossin

In the 1970s, Parisian artists were divided between those who had never really left the barricades of May 1968 and wanted the Revolution, and those who, disillusioned, had returned to their studio and simply wanted to revolutionize painting. Gérard Fromanger wanted to do both. He was one of the few artists who, in the aftermath of May '68, refused to choose between art and revolution, but instead tried to conciliate the conflicting demands of political action with avant-garde practice. While his commitment to the revolutionary ideal led him to create works that invoked the limits of the *républicaine* values of liberty, equality, and fraternity in contemporary France, the painter successfully went beyond political illustration by intertwining social commentary with formal investigation and effectively addressing postmodern concerns with representation, originality, and the exhaustion of painting. Through his friendships and collaborations with Jean-Luc Godard, Michel Foucault, Gilles Deleuze, and other contemporary French intellectuals, Fromanger realized that revolution does not only happen on the barricades but also in the discourses. Their examples allowed him to see the revolutionary potential of deconstructing the established codes of representation, and thereby create truly revolutionary paintings.

As such, Fromanger's work offers one of the most persuasive examples of political art since *Guernica*. By retracing his career since the 1960s and analyzing key paintings, this study will explicate how the artist overcame the tensions between art and politics, whereby he could serve as a model for contemporary artists often trapped between the complicated demands of the contemporary art world and a urgent desire to respond to the world that surround them.

When the massive strikes and students' movement of May 1968 started, Gérard Fromanger was a promising young artist and a member of the Association de la Jeune Peinture, an artist-run organization with strong leftist ties.[1] Since the early 1960s, the Jeune Peinture had undergone an artistic and political radicalization under the combined influenced of the Spaniard Eduardo Arroyo, who raged against the Francoist regime in sarcastic paintings and Gilles Aillaud, a French artist with radical political views who developed a very original understanding of Modernity, Vanguardism, and political art.[2] At the end of the 1964 Salon of the Jeune Peinture, Arroyo asserted: "we are entering a new phase—an art that engages more of the spirit of art than its vocabulary. We intend to participate totally in the real. That is to say, to accuse, to denounce, to cry out, and not to fear taboo subjects such as politics and sexuality."[3]

On May 8, 1968, when the students of the Ecole des Beaux-Arts seized control of the building, artists of the *Jeune Peinture*, Fromanger among them, logically stepped in to help organize the siege and set up collective projects. Their first idea was to make a lithograph and sell the prints to help striking workers. As Fromanger explained: "The idea was to bring them to an art gallery to sell them. But we had hardly stepped out in the streets than the students took them and posted them on the wall. Then we got it: of course, this is the idea; this is how it should be used! We quickly went back to the print shop."[4] The Atelier Populaire of the Beaux-Arts was born at that moment.

The artists working at the Atelier were using the serigraphic technique, then a novelty in France. This technique allowed them to produce a large number of prints quickly and cheaply. The workshop printed on average between two and three thousand prints a day, producing around a million posters in less than two months. The Atelier was a collective endeavor in which there was no room for individual style and personal expression. Artists were at the service of the revolution and the works they created had to serve

1. On the *Jeune Peinture*, see Parent and Perrot, *Le Salon de la Jeune Peinture*.

2. On this transformation, see Dossin, "The Jeune Peinture."

3. Levêque, "Le Salon de la Jeune Peinture écartelé entre Bonnard et Bacon."

4. Quoted in Gervereau, "L'atelier populaire de l 'ex-Ecole des Beaux-Arts 184

a purpose. Every evening there would be a meeting of the General Assembly during which artists would propose designs for posters. These proposals would be discussed and voted on.[5] When Fromanger proposed an image of a bleeding French flag, it was rejected after eight hours of vivid discussion. Accepted designs would be realized that very night.[6]

On June 27, the CRS (French anti-riot police) stormed the School and forced the Atelier to close. Fromanger left the School quickly, taking the screen and the squeegee of the Ateliers under his arm. While the CRS was searching the School to find the heavy equipment responsible for the production of so many posters, Fromanger was creating one last poster: "La police s'affiche aux Beaux-Arts, les Beaux-Arts s'affichent dans la rue,"[7] which was then plastered on the streets of Paris.[8]

In June 1968, Fromanger staged an event in the streets of Paris. In an attempt to bring art to the people and spread the revolutionary spirit, he placed several semi-spheres made of transparent red material on the pavement at Place Blanche. The *Souffles,* as they were called, reflected the people and the city, and he colored them red—the color of the revolution. The shape of the *Souffles* recalled the shields of the CRS. They were shields for the people—red shields to hold against the blue shields of the police. With this temporary installation, Fromanger was not only bringing art to people; he was also offering them a metaphorical protection: the protection of imagination and art against alienation and repression.[9]

On October 12, 1968, when life had returned to normal in the streets of Paris, Fromanger re-installed the *Souffles* at the Alesia subway station. By bringing the red shields back to the streets of Paris, the artist was trying to keep the revolutionary spirit alive and to prevent Parisians from falling back into their comfortable apathy.

---

5. On the organisation of the *Atelier Populaire*, see Parent and Perrot, *Le Salon de la Jeune Peinture*, 76-82.

6. Gervereau, "L'atelier populaire de l 'ex-Ecole des Beaux-Arts," 187.

7. This is a play of words in French, where "affiche" means both a poster and to present oneself or to show up. The statement here roughly translates as "The police show up at the Beaux-Arts school and the Beaux-Arts school shows up in the street."

8. Parent and Perrot, *Le Salon de la Jeune Peinture*, 81.

9. This installation is part of a number of events that were staged in the streets of Paris in the late 1960s, including Le GRAV's *A Day in the City* (1966) and Carlos Cruz-Diez's *Chromosaturation Labyrinth* (1969), which were intended to activate passersby's political consciousness.

Fromanger, who had failed to obtain an authorization to install his work, was arrested when police intervened. Police also destroyed the work, and arrested Jean-Luc Godard, who had come to film the event.[10]

This example of police repression only sharpened the artist's desire to continue political action and keep the revolutionary spirit alive. To this end, Fromanger created a portfolio of prints that summon the revolutionary spirit. For the *Album Rouge*, he went back to his idea of the bleeding French flag that the Atelier's General Assembly had rejected. The result was a powerful image whose simple graphic style evokes, with great efficacy, the limits of the values of liberty, equality, and fraternity. The disruption of the familiar image invokes the blood spilled on behalf of the fatherland, the state's repression against its own people,[11] as well as the march forward of the communist revolution. Using thfe same graphic principle, Fromanger created bleeding versions of other nations' flags. The most powerful image of the series is, to my mind, a print that displays nine flags. The red sections bleed across the page and merge, visually uniting the people of all nations through blood and revolution (figure 9.1).

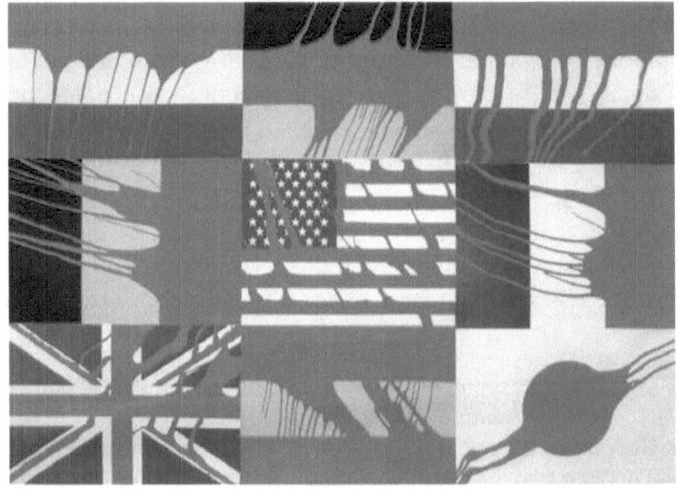

Figure 9.1. Gérard Fromanger, L'album Rouge, *1968. Courtesy Gérard Fromanger.*

10. For an illustrated account of these events, see Ameline and Ajac, eds., *Figuration Narrative, Paris 1960-1972* , 134,136

11. The colors of the French tricolor flag originated from the tripartite division of society during the Ancient Regime: blue represented nobility, white was for the clergy, and red stood for the people.

The remaining prints of the *Album Rouge* were based on photographs of the 1968 events. Fromanger reproduced these images in serigraphy using only two colors, blue and red, with the white of the paper serving as third color. The artist used graduations of blue for the background and the police, and colored the people in solid red. As a result, white and blue merge, and red stands out in its isolation. If the use of flat red depersonalizes the people of the photographs and places them at the same level, it also unites and empowers them: be they street-sweepers or professionals passing by, they all carry with them the possibility of change—the Red. The *Album Rouge* was not a memento to the 1968 revolution; it was a summons to believe in and to carry on the revolutionary spirit.

In the early 1970s, Fromanger created paintings that address problems of contemporary French society, using the formal vocabulary he had developed in the *Album Rouge*. *Fleury-Villandry ou la nouvelle societé dans la France éternelle* (1971), for example, participates in the 1970s critique of the French penitentiary system. In February 1971, Fromanger's friend, Michel Foucault, cofounded the *Groupe d'Information sur les Prisons* (GIP, Prison Information Group) with Jean-Marie Domenach and Pierre Vidal-Naquet, to which Fromanger belonged. A direct response to the recent imprisonments of intellectuals involved in demonstrations and actions against the government, the group aimed at studying life in prison and providing prisoners an opportunity to speak up about their conditions.[12] Fromanger's painting depicts the entrance of Fleury-Villandry jail toward which several people are walking. By exaggerating the verticality of the composition and focusing on the façade, the artist forces viewers to look at the prison's doors and imagine life inside these heavy, opaque walls. What do we know about what happens inside the prisons? What do we know about the penitentiary system and its prisoners? Those questions, which this painting triggered, were also the premise of Foucault's investigation for *Surveiller et Punir* (*Discipline and Punish*).[13] In Fromanger's painting, the people entering the jails are colored in solid red. Through this image of the symbolic Red entering the jail, the painter evokes here again the revolutionary potential carried in each and any citizen, and inscribes the responsibility to take action and change things on them. The title, *Fleury-Villandry or the New Society in the Eternal France* was both a cynical comment on French contemporary society and a call to engage in the shaping of the "new society."

12. On the GIP see Salle, "Mettre la prison à l'épreuve."

13. Foucault, *Surveiller et Punir*.

In 1971, Fromanger created a series on the *Boulevard des Italiens*, based on snapshots taken on the Boulevard des Italiens. For thirty minutes, he took a series of photographs documenting the daily life of a busy Parisian street around lunchtime. The photographs offered a candid portrait of Paris in 1971—three years after the events of May '68, which had promised to transform French society. Working on this series, Fromanger continued painting the figures in unmodulated red, and rendering the background through tonal gradation, but instead of using only blue, he experimented with different shades of brown, yellow, purple, and even green, thereby moving away from the French tricolor palette. By playing with the background colors, the artist was trying to renew what was threatening to become nothing but an autographic style. He might also have been commenting on the return to normal; on the spirit of May '68 progressively sinking into oblivion. It is indeed difficult not to feel a certain disillusionment in these images. However, through his use of color, Fromanger suggests that the Parisians, who are mindlessly window-shopping, queuing at a movie theater, or simply crossing the streets, are still wearing on them, in them, the color of the revolution. One of the paintings, simply titled *Le rouge* (1971), shows a police van with a red prisoner in it. In the background, another red figure, seated at a café, reads a newspaper. Considering that the series was started during the launching of the GIP, this image takes a particular meaning. As explained earlier, the GIP's ambition was to draw attention to the penitentiary system and open French prisons to the press and the public. The man reading the newspaper does not pay attention to the man in the police van, or if he sees the prisoner, he does not question the legitimacy of his confinement. By painting both of them red, the artist erases any differences between those two men and makes us wonder if the man seated at the café is really safe from police and governmental abuse.

In 1971, Fromanger became one of the main leaders of the Front des Artistes Plasticiens (FAP, Plastic Artists' Front), a new association of artists aimed at defending artists' rights and artists' involvement in French political life. The front's major goal was to protest against President Pompidou's plans for Beaubourg (an area in Paris set aside for redevelopment to include high-tech architecture and emblematic buildings), which entailed the demolition of Les Halles, that is, the ancient covered market of Paris, and of hundreds of artists' studios in the vicinity. They also wished to denounce the absence of artists' involvements in decisions regarding the visual arts in France. In 1972, the FAP strongly opposed *Douze ans d'art contemporain en France*, an exhibition organized under the aegis of

President Pompidou. While several members of the FAP had been invited to participate in the show, most of them had been left out for political reasons. To many observers, the choice of artists did not offer an accurate image of the artistic landscape in France. Before it even opened, the show had already caused vivid polemics. On the day of the opening, the Front des Artistes Plasticiens, led by Gérard Fromanger, demonstrated outside the Grand Palais, keeping guests from entering the exhibition. When the arrival of the Queen of England's retinue on the Champs Elysées was announced, police were ordered to break up the crowd. During the clash that followed, several artists were hurt and five arrested. In response, the Malassis took their paintings down and replaced them with enlarged photographs of the police's attack on the artists.[14]

In this context, Fromanger realized a new series titled *Le peintre et le modèle* (1972). At first glance this body of works, with its street scenes, passersby, and shopping widows, is similar to the *Boulevard des Italiens.* In those works, the artist gave up representing people in solid red and started using multiple colors and levels of shading, thereby restoring passersby's individuality and moving away from the revolutionary message. This series represents a moment of transition, when the artist starts questioning his role as a painter in society. On several paintings, the black silhouette of the artist occupies the foreground of the canvas. In the essay he devoted to this series, "Le chaud et le froid," Gilles Deleuze explains that the painter's silhouette does not belong to the street scene but to the studio in which the work was painted.[15] The black silhouette is indeed posed on top of the photographed scene. Fromanger uses an overhead projector to project the black and white photograph onto the canvas. The artist thus works in the dark, and paints the shadow of the photograph on a canvas that is never white. This method also means that his shadow is cast on the canvas. Painting the scene, the painter moves from the lightest to the darkest sections. For Deleuze, this working method completely abstracts the subject matter and deconstructs the composition by focusing on shades and colors—on the opposition between cool and warm colors. In strong contrast to these modulated colors, the silhouette of the artist is painted in flat black—the non-color.[16] As Deleuze explains, the painter is an

14. On these events, see 169–71.

15. Deleuze, "Le chaud et le froid," in *Gérard Fromanger: Le peintre et le modèle.*

16. On Deleuze's reading of Fromanger, see Wilson, "Deleuze, Foucault, Guattari. Periodisations: Fromanger."

essential element of the work but he does not exist in the painting. Expanding on the philosopher's comments, we can add that the painter is not shown working on the painting, but standing still as an observer of the street scene and the painting in the making.

Such *mise en abime* of the artistic process was common in the novels of the French Nouveau Roman and the movies of the Nouvelle Vague of the 1950s and 1960s. The Nouveaux Romans were not stories about heroes launched into adventures. They were writing experiments: acts that aimed at letting language reveal itself. The subject of a book was henceforth the process of its own creation. As Jean Ricardou summarizes, "The novel is not the writing of an adventure but the adventure of writing."[17] The same process of deconstruction was applied to movies by the young cineastes of the Nouvelle Vague, of which Jean-Luc Godard, Fromanger's friend, was a major figure. The new cineastes deconstructed movies to show viewers the codes and conventions that made a movie. Their films constantly reminded viewers that they were watching actors playing in a film. It was, to a certain extent, the pinnacle of realism: a realism that did not try to fool its viewers into believing in a pseudo-fiction, but instead showed them cinematic reality. Such ambition was clearly visible in the techniques used: from natural lighting to actors' directly addressing the camera to *mise en abyme*.[18]

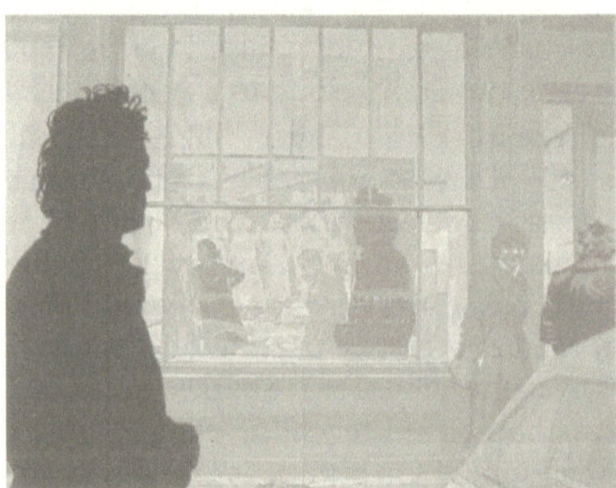

Figure 9.2. Gérard Fromanger, Vert Véronèse, *1972, from the series* Le peintre et le modèle. *Courtesy Gérard Fromanger.*

The silhouette of Fromanger is standing still, pondering what he sees. One of the paintings, *Vert Veronèse*, shows an art gallery in

17. Ricardou, *Problème du Nouveau Roman*, 111.

18. On the Nouvelle Vague see, for instance, Douin, ed. *La nouvelle vague 25 ans après*.

which *Rouge cadmium clair* is displayed (figure 9.2). The two silhouettes of the painter are facing each other. This work certainly comes from Fromanger's discomfort at seeing his paintings being bought and sold in commercial galleries; in other words, being part of the very capitalist system against which he had fought in May '68 and that he still rejected. Disillusioned? Maybe, but by superimposing his image onto the scene, by making himself the witness of the world and of the painting, Fromanger shows that he still believes that he has a role to play, even though he might not know what this role can or should be.

The introspection of *Le peintre et le modèle* was followed by a more overtly political series titled, *Annoncer la couleur* (1973–74), which questions the power of the press. In February 1973, Fromanger's friend, Serge July, founded a new newspaper with Jean-Paul Sartre titled *Libération*, whose ambition was to give a voice to the people. *Qui parle à qui, de quoi?* (1974) shows a man—most likely an immigrant from North Africa—selling the influential daily *Le Monde* in the street of Paris. In the early 1970s, *Le Monde* supported a moderate socialism and appealed to the educated middle class. In this image, Fromanger thus captured the discrepancy between the information and ideas presented in the newspaper, and the reality and preoccupations of the man selling them. The painting and its caption illustrate the absence of representation for the working-class in the press—an absence that *Libération* ambitioned to fill.

Comment dites-vous? (1973) shows the artist standing in front of a newsstand reading *Libération*, the headline of which announces that Great Britain had declared a state of emergency following a massive strike of miners and electricians. Great Britain is also on the front page of the other magazines displayed on the stand. However, the topic of discussion is not the workers' strike but Princess Anne's wedding. *France-Dimanche* claims: "Elle a défié la Cour pour épouser Mark. La triomphale victoire d'Anne" ("She braves the Court to marry Mark. The triumphal victory of Anne"), while *Detective-Special* simply proclaims: "Le triomphe d'Anne" (Anne's triumph). These newspapers feed their readers with princess stories while ignoring the workers fighting for their rights. As the painting illustrates, only *Libération* reports on the life and preoccupations of the working-class. Yet, the clash of headlines was not deliberate on the part of Fromanger. It merely reflects the blunt reality of what was on the newsstand the day he took the photograph.[19]

Despite their obvious message, the works of *Annoncer la couleur*

19. Gérard Fromanger, Interview with the author, March 24, 2013.

are not mere illustrations of political ideas. In this series, Fromanger does not only question the press; he also questions painting. He reflects on the way his painted images, like the printed images of the press, influence public opinion while conveying his personal, thus disputable, viewpoint. Pursuing the reflection he had started with *Le Peintre et le Modèle,* the painter deconstructs the process of creation. Without showing his shadow, he exposed the formal choices he made while creating his image. In *Comment dites-vous?* for instance, he paints close-up views of his face, and of his body in different shades of red. In *Quel est le fond de votre pensée?* (1973; figure 9.3), he creates legends with the swatches of colors and patterns he uses to paint the figures, transforming his painting into a map to be read and analyzed. In the same way as Roland Barthes unveiled the ideology at work in photographs and advertisements, Fromanger took his paintings apart, thereby inviting his viewers to look not only at his but at all images more critically.

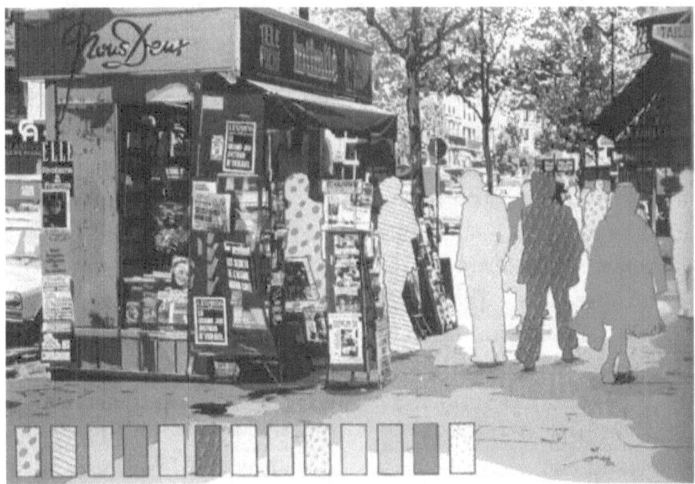

Figure 9.3. Gérard Fromanger, Quel est le fond de votre pensée? *1973 from the series* Annoncer la couleur. *Courtesy Gérard Fromanger.*

In a diptych titled *Comment faire le portrait d'un tableau?* and painted in 1975, Fromanger brought the deconstruction of painting further: the left panel is divided into ten sections that show different stages in the making of a street scene. We can see how the artist first paints the lightest areas in grey (remember his canvas is never white), then proceeds from the darker to the darkest areas, and finishes with vivid green for the background. On the right panel, we see the artist in his studio working on the street scene. The right panel is painted in different shades of red—the trademark color of the artist. In the darkened studio, Fromanger is adding the last touch to a small canvas hung on the wall, also the projected photograph covers it entirely. The artist has selected only a small section of the photograph for his painting. In the text he devoted to Fromanger's work, "La peinture photogénique," (photogenic painting) Michel Foucault analyzes the relationships between photography and painting in Fromanger's work. He explains that the painting is not a reproduction of an event photographed but the creation of an independent event that takes place in the artist's studio.[20] The event takes place when the artist projects the photograph on the canvas, selects the parts he will include, and then short-circuits the meaning of the original event through addition of colors and textures. Through his decisions and actions, Fromanger creates a new image, a "source of myriad surging images."

Composition, colors, and textures inform the message of the work. As T. J. Clark was arguing at the time in his studies of Courbet, sociopolitical and artistic-aesthetic orders cannot be distinguished; they work hand in hand. Style conveys ideology and, as such, has a certain degree of political significance.[21] For the painters, the consequences are twofold: on the one hand, images cannot be trusted and the artist's role is to warn people against them, but in another way it means that style has a role to play in the revolution. At the end of the day, the artist may not have to choose between painting the revolution and revolutionizing painting; he might be able to undertake the revolution in painting.

The possibility of undertaking the revolution in painting was, I argue, attempted and possibly realized in a series titled, *Hommage à François Topino-Lebrun*. Fromanger created this series for an exhibition organized by Alain Jouffroy in homage to the revolutionary painter François Topino-Lebrun, who had been executed during the Directory period of the French Revolution in 1801. In 1971, Jouffroy had rediscovered the revolutionary artist, whose death marked the end of the French Revolution. For Jouffroy, who had been actively involved in the events of May '68, understanding Topino-Lebrun's fate and the failure of the French Revolution was a way to deal with the failure of the 1968 Revolution. It was also a way to reflect on the artist's place in society and the validity of a committed painter. Jouffroy created *Les Amis de Topino-Lebrun*, an association that successfully lobbied for the restoration of his most

20. Foucault, "La Peinture photogénique," and Fromanger, Interview with the author, March 24, 2013.

21. Clark, *Image of the People*.

famous work, *La mort de Caius Gracchus* (Marseille, Musée des Beaux-arts). The painting, which depicts the arrest of Caius Gracchus in 121 BCE, represented in fact the arrest and execution of Topino-Lebrun's friend, François Noël (Gracchus) Babeuf in 1797. To celebrate the restoration of the painting, Jouffroy organized an exhibition in homage to Topino-Lebrun at the Centre Georges Pompidou in June 1977. The series Fromanger presented at this exhibition included five paintings created between 1975 and 1977: *La mort de Caius Gracchus*, *La mort de Pierre Overney*, *La vie des Idées*, *La vie d'artiste*, and *La vie et la mort du peuple.*

The first work of the series is based on Topino-Lebrun's painting, which is reproduced in black and white on the upper left corner of the canvas. Fromanger's homage is a color-coding of the original work. The landscape is thus rendered through zones of black and grey, which systematize twilight. The figures are reduced to silhouettes painted in different combination of colors. As explained in the captions at the top of the canvas, each combination represents a particular individual or group. Gracchus's enemies, for instance, are rendered in black and white strips. Only Caius Gracchus (a combination of purple, yellow, blue, red, green, and orange), his friend (mauve), the herald of the People (mauve and brown), and the People (yellow and ochre), in other words the People and its representatives, are in colors. In the legend, Fromanger identifies the figures for the roles they played in the stories of both Caius Gracchus and Gracchus Babeuf, thereby decoding Topino-Lebrun's painting and unveiling its political message.

A figure in solid black stands out among the angry crowd rushing toward Caius Gracchus. In the caption, Fromanger identifies the figures as Topino-Lebrun. With his turban, the black figure clearly belongs to the eighteenth-century story, and has no equivalent in the ancient story. If there is one, he is not to be found in the past but in the present: Topino-Lebrun's black silhouette indeed brings to mind the silhouette of the artist in *Le Peintre et le Modèle,* thereby bringing the modern period into the story.

The idea that three stories, three moments in history, are colliding in this work is confirmed by the second painting of the series, which represents the death of Pierre Overney. In February 1972, Overney, a young Maoist militant, was killed while handing out tracts outside a Renault factory. Journalists and photographers witnessed his argument with a security agent, which resulted in his death. The tragic incident made the headlines and started a wave of strikes and riots in France. Fromanger used one of the photographs taken after Overney's death. He removed all the details to only keep the face and part of the bust that he paints in an explosion of purple, yellow, blue, red, green, and orange, that is, the colors used to represent the revolutionary heroes in *La mort de Caius Gracchus.* Fromanger transformed Overney into the modern equivalent of Gracchus and Babeuf, beatifying the young man in a flicker of colorful dots and lines that evokes the grains of photographic reproductions in newspapers. Moreover, those thousands of purple, yellow, blue, red, green, and orange dots and lines that the artist spent hours making assert the painterly quality of the work. Here, rather than report on events or critique society, Fromanger aims to talk through painting about the production and reproduction of history and its images.

The third work of the series, *La Vie des Idées*, returns to the question of the press's role in political life. The painting shows the upper part of a *France-Soir* cover dated from Tuesday, September 2, 1975. Fromanger reproduced the recognizable logo, while concealing the articles with rectangles of the same colors used in the first two paintings. In the 1950s and 1960s, *France-Soir* had the largest diffusion among French daily newspapers, selling more than a million copies. As such, it played a very important role in shaping French people's visions of the world. Yet, its populist editorial was exactly what *Libération* and Fromanger opposed. The artist did not cover the letters "GP," which referred to the region of the "Grand Paris" for which the journal was issued, but actually framed it in the revolutionary colors, transforming it into the acronym of the "Gauche Prolétarienne," a Maoist political party founded in 1968.[22]

The fourth canvas, titled *La vie d'artiste*, shows Fromanger working in his studio. The artist, seated at his table, is adjusting the overhead projector, which projects on the wall behind him a photograph taken during the riot at the Toul Prison, to which he had devoted a series in 1974.[23] The rioters, standing on the roof, are painted in solid bright colors (purple, yellow, blue, red, green, and orange) while the rest of the painting is done in monochromatic gradation of green. *La vie d'artiste* represents the artist working in a composition similar to *Comment faire le portrait d'un tableau?* but, in this case, there is no canvas. The work is not about a painting being made but about what is happening in the studio. The entire composition is covered with lines of colors that link the projector, the art-

22. Fromanger, Interview with the author, March 24, 2013.

23. In 1974, at the time of the riots, the artist had devoted several paintings to the event. On this event see Foucault's unpublished manuscript, "La révolte de Toul," available at: http://michel-foucault-archives.org/spip.php?article247.

ist, and the projected images, and expand beyond the frame of the canvas to the real world. The lines represent the artist's intervention and creation of new layers of meaning—or to quote Foucault, of "myriad surging images." The bright colors of the lines place this intervention within the realm of politics and revolution. The painting asserts that the painter and his works have a role to play in the revolution, even though they are only one element in a larger movement.

The final work in the series, *La vie et la mort du people,* shows modern Parisians going by around Place Pigalle, wearing the colors and textures of the Gracchus-Babeuf-Overney story. Unlike the *Album Rouge* or the *Boulevard des Italiens,* in which the people wore the red of the revolution, in this last work most of them wear the non-colors of the establishment as coded in *La mort de Caius Gracchus*. However, the legend of the first painting with its rectangles of colors and explanatory captions gives away to elongated clouds of colors that cover the entire upmost part of the canvas, lightly connecting the present to its revolutionary past. With this final work, the painter invites us to reflect on the way history repeats itself: on the cyclical movement between revolution and counterrevolution—between the life and death of the People. The revolution is unfinished but the possibility of change is there; it is up to the people to make it happen. Standing still among the passersby, the black silhouette of what I am inclined to see as the painter looks at us. He is the witness of his time, who offers a personal vision of history, draws comments and paints connections, but cannot undertake the revolution. The only revolution he can carry out is a revolution in painting.[24]

In 1975, the year Franco died, Fromanger took part in the creation of the Collectif Antifasciste within the Jeune Peinture, the goal of which was to continue fighting Fascism and oppression throughout the world.[25] The first action of the Collectif was to create a poster in response to the killing of Mohamed Laïd Moussa, a young Algerian immigrant. In 1973, Moussa had involuntary killed a Frenchman during a neighborhood quarrel. Released after eighteen months in jail, he was summarily executed by an extreme right commando.[26] The Collectif designed a blue, white, and red silkscreen poster, reminiscent of Fromanger's *Album Rouge*, displaying Moussa's portrait on the left and, on the right, the superimposed silhouettes of his killer holding a gun, a policeman brandishing his billy, and President Giscard d'Estaing standing in the background.

24. See Jouffroy and Bordes, *Guillotine et peinture, Topino-Lebrun et ses amis*, 79.

25. Perrot, *Le collectif antifasciste 1974–1977.*

26. Brino, "Qui est raciste?"; Chabalier, "La loi de lynch à Marseilles."

In the following years, the Collectif and with it Fromanger participated in multiple actions including against racism in France, apartheid in South Africa, military dictatorships in South America, the occupation of Palestine, and Soviet repression of the Polish Solidarity movement. Those collective actions enabled the painter to play an active role in the world beyond his painting, and as such helped him bridge the gap between art and politics.[27]

The First Gulf War in 1991 reopened the question of the artist's role in the world with a new terrible urgency. With disbelief, Fromanger followed the unfolding of the crisis on his television screen, from the invasion of Kuwait in August 1990 to the failure of diplomatic negotiations to the launch and success of *Operation Desert Shield* in January and February 1991. On the night of January 15, which marked the US ultimatum for Iraq to withdraw from Kuwait, he stayed up, watching the news, clutching to the dim hope of a peaceful resolution of the situation. But the war started, bringing with it its toll of destruction and death. As the war ended, he saw with horror US aircrafts chasing and bombing the routed Iraqi army, thinking to himself that it could only be the beginning and not the end of the war.[28]

At that time, Fromanger had started working on a large canvas conceived as a bulletin board covered with rectangles of different sizes and colors that would act as posts-it on which he would paint reminders. As the war progressed, he started filling the colored plaques with black silhouette of weapons used during the conflict such as tanks, submarines, aircraft carriers, and helicopters. Relatively small, those images are kept on the outer edge of the canvas, while the center is occupied by representations of the four elements: water (fish), air (birds), earth (trees), and fire (media spotlights). The rest of the rectangles are filled with images of past civilizations: the Egyptian pyramids, Etruscan paintings, Notre-Dame Cathedral in Paris, the Statue of Liberty, the World Trade Center, and so on. Then at the left of the canvas, on a blue vertical rectangle, Fromanger represented himself, hunched over, holding a brush in his hand and looking at a reclining nude that occupies a large horizontal rectangle at the right of the canvas. The painter and his model are surrounded and separated by the world, present and past.

As in *La vie d'artiste* but on a much larger scale, lines of colors run through the canvas like the circuit board of a TV set, connecting the different elements of the painting. Adding to the visual fren-

27. On the collectif, see Perrot, *Le collectif antifasciste 1974–1977.*

28. Information on this painting comes from a conversation between Fromanger and the author on March 24, 2013.

zy, Fromanger covered the work with splashes and drips of white, black, and red paint, thereby expressing in paint the violence and destructiveness of the world that surrounds him. Beyond the immediate bloodshed of the Gulf War, the red splashes over the painter, and the weapons, the elements, the pyramids, the cathedral, and the Statue of Liberty represent Fromanger's disillusioned vision history and resigned hopelessness for humanity—a hopelessness that led him to paint at the center of his canvas, the terribly foreseeing image of the Twin Towers bleeding.

Yet, amidst the chaos of lines, splashes, and images, Fromanger continues to paint. He paints the nude woman, whose pose stands as homage to Courbet's *Origin of the World* (1866), but also as a statement on painting as an act of resistance to the horrors of the world. For more than a year, Fromanger worked on this painting, trying to make sense of the world that surrounded him. In his mind, he was creating his *Guernica*. Like Picasso, who had used the color scheme of the newspapers through which he had experienced the event, Fromanger used the Technicolor and shape of the TV screen through which he experienced the war. However, while Picasso wished to attract public attention to the bombing of the Basque city, Fromanger was dealing with an event that had been overly present in the media. Rather than propagandist and emotional, *De toutes les couleurs, peinture d'histoire* (1991–92; figure 9.4) was personal and factual. With it he was not so much trying to make people react but trying to come to terms with humanity's incurable destructiveness. The cheerful colorfulness of the title and palette of the work indicate, I believe, Fromanger's success. Free from any illusion about his fellow humans, he embraces the world at its best and worst, creating a multicolor portrait of love, war, and art, lazily watched over by a black cat splattered with red paint.

Years after finishing the painting, Fromanger came across the last paragraph of Claude Lévi-Strauss's *Tristes Tropiques* that so well encapsulated his own views:

> Let us grasp the essence of what our species has been and still is, beyond thought and beneath society: an essence that may be vouchsafed to us in a mineral more beautiful than any work of Man; in the scent, more subtly evolved than our books, that lingers in the heart of a lily; or in the wink of an eye, heavy with patience, serenity, and mutual forgiveness, that sometimes, through an involuntary understanding, one can exchange with a cat.[29]

---

29. Lévi-Strauss, *Tristes Tropiques*, 398.

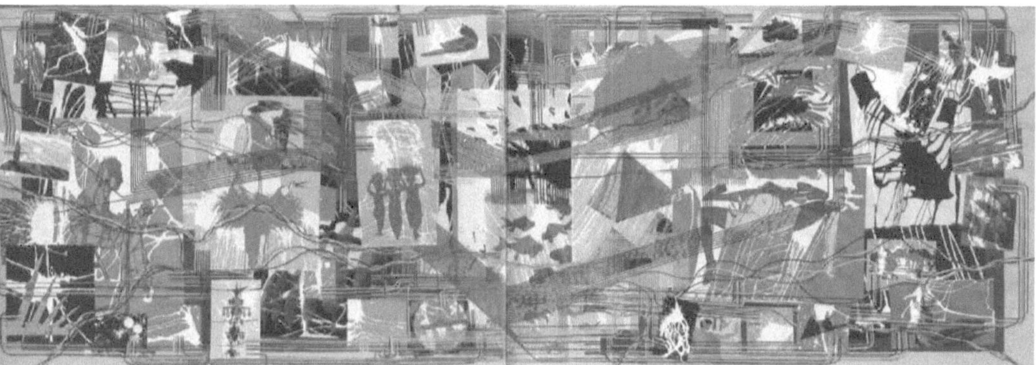

Figure 9.4. Gérard Fromanger, De toutes les couleurs, peinture d'histoire, *1991-92. Courtesy Gérard Fromanger.*

From the 1960s to the present, Gérard Fromanger has striven to conciliate the conflicting demands of politics and art with avant-garde practice. Without ever renouncing either his artistic practice or political engagement, he has never fallen into mere political illustration nor has he indulged in empty formalist pursuit. To use Peter Selz's phrase, he has remained all along engaged with the world and committed to art.[30] In fact, I believe that it is the continuous tension between his engagement with the social and political context of his time and his concomitant commitment to the medium of painting that has enabled him to create a body of works that is both a political act and artistic feat.

Bibliography

Ameline, Jean-Paul, and Bénédicte Ajac, eds. *Figuration Narrative, Paris 1960–1972*. Paris: RMN & Centre Georges Pompidou, 2008.

Brino, Nicolas. "Qui est raciste?" *L'unité*, March 28, 1975, 1–2.

Chabalier, Hervé. "La loi de lynch à Marseilles." *Le Nouvel Observateur*, March 24, 1975, 24–25.

Clark, Timothy J. *Image of the People: Gustav Courbet and the Second French Republic, 1848–1851*. London: Thames & Hudson, 1973.

Deleuze, Gilles. "Le chaud et le froid." In Gérard Fromanger, *Le peintre et le modèle*. Paris: Baudard-Alvarez éditeurs, 1973.

Dossin, Catherine. "The Jeune Peinture: The Parisian Third Way of the 1960s." *In Sweet Sixties. Specters and Spirits of a Parallel*

30. Selz, "Engagement and Commitment."

Avant-garde, 276-88. Edited by Georg Schoellhammer and Ruben Arevshatyan. Berlin: Sternberg Press, 2014

Douin, Jean-Luc, ed. *La nouvelle vague 25 ans après*. Paris: Les Editions du Cerf, 1983.

Foucault, Michel. "La Peinture photogénique." In Gérard Fromanger, *Le désir est partout*. Paris: Galerie Jeanne Bucher, 1975.

———. *Surveiller et Punir: Naissance de la prison*. Paris: Gallimard, 1975. English: Discipline and Punish: The Birth of the Prison. Translated by Alan Sheridan. New York: Pantheon Books, 1977.

Gervereau, Laurent. "L'atelier populaire de l 'ex-Ecole des Beaux-Arts: Entretien avec Gérard Fromanger." *Matériaux pour l'histoire de notre temps* 11 (1988): 184–91.

Jouffroy, Alain, and Philippe Bordes. *Guillotine et peinture, Topino-Lebrun et ses amis*. Paris: Editions du Chene, 1977.

Levêque, Jean-Jacques. "Le Salon de la Jeune Peinture écartelé entre Bonnard et Bacon." *ARTS: lettres, spectacles, musique* (January 15, 1964).

Lévi-Strauss, Claude. *Tristes Tropiques: an Anthropological Study of Primitive Societies in Brazil.* Translated by John Russell. New York: Atheneum, 1972.

Parent, Francis, and Raymond Perrot. *Le Salon de la Jeune Peinture: Une histoire 1950–1983*. Paris: Jeune Peinture, 1983.

Perrot, Raymond. *Le collectif antifasciste 1974–1977.* Paris: E.C. Editions, 2001.

Ricardou, Jean. *Problème du Nouveau Roman*. Paris: Editions du Seuil, 1967.

Salle, Grégory. "Mettre la prison à l'épreuve: Le GIP en guerre contre l'Intolérable." Cultures & Conflits 55 (2004): 71–96.

Selz, Peter. "Engagement and Commitment." In this volume.

Wilson, Sarah. "Deleuze, Foucault, Guattari. Periodisations: Fromanger." In *The Visual World of French Theory: Figurations.* New Haven and London: Yale University Press, 2010.

10

Anti-Espaliú: From Model Figure to Intertext (or, Toward a Larger Cartography of AIDS Politics in the Basque Country and Spain)

Aimar Arriola

With their impressionist language, iconography-centered analysis, transcendent tone, and hackneyed topics, hegemonic historiography and criticism in Spain[1] have made Cordoba artist Pepe Espaliú

---

1. A slightly different version of this text was presented at the symposium related to this book under the not so resounding title: "Contaminate the Paradigm: Reconsidering Espaliú's Actions on AIDS Twenty Years Later." This title has been now modified to fit the actual contents and structure of the final text. Here, "Anti-" refers not so much to a radially contrary or strictly antagonistic position of enunciation, but to a fuzzy set of "oppositional properties," following a broader reading of the Greek etymology of the prefix. In this case, these properties seek to open the closed set of values and meanings traditionally associated with Pepe Espaliú, which will be discussed throughout the chapter, and to introduce new directions in the analysis of his figure.

According to art critic and curator Juan Vicente Aliaga "what prevails in Spain is a criticism that I would call 'impressionist' and, of course, [which] irritates me a lot. That criticism combines elements from the phenomenology of perception with semi-mystical ingredients: the ineffable, indescribable, inexplicable, which respond to ultraprotectionist and tautological positions." See "Una conversación en el Macba," 306. Aliaga tops much of the available literature on Espaliú and is, among other things, responsible for the various retrospective exhibitions on the artist. Deliberately, and with the intention of opening up new avenues of analysis around Espaliú's figure, throughout this chapter I have decided to minimize my references to his textual production. In view of the clashing language used in his quote here, one could claim that no one is free from a certain dose of "impressionism."

(1955–1993) into a figure paradigmatic of the forms of cultural production geared to a critical reformulation of AIDS[2] that emerged in the early 1990s. Espaliú's action/performance *Carrying*, which took place in the summer of 1992 in Donostia-San Sebastián in the framework of a three-month workshop that Espaliú gave at Arteleku,[3] soon became a paradigm for critical action in the face of AIDS, as well as a model for "political art" and its practice.

My statements above are based on the type of coverage that Espaliú received in the media during the final two years of his life and the specific treatment given to *Carrying*, as well as the constructions that the fields of criticism and historiography produced—and continue to produce—around his figure. It is on the basis of those constructions that the specific narrative of the artist's "political commitment" in the face of the "disease" has been bolstered, as has a dense authorial identity. As recently as 2005, the magazine *Lápiz*—representative of the type of hegemonic and traditional criticism to which I refer—published an extensive article that provided, for the umpteenth time, an account of the relationships between "art and AIDS" in Spain,[4] a relationship that, thus far, has been formulated solely in thematic terms in the sense of an "art inspired by the disease," terms that it is imperative to reassess. That article insisted on presenting Espaliú as, "the first person in Spain to work on a non-idealistic expression of AIDS, after being diagnosed HIV-positive in 1991."[5] Further, according to the same article, the performance *Carrying*, signified as his paradigmatic work, was "the first time" a Spanish

2. Each allusion to AIDS in this text should be understood as a joint reference to HIV (the virus) and AIDS (the syndrome). I have opted for the reduced form for the sake of readability.

3. Arteleku (www.arteleku.net/) is the public contemporary art center under the auspices of the Culture Department of the Provincial Government of Gipuzkoa (Guipúzcoa). Inaugurated in 1987, the center initiates and promotes both theoretical and practical interdisciplinary ideas with impact on both the local community and at the national and international level. Arteleku was instrumental, especially between the mid-1990s and mid-2000s, in training and promoting a generation of Basque artists that have had the most international projection.

4. Álvarez Teruel, "Art and Aids in Spain."

5. Ibid., 58. The trace of this idea of Espaliú as a pioneer figure goes back, without any doubt, to the theoretical production of Juan Vicente Aliaga, who devoted himself to Espaliú's work early on: in his words, "Pepe Espaliú's work is paradigmatic for being the first in Spain to be unmasked to talk about AIDS." See Aliaga, "Para los que ya no viven en mi," 77. As the article in *Lápiz* shows, this argument has cast a long shadow.

artist publicly admitted that he was infected with AIDS.[6]

By means of two distinct operations, what I intend to do here is adjust the description of Espaliú as the "inaugural" figure that ushers in a new stage of art in relation to "the political": first, I will indicate the type of rhetorical constructions and discursive hubs that constitute Espaliú's posthumous identity, concentrating on the role that the performance *Carrying* has played in those constructions; second, I will discuss two events: —a little considered group exhibition in which Espaliú took part and an institutional episode both far from and near to Espaliú—that, together, might provide the first lines in a more complex cartography of AIDS politics in the Basque Country and the Spanish state.[7]

The reflections that I am going to share here emerged in the context of a recent project I carried out in the framework of Pepe Espaliú's personal library, which the artist donated to Arteleku shortly before he died, just over twenty years ago, in November 1993. The project took the overall title of *Marginalia* and began as a "a critical laboratory to reactivate the Pepe Espaliú Library";[8] it has taken the shape of four artistic and archival productions by four invited artists and art collectives,[9] as well as research that I am carrying out on Espaliú's figure at the end of his life on the basis of all the documentary material on the artist available at Arteleku. This part of the project is still in process, and hence these reflections are preliminary; they are a preview of a small-scale documentary exhibition that I am pre-

6. Álvarez Teruel, "Art and Aids in Spain," 60.

7. In recent decades, the construction of cartographies, along with the production of dissident archives, has emerged as a major methodological tool for counter-historiographical practices. I myself have resorted to them as a strategy in collective projects such as *Social Dangerousness*, on which see www.macba.cat/en/social- dangerousness-sexual-minorities-language-and-practice-in-70s-and-80s-spain.

8. This is how it was described on the website of Eremuak, an initiative of the Basque government's Department of Culture that funded the project, when it was initiated: see www.eremuak.net/0303marginalia.

9. These artists and collectives are: Jeleton, Antonio Gagliano, Susana Talayero & Pablo Marte, and Equipo re. The first results of *Marginalia* were presented on March 16, 2013 in Arteleku, in a public event in which the four artistic and archival production projects were presented. For more information on both the project and the event please see www.arteleku.net/en/marginalia. In fact, the illustrations used in this paper are part of Antonio Gagliano's *The Free Mimesis Project*, an experimental editorial prototype designed to release and circulate materials "locked" in archives by means of their being copied by hand as drawings, which was initiated in the context of *Marginalia*.

paring for the Ganbara gallery of the Koldo Mitxelena Exhibition Center in Donostia-San Sebastián.[10]

Most of the documents that I will refer to in the following pages are journalistic references that address the relationship between Pepe Espaliú and Arteleku; they come from the center's archives.[11] One of the characteristics of what social anthropologist Ignasi Terradas defines as "anti- biography"—"the *impossibility* of reducing a life to a biographical order, on the one hand, and the simultaneous need to reconstruct or remember that life (as character, symbol, performance, etc.), on the other"—is the limiting of "the phenomena of personal life to a news story."[12] The approach to Espaliú that I will venture here is largely restricted to press materials on the last two years of his life; it does not set out to be an "anti-biography" of the artist (as someone in the margins, in Terradas's terms) but rather to reread his figure in its "intertextual" dimension—in the Barthesian sense, that is, as a polysemic space in which meanings intersect[13]—while evidencing the constructed and media-based dimension of AIDS.

The Author-Function: The Production of Espaliú as a Model Figure

"At what point did we begin to tell the lives of authors rather than heroes?" asks Michel Foucault in "What is an author?"[14] For Foucault, what "we designate as an author (or which comprise an individual as an author), are projections, in terms always more or less psycho-

---

10. At the time of delivery of this text, the exhibition is scheduled to open December 17, 2013.

11. These were compiled as a dossier by the document services company Euro Documentation, and includes twenty-three references in total, covering the period from January 1, 1992 to April 31, 1994, that is, between the months prior to the workshop that the artist gave in Arteleku in the Summer of 1992 and the donation to the center of his personal library after his death. Many of the articles reproduced in the dossier lack original page numbers, so sometimes this information is not included in my text either. The dossier is available for public consultation only on paper in Arteleku's documentation center.

12. Terradas, *Eliza Kendall: Reflexiones sobre una antibiografía*, 9, 19.

13. While it may have been Julia Kristeva's take on Bakhtin that eventually led to the term "intertextuality," it is Barthes who has developed this idea into a key concept of post-structuralism. See, especially, Barthes, "The Theory of the Text."

14. Foucault, "What Is an Author?"115.

logical, of our way of handling texts; in the comparisons we make, the traits we extract as pertinent, the continuities we assign, or the exclusions we practice."[15] The media coverage of Espaliú at the end of his life is the product of those very operations of psychologizing projection and of characterization of the artist as "author"; in that coverage, the common rhetorics of "political commitment" intersect and are interwoven to give shape to Espaliú in conjunction with the practice of art, thus forming a semiotic-moral clutter difficult to untangle.

For instance, an article published in the now defunct newspaper *Diario 16* announcing that Espaliú had been awarded the Andalucía de Artes Plásticas Prize reads: "As the end of the eighties drew near, many artists claimed to deal with the political in their work. Espaliú is one of the few who has actually done so, combining political commitment with aesthetics."[16] Ten years later, in the coverage of the posthumous retrospective exhibition of Espaliú's work at the Reina Sofía Museum in Madrid, the Bilbao-based newspaper *El Correo* sums up his career as follows: "Early on, [Espaliú] had made Neo-expressionist painting of the sort very much in fashion in the mid-eighties, but his illness changed him, and he began to 'speak' from a place of social commitment."[17] In these and other accounts, Espaliú is a model figure for the relationship between the aesthetic and the political. The instant secondary effect of this formulation is the reinforcement of his "author- function," which could be defined, again following Foucault, as the result of, "a complex operation whose purpose is to construct the rational entity we call an author."[18]

Of course, the fact that Espaliú's public circulation has been subject to his dimension as author is by no means unique to him: the author-function has been, as we know, constitutive of most artistic figures since the advent of modernism, from Picasso to Oteiza, and it is still operative. In the case of Espaliú, though, it is paradoxical. In the last two years of his life, after his association with AIDS, he made a great many public declarations geared to "downplaying" the authorial identity that had been bestowed on him from the 1980s on. In an oft-cited 1992 interview with historian Javier San Martín for Arteleku's magazine, *Zehar*, for instance, Espaliú states:

15. Ibid., 127.

16. Fernández-Cid, "Pepe Espaliú y Rogelio López Cuenca, premio Andalucía de Artes Plásticas,"

Diario 16 (Madrid), February 20, 1993.

17. Esteban, "El Reina Sofía recuerda a Espaliú a los diez años de su muerte por sida," *El Correo Español - El Pueblo Vasco* (Bilbao), January 26, 2003, 80.

18. Foucault, "What Is an Author?" 127.

> There is a whole set of stereotypes that I strive to shatter. And one of them is the centrality of the artist in the eighties in a sort of exaggerated individualism . . . I still have a utopian idea of what art is, of collective work. I still believe that art can change things . . . Art is bound to the real, and it has little to do with that sort of eighties paraphernalia whereby all that mattered was creating images recognizable to the market. Of course, art does not solve anything . . . But it is necessary to hold onto that mad trust in the artist's task . . . in the fiction of thinking we can change the world . . . And it is in that sense that I think it is better to work all together than to work in isolation.[19]

Espaliú's reference to the paradigm of "the collective" as a certain way to dissolve the author's subjectivity into the social raises disparate questions. First, we must consider the framework in which those statements were made, the collaborative three-month workshop that Espaliú gave to twenty-some participants at Arteleku in the summer of 1992. That is the specific context in which the conception and political meaning of the performance *Carrying* must be reconsidered. But, at the same time, it must be read in conjunction with other statements from the same interview in which Espaliú refers to *Carrying* not as a collaborative experience or shared responsibility, but rather as an "artist's action" in relation to which the author holds onto all of his symbolic privileges. This indicates the simultaneous coexistence in Espaliú of two regimes of identity: an authorial identity in which the artist's subjectivity comes first; and the non-authorial identity in which the author-function wants to be contaminated by that new horizon of collective agencies that AIDS activism brought on the scene.

The Artist as Work (or the Artist Consumed by His Work): Espaliú and *Carrying*

The public image of Espaliú that lives on into the present has been constructed around two interwoven proper nouns: his name and that of *Carrying*. In this operation, the author does not precede the work and the work does not precede the author; instead, both operate in terms of identification and equivalence. As described earlier, *Carrying* was the action by which, on September 26, 1992, Pepe Espaliú marked the end of the three-month summer workshop he

19. San Martín, "Pepe Espaliú, entrevista," 4–7.

gave at Arteleku; in it, a body codified as "infected"—the body of the artist himself—was made visible by means of a human chain of the workshop's participants and volunteers that went through the city's downtown area, as shown in figure 10.1. From the time of that action on, even into the present, any published reference to Espaliú—the announcement that he had been awarded a prize, that he had died, that his library had been donated, and so forth—would be accompanied by a photograph of the performance; the image acts as both visual register of a collective action and as index of recognition of an individual identity.

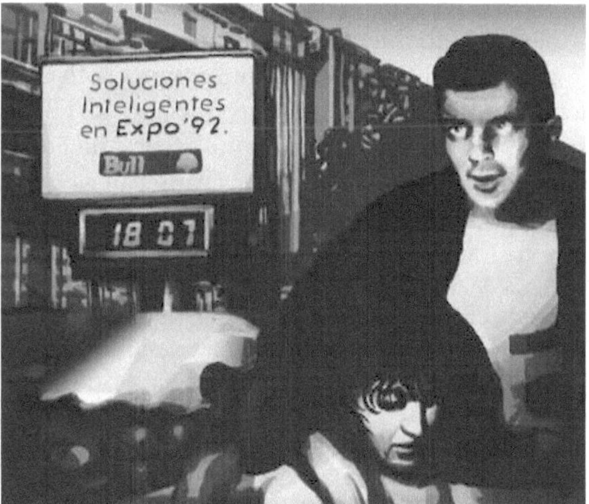

Figure 10.1. Human chain.

The article in *Lápiz* on the relationships between art and AIDS in Spain that I referred to before suggests that in *Carrying*, "Espaliú achieved his greatest media and artistic impact";[20] *Carrying* has been codified as his signature-work, his *Guernica*, and one that—in terms of the principles that, for Foucault, define an "author"—ensures the coherence and uniformity of his entire production.[21] According to the commonly held thesis, it was when Espaliú came into contact with AIDS that his political commitment became explicit;[22]

20. Álvarez Teruel, "Art and Aids in Spain," 60.

21. According to Foucault, the author is defined as a "field of conceptual or theoretical coherence" and "as a stylistic uniformity." See "What Is an Author?" 128.

22. For instance, an article on the artist's death in the newspaper *El País* stated: "since his decision to accept his disease he became an activist." See J. L. Rodriguez and Fietta Jarque, "Las cenizas del artista Pepe Espaliú serán esparcidas en los jarales de Córdoba," *El País* (Córdoba / Madrid), November 4, 1993. This was sentence was reproduced by other newspapers.

thitherto, that commitment, though "present," had been "veiled" and "masked."[23] That commitment would inject intensity and political charge into all his earlier work, as if it were the answer to a retrospective politicizing equation. In these readings, *Carrying* does not mark the beginning of the political in Espaliú, but just makes it visible; it is the artist's political "outing."

Carrying is usually analyzed either as a biographical inflection (on the basis of Espaliú's status as "diseased," his supposed contact with North American activist practices, and so on); or in its symbolic dimension; or in strictly representational terms (with glowing references to religious iconography, such as the theme of The Pietá). Most references to the work focus on its "origins" and "hidden meanings," insisting on Espaliú's alleged contact with the performative production practices of activist groups like ACT UP, in his numerous visits to New York City during the second half of the 1980s;[24] and at the same time subordinating this rather local and contextual action to foreign realities.[25] It is rarely analyzed in relation to the specific context in which it emerged—the experience of the work-

---

23. The figure of the mask as a representation of identity is central in Espaliú's earlier work. References to the mask and the rhetorics of concealment and unmasking would also dominate art writing around the late Espaliú, i.e., see footnote 4.

24. For instance, "The idea for this project came to Espaliú in New York - sometimes it is impossible to avoid the feeling that without New York-based activism, art about AIDS would scarcely exist, or at least, would look very different." in the words of Aliaga, "Para los que ya no viven en mi," 77.Note, also, the following: "his commitment to serving other affected [people] arose after meeting US activist group Act-Up and seeing how they confronted the disease and fought for the rights of those affected."Rodriguez and Jarque, "Las cenizas del artista Pepe Espaliú serán esparcidas en los jarales de Córdoba."

25. Although Espaliú himself has admitted that it was in New York where he got to know the type of symbolic protest actions that the anti-AIDS coalitions would carried out, the claim that he had a greater involvement with groups like ACT UP is doubtful. In fact, in the course of my research on the artist's library in Arteleku, I contacted Gabriel Calparsoro, who was an ACT UP activist in New York in the late 1980s and one of Espaliú's main local collaborators in Donostia-San Sebastián in the summer of 1992, coinciding with the artist's workshop in Arteleku. During an informal conversation, Calparsoro admitted being the one who supplied Espaliú, not in 1980s New York but in Donostia-San Sebastián, with most of the literature on AIDS today available in his personal library; and who, for example, would bring Jon Greenberg, founding member of ACT UP, to the city to give a talk within Espaliú's workshop. Through Calparsoro I recently had access to a sound recording of Greenberg's talk.

shop in Arteleku where, in addition to this experience, two other collective exercises took place that, in my view, must be analyzed jointly.[26]

Espaliú as Intertext: First Steps toward a Larger Cartography of AIDS Politics

Thus far, I have briefly discussed the types of rhetorical operations that constitute Espaliú's posthumous identity as it has lived on through the sum of writings on the last two years of his life, writings that together constitute a network for the distribution of meanings. I have also referred to the sorts of commonplaces regarding art and its comingling with "the political" that his figure epitomizes. The aim of signaling the writings, the set of meanings, and subjectifying projections that give shape to the "Espaliú paradigm" is to evidence his value as "text," that is, as body subject to endless processes of writing and reading, publishing, and archiving. Pondering this with Barthes, a textual analysis of the figure of Espaliú would allow us to reread him as network, as intertext, as an overdetermined and plural field, and thus to salvage him from identification, from the assignment of a sole meaning. It would then be possible to reinsert him in a larger network of proper nouns, dates, milestones, events, and so forth in order to draw that cartography of AIDS politics in the Basque Country and the Spanish state.

My approach here to Espaliú also forms part of the larger and ongoing collective *Aids Anarchive* project.[27] This project, which attempts to reconsider the cultural production that characterized AIDS politics, is being carried out in the framework of *Equipo re*, a collaborative research platform, which I co-founded, that brings together a variable number of actors in an array of contexts. For this project, *Equipo re* sets out to identify, compile, and analyze the aesthetic practices, representations, collective experiences, and perfor-

26. While it is true that Aliaga's previously mentioned text opens with a reference to the set of three exercises that Espaliú developed within his workshop in Arteleku ("Para los que ya no viven en mi," 75), this reference has been lost down the years in the process of " singularization" that is the media treatment of *Carrying*. Indeed, one of the main goals of the small-scale exhibition that I am currently preparing (see footnote 8) is to resituate the experience of *Carrying* in its precise context of emergency: an unparalleled educational experience in Arteleku.

27. Initiated under the auspices of the 2012-2013 Research Residencies at the Reina Sofía Museum, Madrid. For more information on the project, see: www.anarchivosida.org/.

mative tactics that have determined AIDS politics; it is the first project of this sort from a from a "peripheral" perspective. Its aim, in other words, is to set off a process identifying, compiling, and analyzing aesthetic practices, representations, and performative tactics decisive to AIDS politics that addresses cultural production outside the North American geopolitical context.

The final aim of the project is to activate a "counter-archive" or what we have called an "*anarchive*" of AIDS politics that heeds practices on the peripheries of Western centers, in the context of the postcolonial struggles and other struggles for emancipation in different "Souths," and includes a rereading of practices in the Spanish state, the periphery and South of Europe. It is not simply a matter of formulating a new approach to the relationship between "art and AIDS" in the thematic sense I mentioned before, that is, in the sense of an "art inspired by the disease." It is, rather, a question of mapping the sort of displacements, ruptures, and structural eruptions that have taken place in the realm of cultural production around AIDS. Regarding practices in the Basque Country and the Spanish state, this necessarily requires trying to generate a new approach to the figure of Pepe Espaliú, "contaminating" his paradigmatic status.

Gimme Me Your Hand, It's Alright: I Exposición de Arte a Beneficio de la Lucha Contra el Sida

The first of the two pieces in this possible "intertextual cartography" of AIDS politics in the Basque Country that I would like to present here is one rarely discussed, even though Espaliú himself appears in it: The "I Exposición de Arte a Beneficio de la Lucha Contra el Sida" (1st Art Exhibition for the Benefit of the Struggle Against AIDS) in the Basque Country, organized by the Asociación de la Prensa de San Sebastián (Donostia-San Sebastián Press Association), with the support of the Basque government's Departments of Culture and Health.[28] The touring show whose aim was to collect funds for the struggle against AIDS was held in three Basque capitals from December 1992 to March 1993. Some fifty artists, most of them Basque, participated, including Gaspar Montes Iturrioz, Maite Gorostidi, Irene Laffite, Pepe Espaliú, and Jon Salaberria, as well as Nestor Basterretxea, Eduardo Chillida, and Jose Luis Zumeta. The

28. At the time of going to press, evidence of the existence of an exhibition catalog was not found. All data included here come from the numerous press articles in local newspapers that covered the event, and are available for consultation at Arteleku's documentation center.

striking slogan for the exhibition, which received widespread media coverage, was "Dale la mano, no pasa nada" (Give Him or Her Your Hand, It's All Right), which serves as a way for me to introduce one of the rhetorical foundations that activates public discourse on AIDS: the "immunity-contagion" pair.

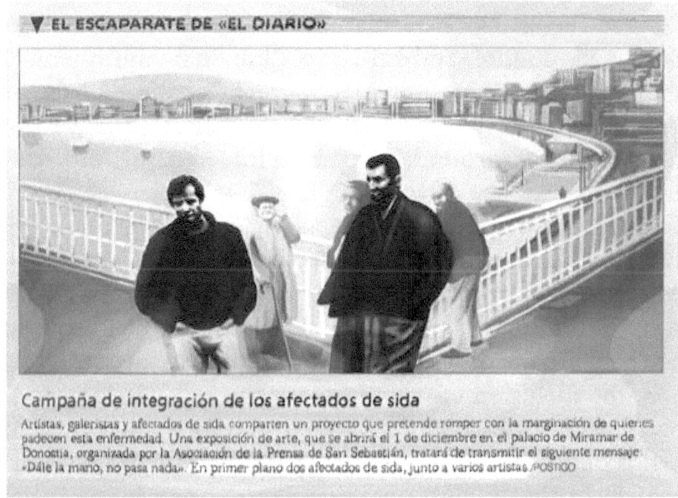

▼ EL ESCAPARATE DE «EL DIARIO»

Campaña de integración de los afectados de sida

Artistas, galeristas y afectados de sida comparten un proyecto que pretende romper con la marginación de quienes padecen esta enfermedad. Una exposición de arte, que se abrirá el 1 de diciembre en el palacio de Miramar de Donostia, organizada por la Asociación de la Prensa de San Sebastián, tratará de transmitir el siguiente mensaje: «Dále la mano, no pasa nada». En primer plano dos afectados de sida, junto a varios artistas./POSTIGO

Figure 10.2. Posed photo of five workshop participants..

Italian philosopher Roberto Esposito points to the logic of "immunity" as the privileged mechanism under which biopolitics, which Foucault defined as the art of governing free bodies, operates. Whereas "common" names—that which is subject to the logic of communication and exchange—can be shared, the "immune" would indicate a space of exclusion.[29] Following Esposito, the rhetorics of immunity and the ideals of protection that characterized AIDS politics were a veiled way of producing zones of bodily exclusion; under the sign of AIDS, common life would be "immunized," that is, interrupted and hindered by means of the reassignment of the limits of a sector of the population. The suspension of the immune space that the slogan of the "I Exposición de Arte a Beneficio de la Lucha Contra el Sida" seemed to decree—its call for contact between bodies with the words "give him or her your hand"—was contradicted by the image that accompanied news stories about the show.

---

29. Roberto Esposito is one of the most prolific and important exponents of contemporary Italian political theory. One of his main theses is that the modern individual—with all of his or her civil and political rights as well as his or her moral powers—is an attempt to attain immunity from the contagion of the extra individual, namely, the community. See especially Esposito, *Terms of the Political.*

The exhibition opened on December 1, 1992, at the Palacio de Miramar in Donostia-San Sebastián. The exhibition's outreach campaign included a posed photograph of five of the participants in the show. The scene, registered from slightly different points of view by photographers from different media, is disturbing: in the foreground Pepe Espaliú and Jon Salaberria are posing in front of the Concha Bay in Donostia-San Sebastián, with Gaspar Montes Iturrioz, Irene Laffite, and Eduardo Chillida behind them. What is it about this image that I find jarring? The caption for the image in the newspaper *El Diario Vasco*, shown in figure 10.2, provides a first clue: in the foreground, "two of the infected," behind, "several artists."[30]

The composition of the image, along with the caption, generates two levels of meaning: Pepe Espaliú and Jon Salaberria, wearing similar black jackets with the typical "red ribbon" as a call for solidarity in their lapels, represent the "immune-deficient" space; behind them are the other artists in the "immune" space, including Chillida, the inclusion of whom here is the second element I find jarring. Worldwide, AIDS reactivated the apparent commitment and sense of solidarity among intellectuals and cultural figures—that which, in the English-speaking world, was labeled "celebrity activism"—and Chillida, who in the 1970s and 1980s had placed much of his work at the service of different institutional causes and social movements connected to Basque issues, could not be left behind.[31] The newspaper *El Mundo*'s coverage of the exhibition revolved around him and included the following quote from Chillida himself in the article's headline: "I am a human being and the least I can do is help."[32] By means of Chillida's presence in the image, then,

30. "El Escaparate de 'El Diario'," *El Diario Vasco* (Donostia-San Sebastián), November 3, 1992.

31. "In the 1970s and 1980s, Chillida would create logos for different kinds of institutions and movements united by a common Basque factor such as the University of the Basque Country, Euskaltzaindia [the Basque Language Academy], Basque Industry, Antinuclear Basque Coast and the Pro-Amnesty Committee. After four decades of Francoist repression, joining nationalist and left-wing causes was obligatory for artists and intellectuals. Enthusiasm for such activism would, paradoxically, herald the swansong of international solidarity causes." Jaio, *A Collection of Prints*, 37. Available at: www.etxepareinstitutua.net/es/artes-visuales/.

32. Andoni Alonso, "Chilida: 'Soy un ser humano y lo menos que puedo hacer es ayudar'," *El Mundo* (Donostia-San Sebastián), November 3, 1992.

AIDS is also signified as a "Basque conflict."[33]

Immune Architecture: The Museum (With and Without Walls)

The following, and here last, two pieces that I propose adding to our "intertextual cartography" of AIDS address the centrality of the museum space in AIDS politics. Indeed, the first involves one of the two extremes in the art-politics configuration that the title of this book refers to (*Beyond Guernica and the Guggenheim: Relations between Art and Politics from a Comparative Perspective*): the Guggenheim Bilbao Museum. The second piece is the collective project The Carrying Society, which was founded by a small group of participants in the workshop that Espaliú gave at Arteleku in summer of 1992. This second piece is diametrical to the first in terms of scale, though close to it territorially and its strict contemporary.

In the cultural practices of the 1980s geared to a critical reformulation of AIDS, theorist and activist Douglas Crimp saw an opportunity to address once and for all the idealist conception of the museum that had been with us since the nineteenth century; namely, it could be displaced, Crimp theorized in the context of his criticism of the function of the contemporary museum, by an institution "without walls," one with greater social relevance.[34] In his article "The Museum Without Walls Reconsidered" (1989), Crimp concludes: "Now that some cultural practices finally begin to find

---

33. The term "Basque conflict" is generally used to define either the broad political conflict between a part of Basque society and the unionist model of the Spanish and French States, or to exclusively describe the armed confrontation between ETA and the Spanish and French states. Here, the expression is used with irony to refer to the character of Chillida as Basque culture icon who is capable of imbuing any current social issue or conflict with a sense of "Basquism" through the mere association with his image or name.

34. The core of Crimp's critique of the role of the museum consists of his two texts: "On the Museum's Ruin",

O and "The Museum Without Walls Reconsidered," the latter of which is, to my knowledge, Crimp's first text published in Spanish (translated as "De vuelta al museo sin paredes"); "The Museum Without Walls Reconsidered" was first read as a lecture at the "Aesthetic Options in Contemporary Art" seminar at the Universidad Internacional Menéndez Pelayo of Seville, on October 4, 1988; then published in the journal *Arena Internacional*; and four years later republished in Aliaga and Cortés, eds., *De amor y de rabia*, 281–95—the first work of cultural criticism on AIDS published in Spain and where I came across this text for the first time.

their way outside the museum's walls, and to articulate a specific relation between aesthetic production and social life [referring here to critical practices on AIDS like those of artist Krzystof Wodiczko and the ACT UP collective], the museum will enter a new phase of its history."[35] Nonetheless, Crimp's diagnosis[36] acknowledged that not all cultural expressions on AIDS worked the same way; specifically, he bemoaned the fact that many of them would resist giving up what he called "idealist" positions on art: "Within the arts, the scientific explanation and management of AIDS is largely taken for granted, and it is therefore assumed that cultural producers can respond to the epidemic in only two ways: by raising money for scientific research [this would be the case of the aforementioned benefit exhibition that brought together AIDS and members of the Escuela Vasca or Basque School] or by creating works that express human suffering and loss."[37] This would be the case of those practices that turn an event—here AIDS—into a "theme," into "a comment on human suffering as universal condition." American artist Jenny Holzer's work *Installation for* Bilbao (1997), on permanent display at the Guggenheim Bilbao, could be seen as an example of this second case.

Since the late 1970s, Holzer's work has been characterized by the use of language as her main form of expression in pieces on a wide range of supports taken from the media ecosystem: posters, electronic LEDs, billboards, and t-shirts. Her work has been interpreted as symptomatic of the 1980s information and consumer society,[38] and her strategies—like those used by her contemporaries, among them Barbara Kruger—would resonate a few years later in the guerilla practices of visual production and communication used by AIDS ac-

35. Crimp, "The Museum Without Walls Reconsidered," 60.

36. I am no stranger to the observation by Jesús Carrillo that, even though "the incisive analysis of political art of the 80s and early 90s performed by Rosalyn Deutsche, along with Douglas Crimp, opened a new way to write critically about art, they seem to lose strength as we go beyond New York." See "Crítica de la crítica," 337. However, in the light of the self-serving institutions that still proliferate—immune to the social reality that surrounds them—the significance of their critical work gains new strength.

37. Crimp, "The Museum Without Walls Reconsidered," 58.

38. "Like other artists who first came to prominence in the 1980s, Jenny Holzer is a product of the TV age and the world of advertising and billboards. Her work reflects a decade in which originality is suspect and, as have many of her colleagues, she employs and aspects of culture to comment on the nature of society and on the way in which art is perceived and received in a consumer society." Waldman, "The Language of Signs," 9.

tivism and the groups of artists associated with this.[39] The text in *Installation for Bilbao* is a variation on *Arno*, a text originally written for a project whose aim was to collect funds for AIDS research and later adapted by Holzer for a collaborative project with fashion designer Helmut Lang for the 1996 Biennale di Firenze (Florence Biennial), that is, just one year before her work for Bilbao.[40]

I acknowledge my ambivalence, even a degree of awkwardness, in referring here to this particular work by Holzer, not so much because I worked at the Guggenheim as a curatorial assistant for almost eight years—an experience that, though fundamental to my early professional development, already feels distant—but because of what might be termed the political ingenuity that, for a long time, marked my relationship to the work. While the reference to AIDS in Holzer's installation is well known and is mentioned in the various informative materials that accompany the work (such as the audioguide or entry of the work in the museum website), it operates mostly on the level of theme, as a "comment on human suffering as universal condition," to return to Crimp's phrase. It is, thus, something like the tree that does not let you see the woods, and in this case, the processes by which micro-politics are depoliticized when they are inserted into the museum space.

I do not want to fall into such ingenuity again and simplify this now classic, though still unresolved, question in terms of binary oppositions—inside-outside, absorption-resistance, and so on. After all, even if the institutional structure we are discussing—the museum as part and parcel of current neoliberal condition—has not exactly abandoned its idealistic aspiration, its walls have been "shaken" by the forces of capital and private interests for some time now. Today, the museum acts as part of a much more complex network of communication and symbolic exchange of which those same oppositional micro-politics form part. At the same time, it is also true that, in the case we are discussing here, the possibility of gleaning

39. This is a recurrent argument and was suggested again in a review of the exhibition that the Carpenter Center for the Visual Arts / Harvard Art Museum, Boston, dedicated to ACT UP, which stated that the collective's graphic work "evoke[s] the contemporary practices of Barbara Kruger, or the truisms of Jenny Holzer." See Merjian, "Act Up New York."

40. This is well explained by the artist in a conversation with Joan Simon, in *Jenny Holzer*, 33. Previous works by the artist also include references to AIDS, such as *Laments* (Dia Art Foundation): "*Laments* came during the AIDS epidemic. I had been writing about unnecessary death of any sort, for example, from bad government or accident" (28).

transformative knowledge from the specific and located experiences that characterized AIDS politics is reduced to a generality: the museum's own website states that "While consideration of the AIDS epidemic provides [Holzer's work with] an immediate and tragic context," it evokes "universal themes of intimacy, death and loss."[41] The potential for the radical transformation of the museum space that Crimp ambitiously envisioned is undone by the fallacy of universal and atemporal experience.

The aim of the initiative *Prospecciones Periféricas* (Peripheral Prospections) by The Carrying Society collective (1992–1998) is diametrical. This work is a strict contemporary of Holzer's project (both are from 1997), and near to it territorially as well, though at a great distance on the level of intention. Founded, as mentioned before, by a group of participants in the workshop that Espaliú gave at Arteleku, The Carrying Society developed a number of projects on art and the public sphere. The public memory of much of their work is patchy and, in the framework of my research on Espaliú's time at Arteleku, I have set out to recollect these experiences. *Prospecciones Periféricas* was formulated in 1997 and developed throughout 1998, before the group disbanded. With this project, The Carrying Society intended to effect a prospective revision of the concept of "museum," one that they introduced as follows: "We are quite skeptical about the art world due to the flashiness it promotes and the marketing techniques that enslave it. Nonetheless, we sense that certain exercises in radical democracy are possible [in art]. From that perspective, we see the museum as a common good funded by public money and, as part of that public, indeed as that public, we feel responsible for its conception."[42]

In what they called "a journey through the museum from outside in and vice versa," the primary aim of the project was to interrogate, by means of a "conversation"-based methodology, "the citizenry's possible conceptions of the public space occupied by museums and contemporary art centers." The project revolved around a series of encounter-workshops held at a large number of public museum spaces, from the Bilbao Museum of Fine Arts to MAAC in Seville, as well as MACBA and the Reina Sofía, in which conversations with persons—from viewers to museum workers and chance passers-

41. At: www.guggenheim-bilbao.es/en/works/installation-for-bilbao/.

42. All quotes on the project (in Spanish in the original) are excerpted from the project's dossier by the collective, available for consultation in Arteleku's archives.

by—were recorded at random.[43] The initiative was geared not only to articulating a commentary on AIDS and what it entailed, but also to transforming a social structure like the museum on the basis of the political experience of AIDS. The project is also pertinent as an early map of the new institutional horizon of the Spanish state in the late 1990s, which witnessed the largest increase in the number of museums planned and built since the nineteenth century, with the opening of a new center in almost every province.

Considered together in this context, The Carrying Society's project and Holzer's work, through the two institutions that sponsored them—Arteleku and the Guggenheim Bilbao Museum—would mark the two extremes of the arc of cultural infrastructures that, in the late 1990, gave shape to the new ecosystem of art in the Basque Country. The relationship between these two extremes, however, would not be a binary opposition, but rather entail a complex system of micro-correspondences, reflections and substitutions.[44]

Conclusions (To Take Shelter)

Throughout this chapter, I have deliberately avoided addressing the complex relationship between "art and politics" in a frontal or direct fashion. I have been careful not to define what "the political" is or to identify where and in what form it appears. Instead, I have chosen to make use of a particular "textual" figure—a specific artist and his practice—to further a general reflection on the sorts of discursive constructions that engine common rhetorics on art and its configuration with the political. On the basis of a handful of specific cases from the intertextual mass that I have called "AIDS politics" I have also tried to address, also indirectly, some of the questions that bring us all here (in other words, those questions included in the organizers' invitation to participate in this book and the related symposium):

43. It seems the group coordinated the project independently so none of the eight art centers that housed this mobile project has any record of the results. Indeed, not even Arteleku, which was the organizing institution, has any record whatsoever. I will soon be reviewing the personal archives of Iñaki Insausti, one of the collective's members who died in March 2013 of complications resulting from AIDS, where I hope to find more on the actual results.

44. "A post-ideological and cynical perversion is the only way to explain how the same political will that in 1986 allowed Arteleku [to be founded] committed itself to the Guggenheim eleven years later: the substitution of faith in the symbolic value of art by faith in the values derived from that intrinsic value." Jaio, "Tout va bien / Garai Txarrak," 61.

To what extent does a given social and political context affect the production of art and artists? To what extent do the personality and character of an artist and/or the strategies that she/he chooses determine the impact of an artwork? To what extent should we analyze artists and their work in a local, collective, or national framework? And what theories and methods can guide us in attempting to understand the relationship between art and politics in contemporary societies? I will be just as careful now not to give a definitive solution to these questions. But if we decided to project them all together on the later work of Espaliú, alone issue would stand out against all others: you cannot answer any question about his paradigmatic status without first taking shelter in the myths generated around his persona,[45] the consolidated narratives on his late practice, and the interpretations that the meaning- reproduction machines that are the fields of art writing and criticism have produced about his configuration to the political. What I have tried to do here is to sketch a first structure for constructing this critical shelter. Needless to say, this shelter is more akin to a precarious but effective hut, temporarily installed in the critical battleground, than a signature building with thick white walls.

Bibliography

Aliaga, Juan Vicente. "Para los que ya no viven en mi. Arte y sida en España." In *De amor y de rabia*, edited by Juan Vicente Aliaga and José Miguel G. Cortés. Valencia: Servicio de Publicaciones, Universidad Politécnica, 1993.

Álvarez Teruel, Cristóbal. "Art and Aids in Spain." Translated by Laura F. Farhall. *Lápiz* 216 (October 2005), 56–67.

Alonso, Andoni. "Chilida: 'Soy un ser humano y lo menos que puedo hacer es ayudar'," *El Mundo* (Donostia-San Sebastián), November 3, 1992.

Barthes, Roland. "The Theory of the Text." Translated by Van McLeod in the Encyclopaedia Universalis, volume 15 (1973). In *Untying the Text: a Post-Structuralist Reader*, edited by Robert

45. I admit borrowing this evocative idea of seeking refuge from myths from the curator and art historian Valentín Roma and his recent project for a critical approach to the figure of Antoni Tàpies, *Contra Tàpies*. In the extended Spanish exhibition press release he stated: "Approaching his trajectory requires building a place safe from the mystifications generated by his figure and even safe from their own words." Available at: www.fundaciotapies.org/blogs/contratapies/nota-de-prensa-larga/.

Young. Boston, MA: Routledge, Kegan, and Paul, 1981.

Carrillo, Jesús. "Crítica de la crítica." In *La crítica de arte. Historia, teoría* y *praxis*, edited by Anna Maria Guasch. Barcelona: Ediciones del Serbal, 2003.

Crimp, Douglas. "On the Museum's Ruin." *October* 13 (Summer 1980), 41–57.

———. "The Museum Without Walls Reconsidered." *Arena Internacional* 1 (February 1989), 54–60.

Esposito, Roberto. *Terms of the Political: Community, Immunity, Biopolitics*. Translated by Rhiannon Noel Welch. New York: Fordham University Press, 2012.

Esteban, Iñaki. "El Reina Sofía recuerda a Espaliú a los diez años de su muerte por sida." *El Correo Español - El Pueblo Vasco* (Bilbao), January 26, 2003, 80.

Fernández-Cid, Miguel. "Pepe Espaliú y Rogelio López Cuenca, Premio Andalucía de Artes Plásticas." *Diario 16* (Madrid), February 20, 1993.

Foucault, Michel. "What Is an Author?" In *Language, Counter-Memory, Practice: Selected Essays and Interviews*, edited by Donald F. Bouchard. New York: Cornell University Press, 1980.

Jaio, Miren. "Tout va bien / Garai Txarrak." *Mugalari* 548, supplement in *Gara* (Donostia-San Sebastián), October 30, 2009, 61.

———. *A Collection of Prints: Visual Arts in the Basque Country*. Translated by Cameron Watson. Basque Culture Series. Donostia-San Sebastián: Etxepare Basque Institute, 2012.

Merjian, Ara H. "Act Up New York." *Frieze* 129 (March 2010). At www.frieze.com/issue/review/act_up_new_york/.

Rodriguez, J.L., and Fietta Jarque. "Las cenizas del artista Pepe Espaliú serán esparcidas en los jarales de Córdoba." *El País* (Córdoba / Madrid), November 4, 1993.

San Martín, Javier. "Pepe Espaliú, entrevista." *Zehar* 18 (September–October 1992), 4–7.

Simon, Joan. "Jenny Holzer." In *Jenny Holzer*, by David Joselit, Joan Simon, Renata Salecl, and Jenny Holzer London: Phaidon Press, 1998.

Terradas, Ignasi. *Eliza Kendall: Reflexiones sobre una antibiografía*. Barcelona: Servei de Publicacions de la Universitat Autònoma de Barcelona, 1992.

"Una conversación en el Macba: Juan Vicente Aliaga, Manel Clot, Menene Gras, Martí Peran y Glòria Picazo." In *Sobre la crítica de arte y su toma de posición*, edited by Glòria Pizaco. Barcelona: Museu d'Art Contemporani de Barcelona, 1996.

Waldman, Diane. "The Language of Signs." In *Jenny Holzer*, exhibition catalogue, Solomon R. Guggenheim Museum, New York, Dec. 12, 1989—Feb. 11, 1990. New York: The Solomon R. Guggenheim Foundation; Harry N. Abrams Inc., 1989.

11

On Art Practices, Feminism, and Gender in the Basque Context

Azucena Vieites

This chapter aims to reflect on the development and evolution of artistic practices in relation to feminism and gender in the Basque Country from the mid-1980s—when there was no feminist tradition in art criticism and practice—to the present.

It is useful to give some clues based on my personal experience as an artist belonging to the generation that started its studies in the faculty of Fine Arts at the University of the Basque Country, in Bilbao, in 1985. After we finished our BA, many of us partly continued our training and professional work in the Arteleku Art Center, in Donostia-San Sebastián.

It is also relevant to introduce the work of the Basque feminist artist group Erreakzioa-Reacción, which I founded in 1994 with Estibaliz Sadaba, as a space to develop the production of activist, feminist, and queer projects in the art world. Our aim was to make visible the work of women artists, to establish genealogies through generations, and to contribute to the expansion of social networks via publications, zines, workshops, talks, videos, and exhibitions.

I was a high school and university student during the 1980s. For university, I moved from Hernani, my hometown, to Bilbao. I would like to mention some issues present in our local context and in our historical time that have strongly influenced me and some other artists of my generation such as Itziar Okariz and Jon Mikel Euba, to name but two. The most relevant historical aspect was that we were one of the first generations of artists and women artists whose formative years happened to take place after the end of the political transition to democracy in Spain. We share a critical approach to certain ideas of the Modern Project such as those that stem from Punk, Postpunk and the Do It Yourself culture. Since there was a strong and visibly organized grassroots feminist movement in the city of Bilbao, feminism was another clear influence for us. Besides, there also existed what we can safely term a protoqueer culture, which allowed us to have other models of gender identification at our disposal rather than just heteronormativity. Finally, music and the cultural phenomenon known as la Movida,[1] which did not just take place in Madrid, was also essential in those formative years. For example, there was a three-women band from Barakaldo, Bizkaia (Vizcaya), Las Vulpes (The Foxes), whose song "Me gusta ser una zorra" (I Wanna Be a Bitch), a version of the iconic Iggy Pop song "I Wanna Be Your Dog," caused a great scandal because of its lyrics and was censored on TV in 1983.

The issues mentioned above have to do with the use of art strategies like appropriation, visual quotations, interventions on the idea of the original and the copy, processes of resignification, multiplicity, fragmentation, breaking the notion of the absolute image and linear narrative forms, an ephemeral and processual work, and the questioning of the idea of "professionalism" or "authority." They all led to creating tools by which to facilitate both personal and collective empowerment.

I consider my work a kind of DIY remix that attempts to represent a memory in relation to a present time and an experience of passage, a memory whose intensity will gradually fade away. This is all reflected in images of the work I produced after I completed my degree in Fine Arts. They are from different decades, from the 1990s to the present. The first images (figures 11.1–5) belong to the series *Juguemos a prisioneras* (Let's Play Prisoners), from 1994 to 1998. The following images (figures 11.6) were done at the beginning of the Millennium. Visual quotations, references to the work of other artists, and events like *If I Can't Dance* or *Ladyfest* play a significant role in these images (figures 11.7–8). The exhibition *Fundido encadenado—Break You Nice* (Cross Dissolve—Break You Nice) took place in the MUSAC Museum, León, Northwest Spain, in 2012 (figures 11.9–10). It was a project that evolved around the idea of editing images in a similar way to that of DIY culture publications.

1. La Movida was a countercultural movement that took place during the Spanish transition to democracy and is typically associated with Madrid.

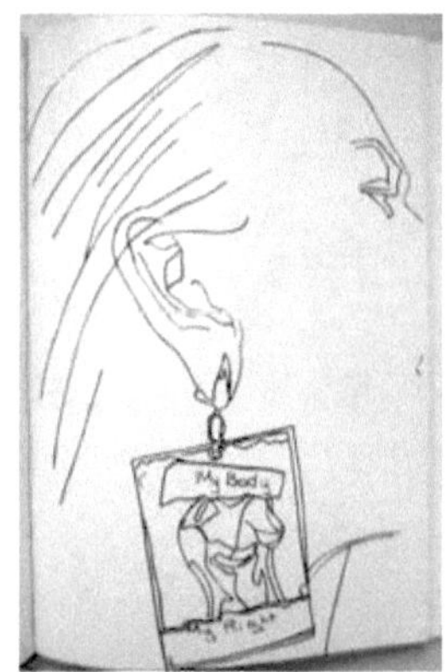

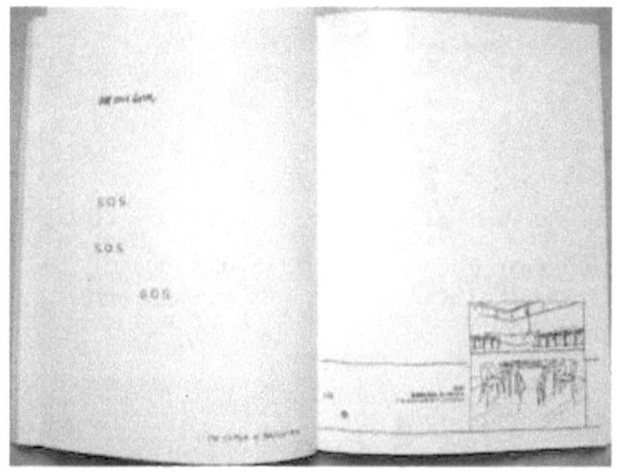

Figures 11.1 (left) and 11.2 (above). Juguemos a prisioneras. *Drawing Book, 1998.*

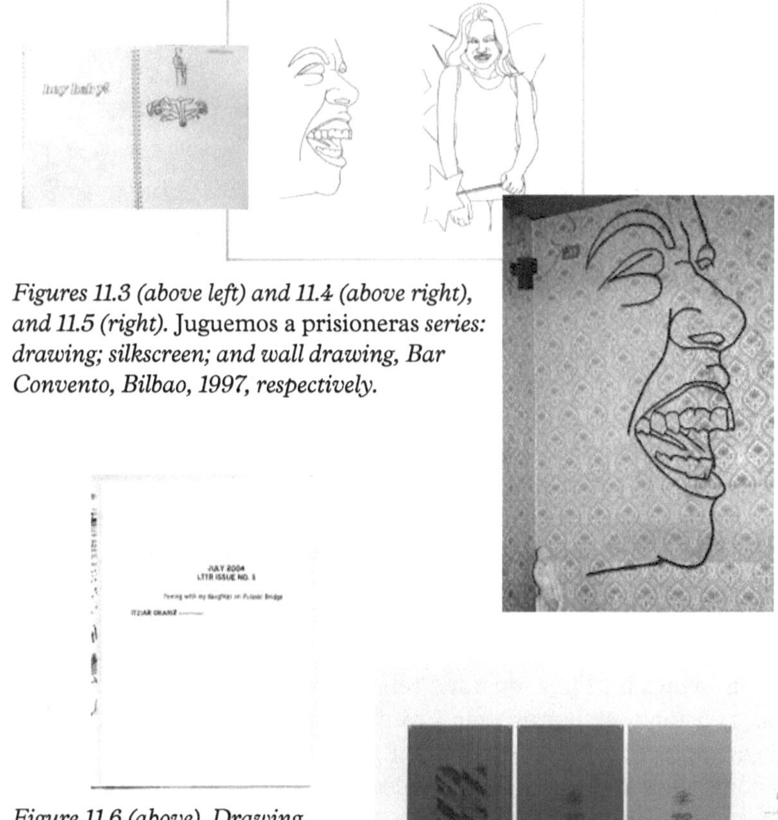

Figures 11.3 (above left) and 11.4 (above right), and 11.5 (right). Juguemos a prisioneras *series: drawing; silkscreen; and wall drawing, Bar Convento, Bilbao, 1997, respectively.*

Figure 11.6 (above). Drawing Book, 2004. Figure 11.7 (right). If I Can't Dance. *Silkscreen, 2009. Photography: Ángel de la Rubia.*

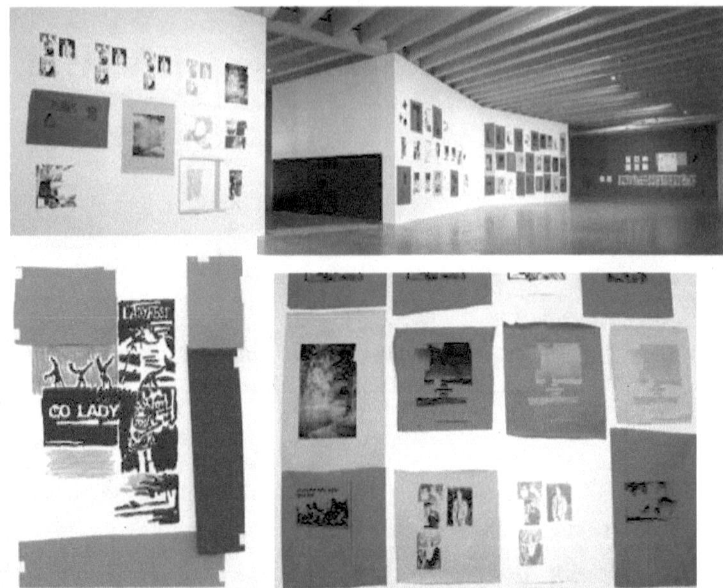

Figure 11.8 (left). Ladyfest—Go Lady. *Silkscreen, 2009. Photography: Ángel de la Rubia. Figures 11.9 and 11.10 (above and below).* Fundido encadenado—Break You Nice. *MUSAC, León (Spain), 2012. Courtesy of MUSAC.*

A Sort of Collage

"A sort of collage" is the name I give to a variety of texts I have written in relation to my work. It includes artistic practices and opinions of other people whose work is close to mine. In an interview, the members of a music group were asked why they played versions of other people's songs. They answered that they normally take songs that inspired them, songs they can give their own angle to. For them, each style of music is an aesthetic, a mood. Similarly, I once wrote a short essay divided into a series of sections, which I could use to put drawings in. They included reflections by other artists: my idea was to bring together aspects I wanted to highlight that connected my own pieces to the work of other people. It can be termed a form of complicity and expanded knowledge.

I remember a powerful show by the Bilbao duo Chico y Chica[2] that took place in 2007. They appeared on stage and when the music started, they stood in front of the public, staring hard at them, without moving for quite a while, mockingly holding their gaze. It

2. At www.chicoychica.com/.

looked like the beginning of something but it was disconcerting—the music went on, but they did not start singing, and the beginning was drawn out for much longer than necessary. The conventional relation to what they supposedly had to be or do was thus revealed: a band ought to sing, their performance has to cover the allotted time space. They might be considered to be imposters in not fulfilling previous expectations or responding to established conventions. However, my experience was that what was represented on each occasion responded to a certain idea of "truth" by calling into question the public's expectations. They did not attempt to contain or fill silences or "empty" spaces, nor did they construct them out of conventions, so I felt I was participating in a highly radical exercise. In the endeavor not to attempt to contain emptiness, certain results come about just where you least expect them, and it is there that representation itself overflows and acquires other layers of meaning and greater complexity.

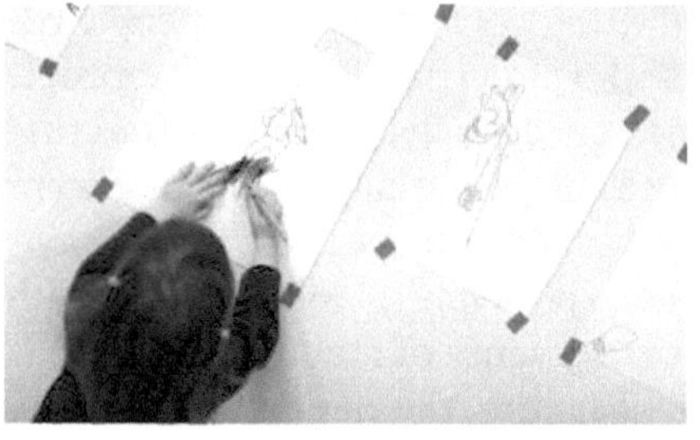

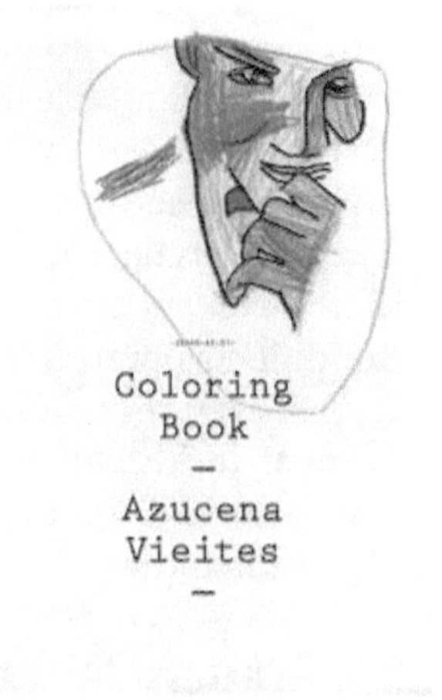

Figure 11.11 (right) Coloring Book. *Zehar-AE-01, 2010. Figure 11.12 (above).* Coloring Book. *Children's Workshop. Valparaiso (Chile), 2010.*

In representations of queer desire, codes change in the fact of representing something to a public. The relationship between artist and audience generates forms of representation and recognition based on attire, gestures, and movements, the gaze, and the body.

Coloring Book is one of my most recent projects. It developed from my interest in looking at the ways children work: their ability to surprise, their lack of conventions and their determination to build language. It could be said that some aspects of these projects are connected to the work of one of my peers, the artist Jon Mikel Euba, who, in a conversation with the art critic Peio Aguirre published in the magazine *If I Can't Dance,*[3] said that when he draws or works he does not do so because he wishes to tell or say something, but because he wants to see something. This will to see is behind *Coloring Book* (figures 11.11–12). Here, I incorporate the idea of translating practice into art, and my effort to understand a particular moment in contemporary culture. I try to represent playfulness and fantasy, and introduce the experience and expectations that are often present in the processes of everyday life.

On the notion of experience and expectation, these usually come to my mind in a series of screenings I saw some time ago on the work of Jack Smith. I was intrigued by how he transformed the ordinary into something extraordinary. In this transformation of the normal into the fantastic, we come across an idea of failure in the sense that nothing works, everything goes wrong. His performances and screenings were structured as follows: You first saw a poster announcing the event, say for nine o'clock, then people turned up and waited for one or two hours, with many of them left thinking nothing was going to happen and when only two or three people remained, Jack Smith showed up with some friends and some props. Sometimes, nothing else happened and, finally, people realized that the performance was over because the song that was playing went on and on. The actors he usually worked with were ordinarily people. They later reflected that their experience in collaborating with Smith in his shows gave them a strong sense of inner freedom.

Smith incorporated the idea of failure, the notion that nothing works, that everything turns out to be wrong by planning deliberate breakdowns in his screenings/performances. This way, he intentionally perturbed the time experience of the performance or the film. He wanted the public to interrupt the illusion that time stands still in the dark, that everything works smoothly.

LTTR, a queer feminist group from NY who were included in the Documenta XII magazine section, titled their third magazine *Practice More Failure.*

One of the posts in the blog about performance coordinated by the artist Itziar Okariz for *Zehar* in 2009 read as follows:

> Joan Jonas is not articulated in the way you expect from crystalline art pieces. She places approximations side by side (a happening, tableau vivant, objects, film, drawings, a camera, etc.), as cumuli. There is something extraordinary

---

3. *If I Can't Dance, I Don't Want To Be Part Of Your Revolution*, Magazine 2, 2008.

in this way of showing how things are registered. The audacity of the register, the difference and similarity between it and the actual occurrence, shares the passion of Houdini for debunking mediums yet being an illusionist at the same time. The sense of possibility is exacerbated. There is a slight displacement, a de-articulation, to be precise.[4]

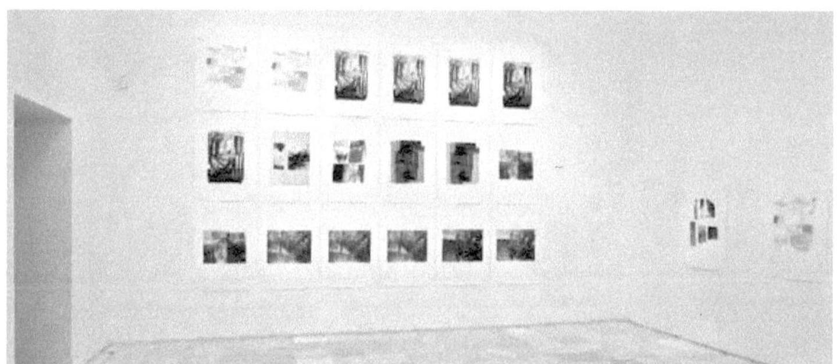

Figure 11.13. Tableau vivant. *MNCARS, Madrid (Spain), 2013. Courtesy of MNCARS.*

Tableau Vivant

In my last exhibition *Tableau vivant* (2013), which took place at the Reina Sofía Museum in Madrid (figures 11.13–15), I lay out a series of silkscreen prints based on preexistent images, along with a series of drawings that were colored in by the participants in *Coloring Book*, the aforementioned children's workshop, which was held prior to the opening of the exhibition. The show also included a video piece and a series of projections, my first incursion in this field, which enter into dialogue with the other two series. My aim in this production was that its multiplicity, fragmentation, and repetition function as a means of breaking away from the absolute image and linear narrative forms. The ephemeral and processual nature of the work is central to it as well. The title, *Tableau vivant,* alludes to painting, to certain ways of dancing, and to an idea of "still" representation in a setting or framework in which a group of characters pose, recreate, or simulate an event or a scene. Other aspects of this work include the idea of entertainment and the construction of a visual iconography in which pleasure, excess, and fantasy are implicit.

4. Itziar Okariz, "Joan Jonas el jueves pasado, *Reading Dante*, in *Performing Garage*," *Blog: Performance Edición*. At www.old.arteleku.net/arteleku/publicaciones/zehar/performance-edicion/2009/12/11/joan-jonas-el-jueves-pasado-reading-dante-en-el-performing-garage.

I am interested in the *tableau vivant* as a way of acting and thinking that relates back to a technique used by filmmakers like Ulrike Ottinger, whose work is a referent of mine. This German filmmaker considers that every film for her possesses a certain form that has to do with colors, with time, with dramatic structure, and with the way of linking the images. And so in every film she works to find the right form.

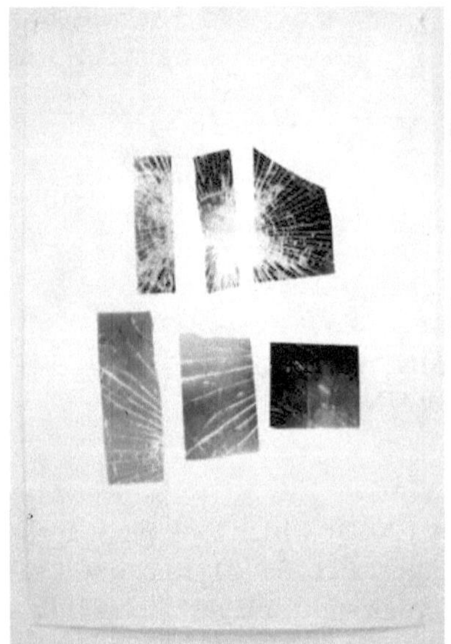

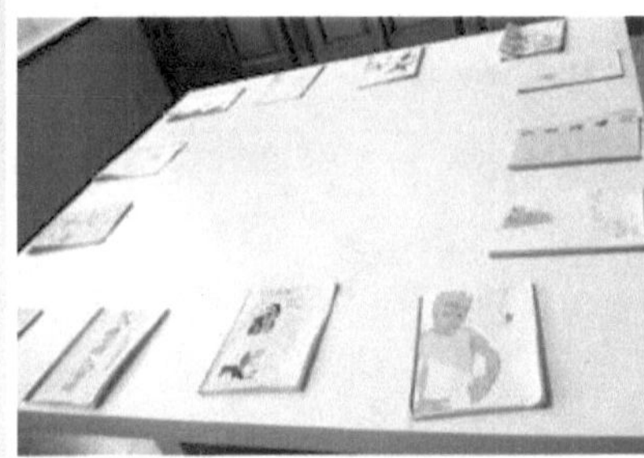

Figure 11.14 (left) and 11.15 (above). Tableau vivant. *MNCARS, Madrid (Spain), 2013.*

The silkscreen prints present a series of collages that might configure a zine opened up on the wall. A zine is a self-produced independent magazine. As an editorial and creative activity, the zine questions the idea of "professionalism" in embracing a project that employs a low-fi aesthetic. It belongs to the DIY Culture, which has its roots in other social and artistic movements like Dadaism, punk, and the feminist liberation movement. These means of expression, which are used by very heterogeneous groups, make it possible to produce and document representation itself. My work with the feminist art project Erreakzioa-Reacción (Reaction) is also framed within these premises; premises that can also be seen in the results of the children's workshops.

The technique of silkscreen allows me to translate images, in this case through the use of four-color printing, and so I obtain a version that casts a new gaze upon them. I think silkscreen allows me to get an image over and over again, and as a technique it allows us to think about the notions of the original, the copy, the unique, and the serial or reproducible artwork. Under the effect of repetition, what is represented changes and fades away. The image is constructed on the basis of that reiterative effect. In the interstices, something occurs that exceeds the representation itself and makes it strange. From my point of view, one of the reasons behind artistic practice has to do with its capacity to provoke a sense of strangeness. I propose a similar dynamics in my work with moving images. The remixing of "any images," which will never be the same as "just any image," gives rise to a video piece whose points of reference range from the most experimental production in the medium to others that are closer to the language of music video clips.

Erreakzioa-Reacción

Erreakzioa-Reacción is a group I created with the artist Estibaliz Sadaba. At the time we felt there was a need to build a space for projects around gender theory, artistic practice, and feminist activism. The name means "Reaction" in Basque and Spanish and we chose it as a means of transmitting an idea of resistance and action. What encouraged us to start Erreakzioa was getting to know what other feminist groups were doing internationally: for example, the Guerrilla Girls and WAC (the Women's Action Coalition) in the United States and (closer to us geographically) Bildwechsel, a video feminist cultural initiative in Hamburg, Germany, that we visited when we decided to start Erreakzioa. We had not heard of any similar project about art and feminism in the Basque Country and in Spain and we thought something of this kind was needed.

From 1994 to 2000, most of our effort was geared to the production of zines. We produced ten publications/feminist zines, an activity that defined our work at that time. Our aim when doing feminist zines (femzines) was to spread feminist thought because we were aware that a feminist tradition in relation to artistic critique and practices was very limited. Femzines were a quick and cheap way to be present in the art scene. So we defined multiple directions that could be taken in this work, some of them just modest interventions in issues and practices in which we thought our context was lacking. We invited women artists to show their work, and we always paid for the collaborations because we believe women's work has to be remunerated; we tried to create a network so similar initiatives of other collectives were presented in our publications and we translated some contemporary texts into Spanish, while at the same time being also aware of the need to translate them into Basque to support the creation of a theoretical feminist corpus in the Basque language. The topics that we covered were sexuality, gender, pornography/post-pornography, the media, labor conditions, violence against women, postcolonial feminism, antimilitarism, music, and transsexual and transgender issues.

Our first femzine (1995) was dedicated to a series of works about gender and included a list of Basque women artists, in order to make visible the huge amount of women present in the Basque artistic scene. Issue number 2, *Construcciones del cuerpo femenino* (Constructions of the Female Body) was presented in Arteleku that same year in the context of a symposium and a video program (figure 11.16). Issue number 3, titled ¿Quién es libre de elegir? (Who is free to choose? 1996) was about antimilitarism: it addresses "Mujeres de Negro" (Women in Black), a world-wide network of women committed to peace with justice and actively opposed to injustice, war, militarism and other forms of violence and "el Movimiento de Insumisión," a social movement against compulsory Spanish military service that was a highly charged political issue at that time (figure 11.17). Besides, many friends of ours were involved in this movement. *Erreakzioa* number 4 (1996) was our collaboration for the exhibition *Nowhere* at the Louisiana Museum in Denmark, curated by Ute Meta Bauer. *Erreakzioa* number 7 (1997) was presented in a video-zine format. And the last edition, *Erreakzioa* number 10 (2000) was about music, female musicians, and feminism. The format of the publications changed, more or less, with every issue and they were distributed in different feminist and artistic events and venues. We printed five hundred copies of each issue. We also received a small amount of money from Emakunde, the Institute of Basque Women, to help with the publishing costs.

In respect to our work editing zines, we love the fact that fem/grrrls[5]/queer zines are a quick, cheap, and direct way to share information and to empower the participants as subjects of action. It enables us to grow in a collective way. We consider feminist zines as part of a social movement. It can also affect processes, ways of doing things. We see ourselves as part of a genealogy in relation to art and feminisms. In this way we have worked into this idea of the DIY punk spirit connected to feminist thought and practices: if you do not like what you see around you, do it yourself; you do not need big

5. "Grrrls" is a term coined by the Riot Grrrls movement. Since it was a movement that young women established, they chose to create a neologism that put together the word "girl" with the onomatopoeic sound an animal makes when angry. The movement was particularly active in creating music and zines in the 1990s.

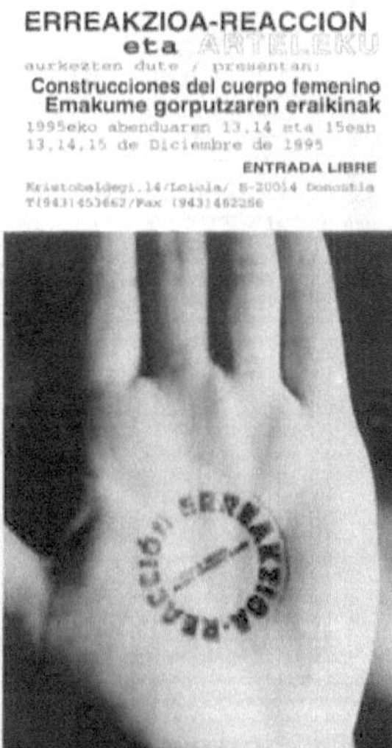

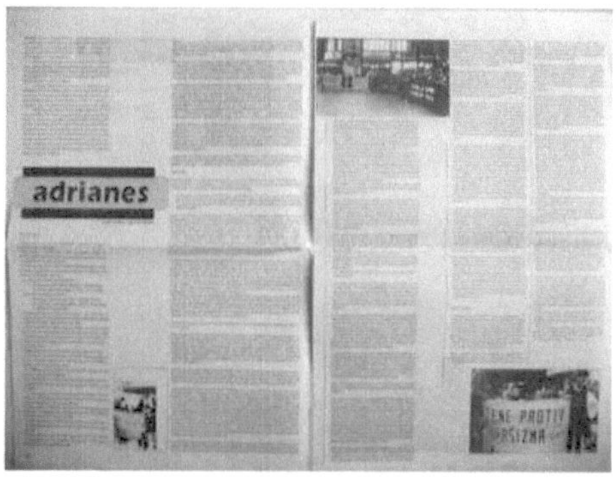

Figure 11.16 (left). Constructions of the Female Body. Erreakzioa-Reacción, *1995. Figure 11.17 (above). Who Is Free to Choose.* Erreakzioa-Reacción *3, 1996.*

infrastructures in order to do something; we can transform the role of the passive object and become the subject of action; we question technical virtuosity as a fundamental requisite to do a project, the idea of "professionalism," of "authority"; we use a low-fi aesthetic technology. It is about to continue with a tradition of generating independent work contexts and networks.

Other activities undertaken by Erreakzioa, besides the zines, have included seminars and workshops. We organized three important seminars and workshops at the Arteleku Art Center: first, *For Your Eyes Only; the Feminist Factor in Relation to the Visual Arts*, in 1997 (figure 11.18). The main theoretical axis of this first seminar was feminism and its political subject, women, although Erreakzioa was already questioning and attempting to break an essentialist or biological idea of the "woman" and the woman/femininity equation. This clearly highlighted the need to leave spaces for new critical feminist interventions constructed in tune with new social, political, racial, and sexual coordinates. Then we created *The Repoliticisation of Sexual Space in Contemporary Artistic Practices*, with María José Belbel, in 2004 (figure 11.19) and *Mutations of Feminism: Genealogies and Artistic Practices* in collaboration with María José Belbel and Beatriz Preciado, in 2005, as an intersection between critical feminism and queer politics. The huge turnout to participate in these activities confirmed our perception that they were very much in demand.

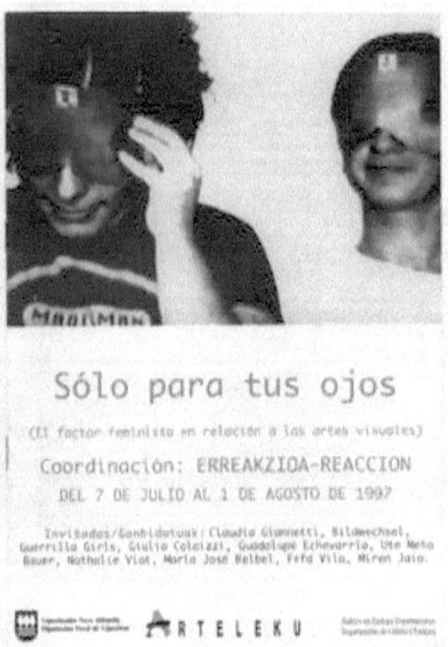

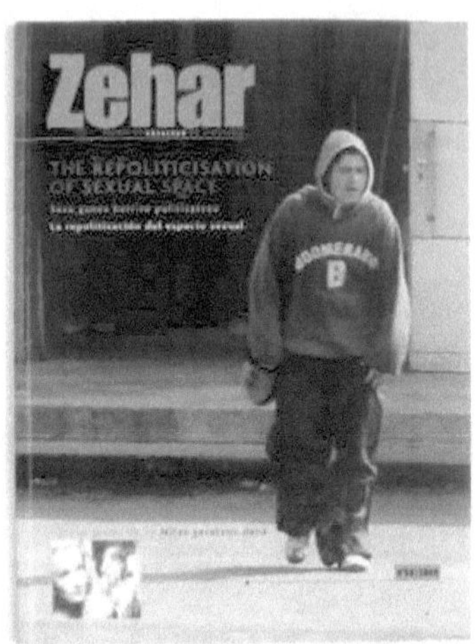

Figure 11.18 (left). For Your Eyes Only. Arteleku, *1997. Figure 11.19 (right). The Repoliticisation of Sexual Space.* Arteleku, *2004.*

In 2008, Sala Rekalde in Bilbao invited us to show our work processes within the scheduling of the space "The Abstract Cabinet." Our proposal for the exhibition *¡Aquí y ahora! Nuevas formas de acción feminista* (*Here and Now! New Forms of Feminist Action*) (figure 11.20) consisted of creating a device designed by the artist Carme Nogueira for presenting different feminist and queer collectives that have also worked with the zine format, given the great number of initiatives that have been developed in this format. We also invited Elke Zobl, who brought a selection of her massive Grrrl Zine Network project.

In addition, we considered it equally appropriate to present an archive that became, at the same time, an exhibition object and also acted as a subsequent transmission platform for the information contained therein (figure 11.21). Because of the open generic nature that this archive aims to have—insomuch as it documents work by women artists from our milieu—we chose to show a most exhaustive compilation possible, rather than a mere selection of works. Although this was already the original aim of Erreakzioa, since we had produced the list of all the Basque women artists that were in the scene, back in 1994, it continues to be equally important nowadays to highlight the presence and work of these artists. This archive does not aspire to be totalizing or absolute, and should instead be understood as the opening up of a process or a kind of permanent work-in-progress. A similar philosophy is present in the project *Edición Múltiple* (Multiple Edition), an exhibition Erreakzioa curated in 2011 at the exhibition galleries of the University of the Basque Country.

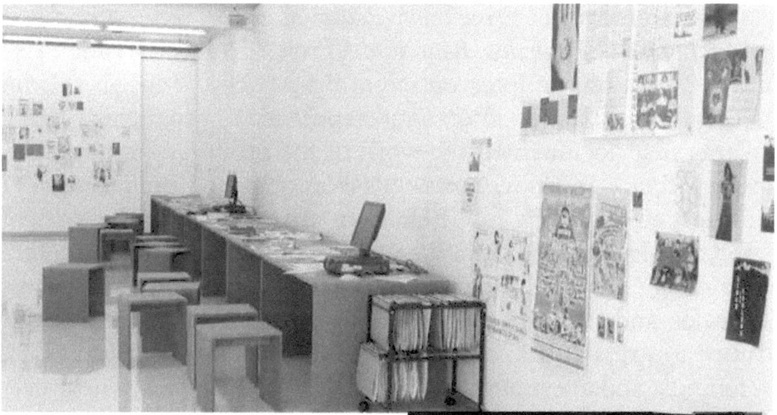

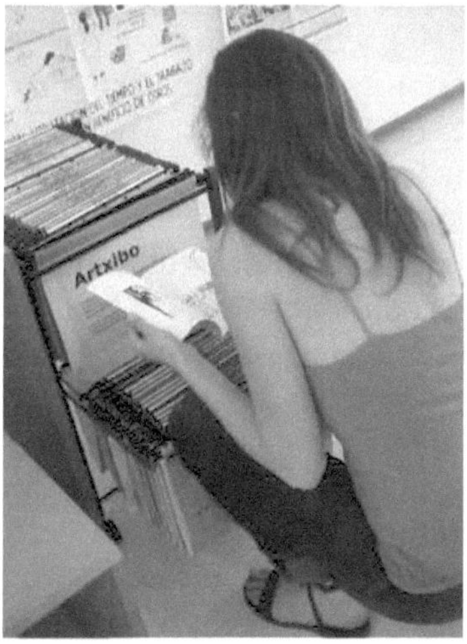

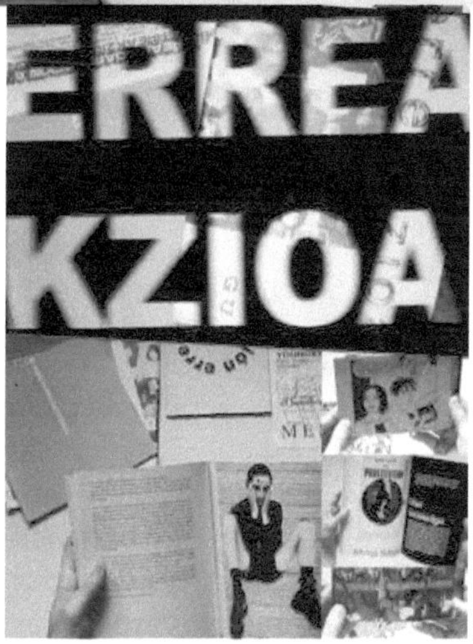

Figure 11.20 (top) and 11.21 (middle left). Here and Now! New Forms of Feminist Action. *Sala Rekalde, Bilbao, 2008. Photography: Begoña Zubero. Figure 11.22 (middle right), 11.23 (below), and 11.24 (inset).* Erreakzioa-Reacción: A Project Between Art and Feminism. *MUSAC, León (Spain), 2012. Courtesy of MUSAC.*

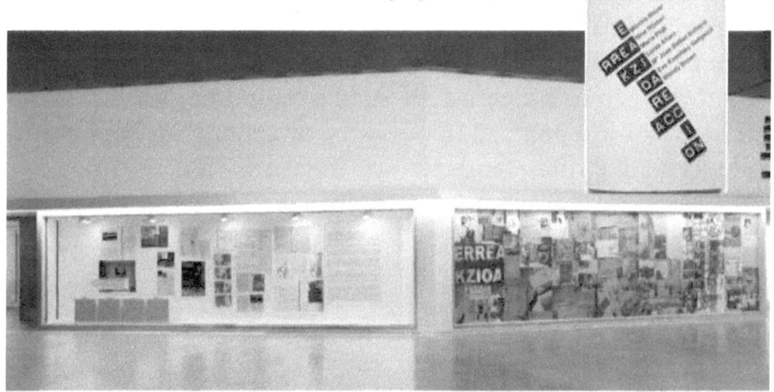

Our latest project *Erreakzioa-Reacción: un proyecto entre el arte y el feminismo* (*Erreakzioa-Reacción: A Project Between Art and Feminism*) (2012) was an intervention at the MUSAC Museum, León (figures 11.22–23). The intervention consisted of producing two big collages that documented the work of the group and a new publication (figure 11.24) with new collaborations and the proposal of the guest editor María José Belbel: an introduction to the work of Eve Kosofsky Sedgwick and Wendy Brown and the translation into Spanish of "Melanie Klein and the Difference Affect Makes" by Sedgwick and "Suffering the Paradoxes of Rights" by Brown. We wanted to stress the importance of the translation of relevant works by feminist and queer authors such as Eve K. Sedgwick, whose only book translated into Spanish so far is the *Epistemology of the Closet* (translated as *Epistemología del armario*), which is now out of print. As for Wendy Brown, she has been translated into Spanish only in compilations. We intend to continue collaborating in the translation and publication of essential works by feminist and queer authors in the future.

We have always thought that feminism is important for any social change, for many disciplines, for many different kinds of people, and not only for women. There is a kind of normalization of feminism at present that could involve its regularization, in the sense of the acceptance of one type of feminism—white, heterosexual, middle class, western—and the exclusion of others. We always have thought that our production and practices should be alert to and critical about this. We started our group when there were no other such initiatives around us. Fortunately, there is now a greater diversity of proposals and debates than our generation encountered. On the other hand, we know through history that changes are not forever, as the attack of the governing Popular Party (PP. Partido Popular) in Spain on abortion rights is showing us at present. In the new scene we see our work as involved in collaborations with new groups. It is important to note that we have been working on the project for twenty years, and it is not very usual for this kind of group to remain in existence for such a long time. We have always been aware of the political importance of generating contexts in a fragile scene that often tends toward fragmentation.

12

Engagement and Commitment

Peter Selz

"Ethics and Aesthetics are one."
—Ludwig Wittgenstein, in *Tracticus Logic-Philospheсus.*

We are going to look at art with political content. We must be cautious when discussing political art. We know what happens when art becomes subject to political machinations, when evil politics produces atrocious art. At the extreme of course was the nationalist art of Nazi Germany, which looked very much like the socialist realist art of the Soviet Union and, incidentally, not totally different from the isolationist American Regionalism of the 1930s. The Mexican muralists did a lot better in creating fine art of historic-political content. With great assistance from their federal government, they painted their subjects, mostly Meso-American culture and contemporary life, with a clear knowledge of modernist art, and each artist worked in his (no women among them) highly personal style. To a large extent their art excelled because of their awareness of formal composition, such as consideration for shape, color and light.

But I cannot agree with Formalist critics like Clive Bell and Roger Fry, who early in the twentieth century maintained that there was no real disparity between a picture of the Madonna and a painting of apples; as Clive Bell puts it, "The representative element in a work of art . . . always it is irrelevant. . . (T)o appreciate a work of art we need bring with us nothing from life, no knowledge of its ideas and affairs, no familiarity with its emotions. Art transports us from the world of man's activity to a world of aesthetic exaltation."[1]

Thus I believe that the more we know about the artist, their life, and the art they looked at, the better for our appreciation of the

1. Bell, *Art*, 27.

work. Formalist criticism was brought to the absurd by Clement Greenberg who claimed that the purpose of painting was ultimately nothing but the presentation of a flat color surface, since two-dimensionality is the hallmark of painting. However, I think it was Theodor Adorno who said: "When art is experienced purely aesthetically, it fails to be experienced even aesthetically." Fatuous as it now appears, there was nonetheless little dissent from the theory by many art historians and critics. Indeed, Formalism was accepted by many of my colleagues for too long a time. Art has to do more than just feed on itself.

I do believe that subject matter is important in a work of art. Mark Rothko, abstract as his canvases may appear, was one of the so-called Abstract Expressionists who, in 1950 founded a school in New York called 'Subjects of the Artist." At times the subject may not reveal itself without the input of the viewer who completes the aesthetic act. Rothko 's paintings are not just color fields; they are works that deal deeply with human emotion. What matters most is how the artist deals with his subject. There is a reason why Leonardo's *Last Supper*, wrecked as it has been for almost its entire existence, has captivated viewers for all these centuries. Instead of depicting twelve men in Renaissance clothing sitting around a table, as was done by many of his contemporaries, he not only gave each of the apostles an individual character, but created a work in which the figures, their position, and the treatment of light and space has resulted in a painting of structural harmony.

In this chapter, I wish to discuss works by artists who were (or are) *engaged* on matters of politics, while being totally *committed* to the creation of art. I plan to focus on two California artists with whose work I am very familiar and with whom I am have curated shows: William T. Wiley and Enrique Chagoya. These two artists have, I believe, enriched and expanded the repertoire of political art, often by making use of drama, comedy, sarcasm, and irony in their creation of unusual paintings.

But before talking about them, let us look first at a truly great painting, which I think meets the maxims of political art superbly. In 1830, the French painter Eugène Delacroix produced his *Liberty leading the People*. It is a very large picture: almost eleven inches across and is certainly commanding. Every time I see it, first in the Louvre and then in the Musée d'Orsay, there are art students copying it and viewers looking with unusual attention. It pictures a contemporaneous event. It was painted during what had been called "the glorious days" of the July rebellion against King Charles X. In front, at our feet, we see men of the people, fallen soldiers, done with journalistic observation, and a wounded man who raises himself to war with the glorious figure of Liberty. On the left is a citizen in top hat, brandishing a musket, actually a self-portrait, and another citizen flashes his sword. On the right is a spunky young boy in a beret with a pistol in each hand. In the center, the passionate female leader wields a bayonet and waves the tricolor of the French Republic, whose brilliant colors are meant to stand out against the general drab colors of the painting as a whole. In the right background, looking through the mist of battle, one can see the towers of Notre Dame—religion joining the revolutionary battle as it were. Liberty at the apex of the human pyramid stands for rebirth conquering death striding forward into the viewer's space with her brilliant flag as the symbol of hope. This goddess of liberty is traditionally female, but it is worth noting that the artist chose to paint her in this victorious stride. Delacroix was a close friend of the Frenchwoman writer, Georges Sand, who urgently promoted woman's rights of social and intellectual equality with men. But he was not a revolutionary; he was a member of the upper bourgeoisie, simply inspired by the rebellion to create this masterpiece.

Some hundred years later Picasso was deeply moved by the tragedy of the Spanish Civil War and the bombing of Guernica (Gernika in Basque). His work evolved from his great etching series *Dream and lie of Franco* (1937) to the creation of *Guernica.* He created this incomparable painting of outrage and anger, painting the great mural for the pavilion of the Spanish Republic at the 1937 Paris World Fair. For the first time in his career, Picasso was fully engaged in a political act. At the same time he was totally committed to the task of painting, he adapted the familiar figures, the women in his life, the horse, and the bull, to create this post-Cubist composition to a work that became the most important, the most fully realized modernist painting.

Moving with speed from the early nineteenth to the late twentieth century, from painting to photography and from poetic allegory to reportage, let us look now at Richard Misrach's photo called *Swamp and pipeline, Geismar, Louisiana* (1998). Misrach, when a student at Berkeley, and a long time before he became a celebrated photographer, was active in the antiwar student movement at Cal. He never forgot the power of photography in many of his series such as the documentation of ecological damage to millions of acres of public land in Nevada done by US Navy airplanes dropping high explosive bombs leaving horrendous craters. Misrach also took a series of photos documenting the destruction of the Los Angeles environment by 26,000 miles of pipelines for the oil industry. These pictures are part of what the people there called "Cancer Alley." One photo depicts what was once a thriving swamp behind a hazardous small bore pipe, which appears like a man-made horizon line. It points to the much more massive threatened XL pipeline that would bring some of the dirtiest crude oil all the way from Alberta to Louisiana.

The two artists I want to discuss now engaged in political issues with both artistic skill and gentle persuasion. This may well be the reason for their acceptance by the public with numerous international exhibitions and prestigious teaching positions at the University of California and Stanford respectively.

Wiley was born in Indiana in 1937, attended high school in the state of Washington where, at the Seattle Museum, he was impressed with its fine Asian arts collection and paintings by Mark Tobey and Morris Graves. He then want to art school at the San Francisco Art Institute (now the California School of Fine Arts) during its glory days, studying with Elmer Bischoff, Nathan Oliveira, and Frank Lobdell, among others. Richard Diebenkorn was also on the faculty at that time. Among his fellow students were Manuel Neri and Joan Brown. In the SF museums he would have seen exhibitions by the Abstract Expressionists—prior to their being shown in NY museums—and of the Surrealists. San Francisco was clearly a center of the arts with Beat poetry among its best-known achievement. In 1959, he produced a bold painting, *Flag song*, which can be read as a figure on a dark area with outstretched arms and a white heart, on the boundary between abstraction and representation.

In 1963, Wiley was appointed to the art faculty of UC Davis, joining artists Roy de Forest, Robert Arneson, and Manuel Neri, and outstanding students such as Bruce Nauman and Deborah Butterfield. These were the artists who were at the core of Funk. Funk, a term borrowed from Jazz, was very different from the contemporaneous Pop. It ridiculed the prevailing culture rather than glorify it. In 1967, I curated a now historic exhibition at the Berkeley Art Museum, called Funk. Funk art, I explained, is "hot rather than cool, committed rather than disengaged, bizarre rather than formal, sensuous and frequently quite ugly."[2] Funk artists knew too well that a fraudulent morality is a fact of the world, and, having no illusion that they could change it, they exposed it. Or, as the artist Harold Paris put it: "The casual irreverent, insincere California atmosphere, with its absurd elements—skinny-dipping, do-it your-

2. "Sculpture: Up with Funk," *Time Magazine* 89, no. 18 (May 5, 1967), 85.

self hobby craft, sun-drenched mentality, Doggie Diner, perfumed toilet tissue in the land of Funk."[3]

A prime funk object was the "Slant Step," which Wiley and his student Bruce Nauman discovered in a salvage shop. It looked utilitarian but how to use thus object? Wiley bought it for 50 cents, gave it to Nauman, and it became sort of a cult object at Davis. They all proceeded to make all kinds of "Slant Steps." Wiley produced *Slant Step becomes Rhino* (1966) with a rhinoceros horn emerging from the slanting platform, creating a phallic object, subject to different interpretations. The NY critic John Perrault described Wiley as a "Metaphysical Funk Monk." At any rate, Richard Serra, before he became the famous sculptor, saw the "Slant Step" and took it away to NY. It is now under the auspices of the New York Society for the Preservation of the Slant Step in upstate New York. In 1971, we at the Berkeley Art Museum organized Wiley's first museum show, which we sent on to museums in Philadelphia and Boston. Wiley's horizons were wide open. He told us at the time of his admiration for artists as different as Clyfford Still, Marcel Duchamp, and H.C. Westermann. The works we were showing were like the watercolor *Lame and Blind in Eden*, which shows a Garden of Eden, despoiled by humans with instruments; a painting on an easel can be seen in the left background. Beautifully painted, the watercolor does not give us much hope. There were assemblage constructions like *Art Official Peace Plan*, which indicates Wiley's opposition to the Vietnam War. The vertical member is a denuded Christmas tree, alluding to what the US did to the forests with Agent Orange. The Peace sign on top is also a slingshot. The black triangle is sort of a Wiley signature sign. Bill Wiley is amazingly productive, and, over the years, he has shown his work throughout the US as well as in Argentina, Australia, France, Germany, Italy, Spain, and Switzerland. I am currently co-curating a show of his paintings and sculptures of the twenty-first century.

Wiley continues to paint, to make sculpture, and to sing songs accompanying himself with his guitar. He loves verbal as well as visual puns, and makes up new ones all the time. His work is interpretive, ironic, illusive, and irreverent and often it is about art. Over the years, he has become increasingly concerned with world events, sociopolitical and environmental issues. And like many artists, he looks at the art of the past to find what would be of use for his own work. As Cezanne said: "The Louvre is the book in which

3. Paris, "Sweet Land of Funk," 98.

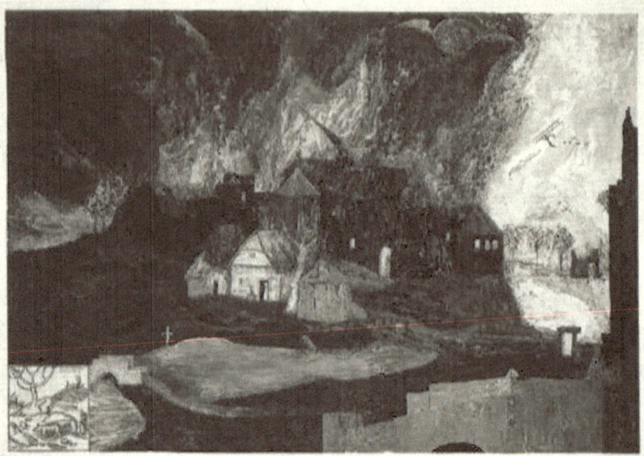

Figure 12.1. William T. Wiley, Grebeny—the burning village (after Bosch). *Courtesy of the artist.*

we learn to read."[4] In 1996, the de Young Museum in San Francisco mounted a show called Nothing Lost from the Original with paintings after Winslow Homer, Eduard Manet, Leonardo, Whistler, Breughel, and Bosch. Wiley's painting *Grebeny—the burning village (after Bosch)* (figure 12.1) depicts the village of Grebeny, which was contaminated by the nuclear meltdown at Chernobyl in 1986, and is based on a detail of Bosch's *Temptation of St. Anthony*. Another painting, entitled *The city after Bosch after Chernobyl* has the two castle towers from Bosch's panel. The tower, painted in menacing grey, has a fire emerging from the top, and we see ominously weighted scales on the dome of the yellow tower. When he exhibited this canvas as the Meridian Gallery he added his "Yum Yum Song":

> Then tell my brothers and sisters
> Do you know what to do with plutonium yet?
> They were gonna hid it in the mountains
> And bury it in the sea
> Or maybe on some indian reservation
> That's not near you and me.
> So tell me about advanced technology
> And virtual reality.
> Then tell my father and mother
> what they gonna do with you and me?
> And does it matter how smart you are?
> And does it matter how dumb?
> Cause nobody on this little planet
> Know what to do with plutonium. Yum Yum

4. Quoted in Rewald, ed., *Paul Cézanne, Letters*, 315.

And, looking at another Bosch painting, he produced *No fault insurance* (2000) to express his outrage at the NY police killing an innocent man. The cop was exonerated because the man "looked guilty," much like the pardons granted by the Middle Ages when it so pleased the Church authorities; or recent government officials like Donald Rumsfeld and Dick Cheney sending men to Guantanamo. Reporting on world events is a strategy employed by the artist. In *9/11/01 #1* (2001), he depicted the before and after in a charcoal drawing. Then in *9/11/01 #2*, he painted it on caves with a view of Lower Manhattan including Statue of Liberty, but now he inserted a frightening image based on Gustave Doré's illustration for Edgar Allen Poe's *The Raven*. Above the towers is a grotesque horned monster, which resembles a medieval gargoyle. There are circles floating in the air and many hard-to-decipher texts in this painting.

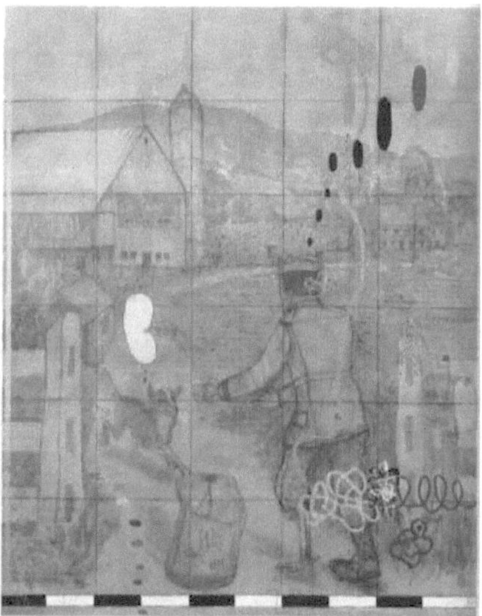

Figure 12.2. William T. Wiley, Sold your returns. *Courtesy of the artist.*

In 2003, in response to all the soldiers and civilians wounded in George Bush's war in Iraq, he turned to a popular drawing by N.C. Wyeth, called *The Homecoming*, depicting a happy occasion after a solder returning home from World War II—but in Wiley's painting called *Sold your returns* (figure 12.2), the soldier's left hand is a hook and his amputated left leg is a prosthesis. There is a lengthy text, hard to read as is his wont, written in the painting and set against Wyeth's sentimental drawing. Wiley added it in a grid overlay and wiggly strands of paint on its surface.

We also have a nice little old schoolhouse in a 2003 painting, called *School of the Americas*. The text refers to the US Army School of Ft. Benning, Georgia, which was set up to fight so-called communist dangers and trained soldiers from many South and Central American countries to fight against putative dangers such as Liberation Theology. But, as mainstream papers like the *Washington Post* and *New York Times* reported, the school taught "coercive interrogations techniques," that is, ways of torture. It was renamed the "Western Hemisphere Institute of Security Cooperation" several years ago. Much of this we find in Wiley's text, which also has scribbled "Georgia on my mind" on his hand-carved frame, and there is an hourglass painted with the text. The interrelation between the visual and the verbal was important to Wiley. In both this painting and in *The Homecoming*, he de-romanticizes old worn-out idylls with harsh reality, all done with a fine painter's craft, and questions our ways of thinking and seeing, which, of course is one of the functions of art.

Enrique Chagoya shares with Wiley the Brechtian the concept that a work of art—be it a play or a painting—should have the potential to create a shock of realization in the spectator. This is similar to André Breton's command: "Surprise me." True, it is by no means easy to create a shock in these postmodern times, yet I think both artists manage to create works that are astounding, often brought about by their sense of wit.

Enrique Chagoya was born in a cultured environment in Mexico City in 1953. In high school, he read Hermann Hesse, Franz Kafka, Rosa Luxemburg, and Karl Marx. In 1968, the young boy was acutely aware of the killing of some five hundred students (nobody bothered to count the bodies) by the Mexican police. Three years later, Chagoya himself participated in an uprising against the federal government and was lucky to escape another massacre by the police. At university, he studied political economy, but after a few years he made the decision to become a visual artist and moved to California and attended the San Francisco Art Institute, and then University of California, Berkeley. While still at the Art Institute, he took part in 1984 in an exhibition called Artists, call against US intervention in Central Americas, which was the occasion when I first saw his work and bought one of his prints from the Goya series.

He had embarked on producing an astonishing group of intaglio prints based on Goya's *Disasters of War*. Goya's etchings, addressing the horror of the Napoleonic invasion of Spain were testimonies of chaos, bestiality, and terror. Chagoya's prints, entitled *Homage to Goya* (figure 12.3) look at first glance like forgeries of the real thing.

But, as Picasso once said, "good artists borrow, great artists steal." Chagoya's prints certainly have the feel of the master. His series, he said, are based on "How would Goya have portrayed events in the 20th Century." These contemporary prints avoid all the horror of torture and killing shown by his predecessor, preferring presentations with a more humorous touch. Among their cast are Pope John Paul II, Fidel Castro, but especially Americans, such as the segregationist Jesse Helms, Henry Kissinger, Bill Clinton with Monica Lewinsky, and, in particular, many images of Ronald Reagan. One example is *Against the Common Good*, based on Goya's number 71 etching. Goya showed an evil monk with talons on his feet and hands and vampire's wings in place of his ears, writing who knows what in his big book. And Ronald Reagan is depicted as doing the same.

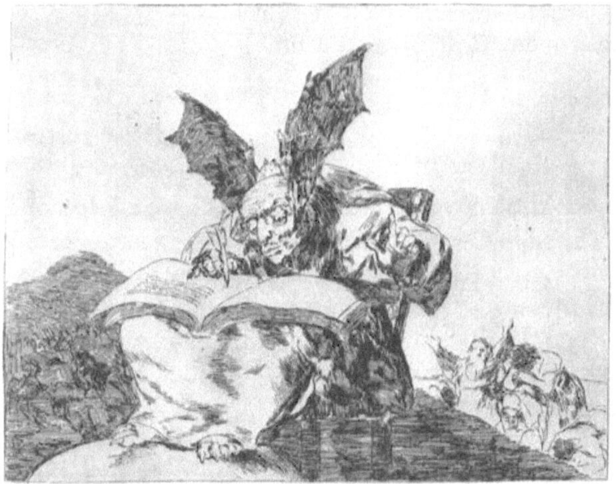

Figure 12.3. Enrique Chagoya, Contra el bien general *from the* Homage to Goya *series. Courtesy of the artist.*

Chagoya produced many codices, using the accordion format of the ancient Aztec books, many of which had been destroyed by the conquistadors. In these, he merges pre-Columbian images, Christian colonial art, and American popular pictures. An example is this detail from *Tales from the Conquest* (1992). He has done many codices in which he "cannibalized" (as he calls it), taking history as ripe for plucking, and created his own work by cobbling together alternate histories in a collage of visual language.

He applies the same ideology to large paintings on amate paper (a bark paper was used by Aztecs for codes books). An example is *The Governor's Nightmare* (1994), which deals with the clash of cultures in a biting sardonic manner. Syncretically fusing aspects of Meso-American culture with the political situation in California during Pete Wilson's administration, Chagoya depicts the Aztec lord of the Dead, sitting on a pyramid, exhorting people to cannibalism. He sprinkles salt on a terrified Mickey Mouse, who is tied up on a plate. Stereotyped Aztec men sit around, devouring parts of a human body, presumably Pete Wilson's, who was known for his anti-immigration stance. Providing a balanced reading of history, the artist also included a small reproduction in the upper left corner of a Colonial era picture showing the drinking of the blood of Christ at Holy Communion.

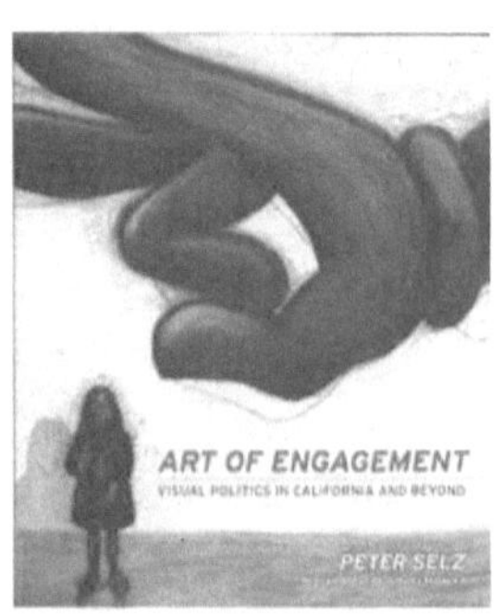

Figure 12.4. Enrique Chagoya, When paradise arrived, *used as the cover for* Art of Engagement. *Courtesy of the artist.*

His best-known works are very large charcoal drawings such as *US intervention in CentralAmerica.* It features a large Ronald Reagan and a small Henry Kissinger, both versions of Mickey Mouse, writing graffiti messages from buckets of red blood/paint with Reagan's slogan "Keep Ruskies and Cubans out of Central America" and Kissinger's "By the way, keep art out of Politics." Addressing the border issue, Chagoya produced his now famous *When Paradise Arrived* (figure 12.4) echoing Mickey Mouse (together with Coca Cola America's unofficial ambassadors). Here the mouse's gigantic hand, with "English Only" imprinted discreetly on one finger, is about to flick away a young Chicana with a little red heart painted on her body.

This artist, taking everything he can find for his own enterprise, could not neglect Andy Warhol and his now iconic soup cans, as exemplified in one work consisting of a pyramid of Campbell, now called CanibBULL soup cans. Now he implicates the whole art world, the art collector, the museum director, the dealer, and the art historian like your author here.

Bibliography

Bell, Clive. *Art*. London: Chatto and Windus, 1914.

Paris, Harold. "Sweet Land of Funk.," *Art in America* 55 (March–April 1967): 94–98.

Rewald, John ed. *Paul Cézanne: Letters*. London: B. Cassirer, 1976.

13

Art and Telos: Aesthetics, Politics, and Limited Action

Fernando Golvano

"With art and with politics, inventions and subjectifications constantly reconfigure the landscape of what is political and what is artistic."
— Jacques Rancière

This chapter is structured as a sequence of theoretical positions, through which I expose in a brief and fragmented manner some problematic points on art, politics, and the aesthetic and political dimensions of different social and historical contexts. There are no aesthetic criteria of universal scope, only creation that is always open to actions and imaginaries that take place under the different denominations of art. The historicity of categories affects the creation, reception, and theorization of works. Given that there exists no art without implicit or explicit telos, finality, the political dimension cannot be reduced to all artistic practice. As a consequence, the finality of art unavoidably becomes a subject of debate.

Schiller and the Humanity to Come

From art and beauty to liberty: this is the thesis that Friedrich Schiller (1759–1805) had for the origin of European modernity. He transgressed the conventions of literary genres and disciplinary boundaries, foreshadowing a feature that would be common in the experience of modern vanguards. He wanted to go beyond the autonomy of the specific domains of reason and sensibility, in such a way that poetry and the arts may sublimate a desire inseparable from rationality. For art, Schiller writes in his *On the Aesthetic Education of Man* (1794), "has to leave reality, it has to raise itself boldly above necessity and neediness; for art is the daughter of freedom, and it requires its prescriptions and rules to be furnished by the necessity of spirits and not by that of matter."[1] This telos manifested itself in other avant-garde attempts in the first decades of the twentieth century; it was present in a refined way in subsequent projects like that of Jorge Oteiza. Simón Marchán Fiz observes how Schiller lengthened an illustrious tradition (that stretches from Shaftesbury to Lessing), which conceived of art and aesthetic experience as paradigms of the formative activity of the human spirit, as mediations that emancipate it from alienation.[2] For Schiller, the action of art may affect the emergence of an aesthetic state such as aesthetic rationality; it is thence that the finality of art should be "the exposition of the supersensitive." In diverse contexts this may variously mean enlightened design, utopian promise, the absolute, or the ineffable. Beauty, because of its genuine indeterminacy, procures for human beings their liberty, and confronts them with their propulsion to the unlimited or the divine.

Mallarmé and Limited Action

In Stéphane Mallarmé (1842–1898) we see a movement from symbolist and Orphean to proto-avant-garde poetics. What was at stake in this transition—which proposed to invent "a language that must necessarily spring from a very new poetics"[3]—was the legacy of inherited aesthetics: a mode of correspondence between poetic (or artistic) languages and the order of the world. Mallarmé assumed the precarious state of all representation, the crisis of meaning that is proper to it, and its power to be engrossed on the white page or in the silence. One could say that he was moved by a desire to search for the absolute first through the Romantic course, and later from the perspective of the rupture of the inherited syntax. He wanted to access pure poetry by other means, by the fragmentary that opens other combinations toward the infinite. Jacques Rancière observes that his poetry tended toward the sacralization of literature, as in the cases of Gustave Flaubert, Maurice Blanchot, and German Romanticism.[4] Consequently, there is the imperative of creative liberty that challenges received tradition; and at the same time the retreat in formal construction as a political imperative. Jean-François Chre-

1. Schiller, "Letters Upon the Aesthetic Education of Man," at www.fordham.edu/halsall/mod/schiller-education.asp

2. Marchán Fiz, "A través de la belleza se llega a la libertad," 198.

3. Letter to Cazalis, October 1864. Translated by Henry Michael Weinfield, quoted in Mallarmé, *The Collected Poems of Mallarmé*, with commentary by Henry Michael Weinfield, 169.

4. See Rancière, *Mute Speech*.

vier argues that Mallarmé, in his essay "Limited Action" (1897), describes the limits just as much as the concentration of poetic action:

> At the end of the nineteenth century, after the death of Victor Hugo, the poet can no longer claim to operate directly in the political arena or even designate himself as moral conscience. He can mention the world, but he cannot change it. His activity, however, is not purely contemplative. He realizes an action in a restricted but essential field, which does not belong to him but which he can reevaluate and even redefine. This is the field of language and languages; it is the space of the book as a "spiritual instrument."[5]

This aesthetic revolution brings about the recognition that there is a poem everywhere, or that one can see beauty: "I think this is the important core: this idea of equality and anonymity."[6] Mallarmé`s opening, his attempt at the infinite book dislocated the world of prose: all a political manifesto concentrated in the form of a poem or literature.

Historical Avant-Gardes: New Fires

After the experience of the Paris Commune, in a *Letter to Paul Demeny* (1871) Arthur Rimbaud vindicated the poet`s role as a clairvoyant by virtue of "a long, gigantic and rational *derangement of all* the senses"[7] in order to reach the unknown. After the radical experiences of World War I, in 1918 another poet, Guillaume Apollinaire, wrote a poetic manifesto that condensed an avant-garde finality present in poetic and artistic action during the first decades of the twentieth century:

> We are not your enemies
> Who want to give ourselves vast strange domains
> Where mystery flowers into any hands that long for it
> Where there are new fires colors never seen
> A thousand fantasies difficult to make sense out of
> They must be made real.[8]

---

5. Catalogue of *Art and Utopia*, Museu d'Art Contemporani de Barcelona MACBA, Barcelona. At www.undo.net/it/mostra/19995.

6. Rancière, *El tiempo de la igualdad*, 203.

7. Rimbaud, "Letter to Paul Demeny," at http://iclosemyeyes.withtank.com/lostfound/2012/08/22/arthur-rimbaud-letter-to-paul-demenycharleville-15th-may-1871/.

8. Apollinaire, "The Pretty Redhead," in *The Random House Book of Twentieth Century French Poetry*, trans. James Wright.

And spoke about new "fires" and "fantasies" that were difficult to make sense of—did these objectives not manifest themselves under diverse practices and poetics in the projects of artistic vanguards? Sometimes, under theoretical buzzes or explicit subscriptions to Marx (as in Soviet constructionism or some surrealist currents), to Nietzsche (like in Dadaism) and to Freud (as in Surrealism), such movements wanted art and life to converge in a project of emancipation. The case of Italian futurism also belongs here, which was dedicated to a dynamics of vital, charismatic, and elitist sublimation of artistic-political action. The avant-garde sublimation of progress and of the aesthetic of the new suffered from the necessary critical contestation to industrial and scientific rationality that underscored the civilizational model of capitalism accelerating its global expansion. The failure of avant-garde attempts added yet another link to the chain of dissatisfied reason. As Marchán Fiz observes, "productivism and surrealism demonstrated, although for different reasons, both that the relationships between aesthetic and social emancipation are never mechanical or linear, and that the first is not an appendix to the second."[9] In this social and historical context, when those new and chimerical fires softened to a considerable extent, Picasso's *Guernica* (1937) became a symbol of a renewed convergence between art and politics, as well as of the paradoxes that affect images and their reception. Let us consider for a moment the debates that this work generated. Andrea Giunta calls this celebrated mural an *image-manifesto*.[10] Such was its power to catalyze, in the course of historical time, a dissenting meaning that this is manifest in its formal construction.[11] Its representative power recreates itself as emblem of the action of art to denounce barbarism. Nevertheless, its importance lies in the fact that this symbolic power, which is "reactive with regards to distinct presents,"[12] recreates itself without closing the debate about the interpretation of the figures represented on the mural. The symbolic power it was invested with in the 1940s and 1950s was also conditioned by the context of the Cold War between the two hegemonic blocks. Through form, *Guernica* as a critical image gives an account of its original power. There are the other figures of art history (Delacroix, Géricault, and Goya, for example), there are other Picassian motives, and there are his tu-

9. Marchán Fiz, *La estética de la cultura moderna*, 201.

10. Giunta, ed., *El* Guernica *de Picasso*, 12.

11. On the controversies regarding *Guernica*, see Rocío Robles Tardío, ed. *Picasso y sus críticos I*; and Giunta, ed., *El* Guernica *de Picasso*.

12. Giunta, ed., *El* Guernica *de Picasso*, 19.

multuous amorous adventures; but all this configures in a new form that cannot derive from any previous work. The result was a free composition that lives by its own rules. This would generate incomprehension and criticisms, like that of Max Raphael in his article "Discordance between form and content" (1947).[13] A paradoxical Picasso. Affiliated with the French Communist Party in 1944, and despite his sensitivity to translate with urgency the bombing of Gernika on a mural whose topicality would always become unseasonable, Picasso was incapable of taking a position against the *gulags* of Soviet totalitarianism. This blindness was shared by other artists and intellectuals as well in the 1960s and 1970s, with Jean-Paul Sartre being the most famous example.

Critical Theory: Benjamin, Adorno, Marcuse

In the mid-1930s, Walter Benjamin's hopes as regards both the democratization of art through its massive diffusion allowing for new conditions to reproduce works of art and a revolution of the social function of post-aura art were soon curtailed. In his celebrated essay *The Work of Art in the Age of Mechanical Reproduction* (1937) he maintains that, given the new superstructure of capitalist development, the traditional foundation of works of art in ritual was being replaced by a political foundation that was inherent in its secularizing dynamics.[14] He postulated with excessive optimism that mechanical reproduction would bring about the liberation of art from all elitist and national interests. The new statute of the work of modern art would thus distinguish itself from the traditional concept of art, and would remain defined by three emergent factors: the dissolution of the autonomy of art regarding life, the disappearance of aura and in a way of an artistic experience associated with it, and the novel convergence between art and political practice, as in case of surrealism and constructivism, the Italian futurists, and the German Dadaists. Against the political aesthetization that Nazism promoted, he supported a politicization of art so that it would converge with revolutionary politics. Yet we know that the aesthetization of politics is present in every form of totalitarianism, and not only in fascism, as Theodor W. Adorno reproached him for. Because the situation of post-aura art did not necessarily involve a rupture with autonomy, and the over-valuation of massively reproduced art did not necessarily grant it more critical value (as Adorno reproached

13. Article compiled in Robles Tardío, ed. *Picasso y sus críticos*, 236–47.
14. Benjamin, "The Work of Art in the Age of Mechanical Reproduction."

him for again in the correspondence they maintained during these years), it became necessary to explore other avenues for critically implicated art.

After World War II Adorno wrote *Minima Moralia* (1948), in which he warns that "the task of art today is to bring chaos into order,"[15] that is, to create the non-identical, the new that resists any instrumentalization of technocratic reason. With the embers of new controversies still smoldering (for example, Sartre and his thesis on the political link of literature), Adorno wrote his "Commitment" (1962), in which he affirms: "A work of art that is committed strips the magic from a work of art that is content to be a fetish."[16] Adorno challenges as false the election between the alternatives of committed art and art for art`s sake, given that "each of the two alternatives negates itself with the other,"[17] and they carry the sign of one-sidedness. The art thus only states alternatives through nothing but its form, therefore "every commitment to the world must be abandoned to satisfy the ideal of the committed work of art—that polemical alienation which Brecht as a theorist invented, and as an artist practiced less and less as he committed himself more firmly to the role of a friend of mankind."[18] He postulated as most urgent the defense of autonomous rather than committed art, thus distancing himself from the historical vanguards. In his *Aesthetic Theory* (1970), he attributed a capacity of knowing, redemption, and salvation to art and to the powers of the aesthetic: through the negative dialectic, art would challenge modern rationalization and its specialized domains. It was his way of taking advantage of its paradoxical autonomy, and above all of emphasizing that the critical possibilities of art reside in its form that is not founded in external references, whether they be of a mythical, metaphysical, religious, philosophical, or political nature. He acknowledges that the relation between art and social praxis is always variable, as both have changed profoundly throughout the twentieth century.

> If in art formal characteristics are not facilely interpretable in political terms, everything formal in art nevertheless has substantive implications and they extend into politics. The liberation of form, which genuinely new art desires, holds enciphered within it above all the liberation of society, for form—the social nexus of everything particular—rep-

15. Adorno, *Minima Moralia*, 222.
16. Adorno, "Commitment," 177.
17. Ibid., 178.
18. Ibid., 191.

> resents the social relation in the artwork; this is why liberated form is anathema to the *status quo*.[19]

Formal construction aspires neither to permanence nor to the mystified coherence of full significations: Adornian negation requires dislocating the total or closed form through deconstructing traditional material. It is therefore not surprising that he would identify, in the dissonant music of Arnold Schönberg and in the literature of Samuel Beckett, the clearest manifestations of his aesthetic theory. In his aspiration to preserve the autonomy of art, which at the same time is a kind of sovereignty, he requires a critical twist of art on itself. Currently, the legacy of this thinker is also manifested in that "art today cannot ignore the commination of having to be 'critical,' be that as it may," as Anne Cauquelin argues.[20]

In the context of critical theory, Herbert Marcuse also discussed an unresolved contradiction in the attempt to liberate the political or subversive potential of art: how to transcend and at the same time deny established reality? His answer is that "art can express its radical potential only *as art*, in its own language and image."[21] For Marcuse, therefore, "the political 'engagement' becomes a problem of artistic 'technique,' and instead of translating art reality is translated into a new artistic form. . . . Permanent aesthetic subversion: this is the way of art."[22] We should note the interpretation of Jürgen Habermas, when he affirms that, "only as art can it express its radical potential. The subversive truth of art appears only in the transformation of reality into illusion,"[23] that is, in aesthetic form.

Oteiza: Poetic, Political, and Religious Finality

Jorge Oteiza was a paradigmatic case of a genuine ability to maneuver between the aesthetic and the political. He aimed to reconcile an objective aesthetics of scientistic bases with mythical-poetic cosmo-visions. He became interested in the Greek myth of Prometheus, who symbolizes rebellion against injustice and the promise of human liberation, with a view of justifying his project *Monument to the Unknown Political Prisoner* (1952), which he presented at an international competition in London. In the words of Oteiza,

19. Adorno, *Aesthetic Theory*, 255.
20. Cauquelin, *Las teorías del arte*, 70.
21. Marcuse, *Counter-Revolution and Revolt*, 103–4.
22. Ibid., 106–7.
23. Marcuse, "On Art and Revolution," 166.

> The monument intends to be the expression of a double image of Prometheus: the bound Prometheus, and the Prometheus converted into victory, into an example and symbol of salvation. A statue of iron of a multiple Prometheus, at the feet of a total Prometheus, final and transcended, in stone. The sentimental articulation of both corresponds with that of the Sacrificed with the Mother of the representations of the Pietà.[24]

With Oteiza, the construction of a monumental form is inseparable from its aesthetic, political, and religious attributes, which in turn all interweave into a finality of redemption: "a monument will be nothing but a bunch of stones (or a reel of wire), if it fails to contribute to the realization of the mystery of a superior man."[25] The image of the triumphant Prometheus is the promise that his project proclaims in harmony with the Schillerian analogy: art and aesthetic education prefigure an emancipated identity, the convergence of reason, and sensitivity in a new form of aesthetic rationality. In Oteiza, the formal innovation that the utilization of the hyperboloid and the fourth dimension meant is at the service of a metaphysics of art, whose promise of human salvation emanates from this void. And this idea would continue to evolve later in his experimental proposal through the dis-occupation of the cylinder, the sphere, and the cube, and whose corollary was his abandonment of sculpture in 1959. Aesthetic action would continue to feature in his poetic work, in its collaboration with architectural interventions and in a theoretical, anthropological, and political praxis.

In the mid-1960s the groups Gaur ("Today"),[26] Emen ("Here"), Orain ("Now"), and Danok ("All") were established. The manifesto of the Gaur group emphasized collective aesthetic action ("we all come together as if in a cultural front or a school, a Company of new Basque artists") for an ethical-political program dissenting from the Francoist regime ("we take this agreement as spiritual and econom-

---

24. Oteiza, "Memoria del proyecto del escultor Jorge Oteiza," 48.

25. Ibid.

26. Gaur was presented in the spring of 1966 at the Barandiarán Gallery in Donostia-San Sebastián (a site that existed between 1965 and 1967). The Gaur group, consisting of Amable Arias, Rafael Ruiz Balerdi, Nestor Basterretxea, Eduardo Chillida, Remigio Mendiburu, Oteiza, Jose Antonio Sistiaga, and Jose Luis Zumeta. A copy of the catalogue and a review of this group may be found in the catalogue *Constelación Gaur* of the exhibition of the same name curated by Fernando Golvano and Juanma Arriaga, Caja Vital Kutxa Foundation, Vitoria-Gasteiz, 2004.

ic protection of our people and our Basque Country"). The common paradox that these different groups faced was the demand for a free and transgressive practice and avant-garde imaginary in such a hostile context like that Francoism. In some notes written during the early 1980s and published in his book *Ejercicios espirituales en un túnel* (Spiritual Exercises in a Tunnel; originally written in 1965 but not published, because of censorship in Spain, until 1983), Oteiza examines his poetic conceptions: "I was struggling with a problem of rationalist heritage, which was about contents and definitions of a normative and general aesthetics for behavior. For me there existed two poetics: a naïve one concerned with aesthetic and experimental preoccupations, and with socially committed investigation; and the other, a post-experimental Poetics, poetics 2, in which a person that has been re-designed leaves art."[27] All in all, his requirement to produce the radically new in art and in life moved him away from the system of art and its progressive institutionalization. One could contrast the *Homage to Mallarmé* (1957), which forms part of an experimental proposition with action reduced to language, to his later *Portrait of an armed gudari* [Basque soldier] *called Odysseus* (1975), which came about as a variation of this piece, and whose political and ethical significance is more associated with Schillerian analogy. Oteiza gave this work great importance, to the point of comparing it to Picasso's *Guernica*.[28]

The dissenting *humus* of the mid-1960s favored the collaboration or implication of artists who most stood out for their creation of a new imaginary of *agit-prop*.[29] Oteiza had deployed political analogies since his experimental laboratory, which he started again in 1973: on the basis of his minuscule chalk works he produced his

27. Oteiza, *Ejercicios espirituales en un* túnel, 432–33.

28. One could say that his *Odysseus* is a self-portrait depicting him as heroic artist of the Basque avant-garde. In 1990 Oteiza evaluates it as "the most important sculpture of our final vanguard of contemporary art" in Spanish art. He supported its inclusion in the permanent collection of MNCARS and its exhibition close to *Guernica*, as "without a doubt it is the work that, with most historical sense and dignity, deserves to be situated close to *Guernica*, to which it is related for its approach evident in its title." See unpublished text in the Archives of the Oteiza Museum, registration 15088.

29. On the critical and descriptive approach to the forms of artistic, cultural, and political activism in the 1970s in the Basque context, there are two publications on two exhibitions that I curated: see the catalogue of *Disidentziak oro / Disidencias otras* and that of *Laboratorios 70 - 70eko hamarkadako laborategiak*.

Navarra as labyrinth (1972) and the *Funeral wake indicating the proximity of Lemóniz* (1973). His desires wavered between militant action and spiritual retreat. In 1974 he presented works in the Txantxangorri Gallery; in the accompanying catalogue he expressed his desire not to exhibit anymore and to take refuge in Alzuza (Navarre) for poetic and theoretical elaboration. The failure of Gaur accompanied him as a specter: "We are left with a single objective of great interest and urgent preoccupation for all. I think that it is our physical defense (nuclear centers whose location and whose future is the same, the desert), territorial and ecological defense, and our country."[30] Political-cultural praxis would become a kind of urgent discharge for the failures of the past through his sporadic collaborations with the diffuse Basque Cultural Front within the orbit of ETA. In an agonic and dictatorial context like that of these years, Oteiza proposed a "Project of military school of Basque artists"[31] (November 1975), whose objectives were of "a cultural order as operations of urgency." He summarized them as 1) pedagogical missions through art expositions 2) Basque theater as compound art consisting of popular languages 3) Basque physical training oriented to education in the ikastolas and as propaedeutic for experimental theater, and 4) an experimental ikastola. Between declarations of abandoning the sculpture project concluded in 1959, and the affirmation of vital and political action, the Oteizian utopia of the new man remained paradoxically modulated by atavistic, mythical, and metaphysical elements. In the 1960s he sympathized with Marxism: he associated his *Law of changes* with Maoist dialectics, as he explained in his text *Kinship with Mao* (1975), and sketched a book of essays that would be titled *Art and Revolution*.

The 1960s: The Laboratory of Creation and Dissidence

Besides Oteiza, other artists also played an important role in the artistic and antagonistic scene of the 1960s and 1970s. Eduardo Chillida remained independent and went against the tide, although sometimes he participated in various collective initiatives. Centered on activity restricted to sculptural language, he composed a poetics of the limit, of the memory of the vernacular in dialogue with the universal, and of the murmur of interior space with musical reso-

30. Oteiza, in the catalog *Oteiza*.

31. Oteiza, unpublished text, Archive of the Oteiza Museum, registration 9447.

nances, which was attentive to the gravitation of the material, or to a certain mystical desire. But Chillida did not stay on the margins of the social-imaginary significations that emerged with great force in the social milieu of those years. He designed some of the most significant logos of Basque political counter-culture, like that of the anti-nuclear movement (1974) and the Pro-Amnesty Committee (a movement created to lobby for the release of Basque political prisoners, 1975). In his graphic series *Euskadi* (1975–76) or *Enda* (1979), he recreated the imaginary of an identity of a Basque Country in construction. Agustín Ibarrola, meanwhile, provided cultural mobilization and the workers` movement with critical images: for example, his fists, workers' figures intertwined in one body, and a graphic series titled *Landscapes of Euskadi* (with references to Picasso's *Guernica*) are particularly well-known. Ibarrola was one of the most militant artists of his time (he was imprisoned by the Francoist dictatorship in 1962–65, 1967, and 1973), and he was one of the most active proponents of the Groups of the Basque School in the 1960s. Previously, in the 1950s he had been one of the founders of the 57 Group, which had rationalist and constructivist tendencies. Interested in making artistic experience social, he supported a realist and committed art through the group Popular Prints of Bizkaia (Estampa Popular de Vizcaya). His painting of social content and expressionist figuration eventually gave way to a sculpture that used found materials. Nestor Basterretxea was another artist who reconciled a constructivist-experimental program with a choral participation in projects that gave new meaning to unique Basque, *Euskaldun* (Basque-speaking) belonging. Starting from drawing, he deployed a diverse, creative domain that included painting, graphics, collage, reliefs, sculptures, industrial design, film, and architectonic volume. Most significant of all were his sculptural series *Basque cosmogony* (1972–78) and the design of posters and logos for popular causes. Co-author of the Gaur manifesto in 1966, Amable Arias engaged in a creative liberty and a critical distancing from the controversies between the abstract and the figurative. "There is not just one kind of art," he used to say. But it was through making a figuration real that he sometimes had an evident surrealist resonance, in that he created a universe inhabited by strange and tiny beings, personages extracted from reality, zoomorphic, hybrid, spectral, or fantastic figures, whether loveable or fearful bestiaries. It is a world that, behind an ingenious and trivial appearance, affirms an ironic and critical distancing from the given reality. He exercised limited action in another way. In the convulsed decade of the 1970s, he took a stance through writing (poems, dramatic sketches, and short essays) as well as drawings, comic strips, collages, paintings, and postal envelopes. One of Amable's exceptional projects was an intervention in the depths of his library over the 1860s and 1970s: drawings, miscellaneous texts, and commentaries created a private-public universe of forms of the thinkable. Esther Ferrer was one of the pioneering figures of action art from 1966 on with the Zaj group, in the company of Juan Hidalgo and Walter Marchetti. In her long career in performance art, she never ceased to innovate and transgress this ephemeral practice through the creation of novel, reflexive, and upsetting situations for her audience. Besides, she also produced a series of conceptual works like *The poem of prime numbers* and the *Triangle of Napoleon*. *Euskadi Sioux* (1979) was a caustic counterpoint in the mixed-up landscape of the 1970s. This collective, which published seven editions of a journal with the same name,[32] sprang forth with the pessimistic and intelligent sting of satire, and with the optimism of ludic desire. They did so "without any intention of salvation or redemption." All this creative and anti-establishment milieu emerging as a partial and fragmentary sketch revealed a genuine complexity, linked to the social-historical context of the 1970s and the imaginary significations that occupied the scene.

Commitment and Criticism: Attempt Done and to Be Done

In the history of Basque contemporary art, one of the lines of rupture with the modern project led by Oteiza, Ibarrola, and Chillida could be situated in the exhibition titled *Myths and crimes* (1985), in which the new generation of Basque sculptors (Angel Bados, Txomin Badiola, Juan Luis Moraza, Pello Irazu, and others) certified the "symbolic death" of the founding fathers of Basque sculpture. At this moment, one dimension of the transformation was finalized. But others remained under new forms of the thinkable and the transformable. The political transformation brought new institutions and politics that affected the configuration of the institution of art and the emergence of other artistic practices situated

32. The artists and writers who participated in the journal included José María Aguirre, Vicente Ameztoy (who was charged with design), Rafael Castellano, Juan Carlos Eguillor, Fernando Illana, Ernesto Murillo, and Iván Zulueta. In 2001, I curated a retrospective on *Euskadi Sioux* in Bidebarrieta Kulturgunea (Bilbao); now, one can access the content of all seven published editions at www.euskadisioux.org, produced by KM Kulturunea, Donostia-San Sebastián.

in what could be termed institutional criticism. Old dilemmas took new forms. As Chantal Mouffe confirms, "one cannot differentiate between political and non-political art. All forms of artistic practice either contribute to the reproduction of a given common consciousness—and in this sense they are political—or contribute to its deconstruction or criticism. Every artistic form has a political dimension."[33] This question has been problematized by the emergence of feminist activism and criticism in art (conceptual, performance, and the visual arts), especially from the 1970s on. Mary Kelly, Cindy Sherman, Martha Rosler, Barbara Kruger, Esther Ferrer, and the Guerilla Girls are just some of the referential names to represent this pioneering critical stance. In the Basque and Spanish context, it was during the following decade that more people were responsive to issues of gender, sexual identities, and political action and consequently produced new perspectives.[34]

In the 1980s, in a context of the crisis associated with late modernity and with postmodern theory and dynamism enjoying its dramatic arrival on the scene, Hal Foster took a key stance in his *Recodings: Art, Spectacle, Cultural Politics* (1985).[35] Specifically, he warned that political art should consider the concepts and displacements of class and production articulated through new forms of power, as Foucault theorized it, and which structured social existence. Foster describes two contrasting positions: one, he conceives of culture as a place of conflict and contestation. Therefore, the strategy to follow should have the form of a "neo-Gramscian resistance or interference—here and now—to the hegemonic code of cultural representations and social regimens"; and the other he terms "Baudrillard's endgame" that sustains the futility of resistance given that the system is total.[36] In harmony with institutional criticism, he challenged the strategy of the modernist avant-garde in order to replace it with a new critical strategy from the inside the system and its institutions. The political artists of the day would thus see themselves propelled to investigate the processes and apparatus that control the creation of representation and forms.

---

33. Mouffe, *Prácticas artísticas y democracia agonística*, 26.

34. See Tejada, "Prácticas artísticas y feminismos en los años 70," Mayayo, "¿Por qué no ha habido (grandes) artistas feministas en España?" and the analyses and case studies conducted by the project *Desacuerdos*, produced by Arteleku, Macba, the UNIA, and Centro José Guerrero. In the mid-1990s in Euskadi, Estibaliz Sádaba, Azucena Vieites, and Yolanda de los Bueis created the group *Erreakzioa-Reacción*, which was dedicated to art and feminism.

35. See Foster, *Recodings*.

36. Ibid., 146.

From the opening of art to its entire means, the new political dimensions of contemporary art also passed through forms of appropriation, reference, and dialectical image. The primacy of intertextuality and appropriation came to dominate contemporary art. In this maelstrom of current art, it is worth recalling Tania Bruguera's warning: "Much of the political art that is done today is rather a gesture of referencing than a political gesture."[37] But there have been emergent artists in the Basque context that have managed to reconcile this tension between the artistic reference and critical politics like, for example, Asier Mendizabal, Ibon Aranberri, Juan Pérez Agirregoikoa, and Azucena Vieites. Thus the forms of re-politicizing art are manifest in very diverse strategies and practices. One paradox defines the aesthetic regime of art:[38] The "politics of art" is made of the interweaving of three logics: aesthetic experience, the logic of fiction, and metapolitical strategies.[39]

The politics of art cannot control its paradoxes under the form of an intervention outside of its place, in the "real world." What space is left for critical art? This for Rancière may take multiple forms in the consensual fabric of the real, one classic form being that which separates document from fiction. Since there exist no models as to what political art should be like at the present the meta-politics of a resistant form oscillates for this French philosopher between two positions: on the one hand, the politics of the becoming-life of art, which ascribes to art a finality oriented to the construction of new forms of life in common, thus eliminating its autonomy and self-sufficiency; and on the other, the politics of the resistant form, which challenges its transformation into a form of life maintaining its autonomy or separation.[40] He maintains the need to return the inventions of politics and art to their difference, this, "entails rejecting the fantasy of their purity, giving back to these inventions their status as cuts that are always ambiguous, precarious, litigious. This necessarily entails divorcing them from every theology of time, from every thought of a primordial trauma or a salvation to come."[41] The action of art may continuously upgrade its potential to give form to chaos; it can

---

37. See España, "Entrevista a Tania Bruguera," 39.

38. In his *The Politics of Aesthetics*, Rancière calls the aesthetic regime of art that which "strictly identifies art in the singular, and frees it from any specific rule, from any hierarchy of the arts, subject matter, and genres" (18–19).

39. Ibid.

40. Ibid.

41. Rancière, *Aesthetics and Its Discontents*, 132.

construct new forms of subjectivity. It is from here that the proposal of Félix Guattari to establish "transversal junctions between political, the ethical and the aesthetic"[42] from the practice of art should be considered. To produce subjectivity, "capture it, enrich it, and permanently reinvent it in a way that renders it compatible with Universes of mutant values."[43] that is, for the re-singularization of subjectivity: that is where the liberating potential of art, its genuine political dimension, resides. Nevertheless, what should be avoided is the temptation to transform critical art in any of its institutional or non-institutional forms into a kind of privileged artistic tendency, with its permitted paradoxes and relational drifts.

Bibliography

Adorno, Theodor W. *Aesthetic Theory.* Edited by Gretel Adorno and Rolf Tiedemann. Translated and introduced by Robet Hullot-Kentor. London: Athlone, 1997.

———. "Commitment." In *Aesthetics and Politics: The Key Texts of the Classic Debate within German Marxism.* Authors Theodor Adorno, Walter Benjamin, Ernst Bloch, Bertolt Brecht, and Georg Lukács. London: Verso, 1977.

———. *Minima Moralia: Reflections on a Damaged Life.* Translated from the German by E.F.N. Jephcott. London: Verso, 2005.

Benjamin, Walter. "The Work of Art in the Age of Mechanical Reproduction." In *Illuminations: Essays and Reflections.* Edited and introduced by Hannah Arendt, translated by Harry Zohn. New York: Schocken, 1969.

Cauquelin, Anne. Las teorías del arte. Buenos Aires: Adriana Hidalgo Editora, 2012.

España, Pablo. "Entrevista a Tania Bruguera Tania Bruguera. In *La promesa de la política / The promise of politics.* Pontevedra: Fundación-RAC, 2001.

Foster, Hal. *Recodings: Art, Spectacle, Cultural Politics.* Port Townsend, WA: Bay Press, 1985.

Giunta, Andrea, ed. *El Guernica de Picasso: El poder de la representación.* Buenos Aires: Editorial Biblos, 2010.

Guattari, Félix. *Chaosmosis: An Ethnico-Aesthetic Paradigm.* Translated by Paul Bains and Julian Pefanis. Bloomington: Indiana University Press, 1995.

Mallarmé, Stéphane. Collected Poems of Mallarmé: A Bilingual Edition. Translated and commentary by Henry Michael

42. Guattari, *Chaosmosis*, 134.
43. Ibid., 135.

Weinfield. Oakland: University of California Press, 2011.

Marchán Fiz, Simón. "A través de la belleza se llega a la libertad: La estetización étnico-política en Shiller y sus derivas." In *Ilustración y modernidad en Friedrich Schiller*. Edited by Faustino Oncina and Manuel Ramos. Valencia: Universitat de Valencia, 2006.

———. *La estética en la cultura moderna*. Madrid: Alianza, 2007.

Marcuse, Herbert. "On Art and Revolution." In *Philosophical-Political Profiles.* Translated by Frederick G. Lawrence. Cambridge: The MIT Press, 1983.

Mayayo, Patricia. "¿Por qué no ha habido (grandes) artistas feministas en España: Apuntes sobre una historia en busca de autor(a)." In *Producción artística y teoría feminista del arte: nuevos debates I*. Edited by Xabier Arakistain and Lourdes Méndez. Vitoria-Gasteiz: Centro Cultural Montehermoso, 2009.

Mouffe, Chantal. *Práctica artísticas y democracia agonística*. Barcelona: Museu d' art contemporani de Barcelo, 2007.

Oteiza, Jorge. *Ejercicios spirituales en un túnel: En busca y encuentro de nuestra identidad perdida*. Iruñea-Pamplona: Museo Oteiza, 1983.

———. "Memoria del proyecto del escultor Jorge Oteiza presentada al Concurso internacional para el Monumento al prisionero político desconocido y protesta ante el jurado." *Revista Nacional de Arquitectura* 138 (1953).

Rancière, Jacques. Aesthetics and Its Discontents. Translated by Stephen Corcoran. Malden, MA: Polity Press.

———. *The Politics of Aesthetics: The Distribution of the Sensible.* Translated by Gabriel Rockhill. London: Continuum, 2004.

Robles Tardío, Rocio, ed. *Picasso y sus críticos, vol. 1: La recepción de* Guernica, *1937–1947*. Barcelona: Editiones de la Central, 2011.

Tejeda, Isabel. "Prácticas artísticas y feminismos en los años 70." In *De la revuelta a la postmodernidad (1962-1982)*. Madrid: Museo Nacional Centro de Arte Reina Sofía, 2011.

Wright, James, ed. *The Random House Book of Twentieth-Century French Poetry.* New York: Random House, 1982.

Part 3

Exhibitions and Curating

14

Denouncing Violence against Women: An Experimental Seminar and Poster Art Exhibition

Selma Holo

Beyond Guernica and the Guggenheim bears a provocative and expansive subtitle, "Relations between Art and Politics from a Comparative Perspective," which implies an openness toward the consideration of political art created outside of the Basque Country and Spain. As such, it inspired me to relate and frame my concurrent experience teaching a curatorial studies course in art history in such a way that it could profitably be considered through a comparative lens.

Denouncing Violence against Women, a yearlong graduate student exhibition project was mounted on April 3, 2013, a month before the CBS conference, by the USC Fisher Museum of Art. It was the end result of a complex experiment in teaching: a multilateral, trans-disciplinary collaboration including USC's Shoah Foundation (The Institute for Visual History and Education); the Center for the Study or Political Graphics (CSPG), an independent poster archive in Los Angeles; the USC Art History Department; and USC's "Visions and Voices" (a university-wide initiative intended to expose all of the university's students to the Arts and Humanities). *Denouncing Violence Against Women* began as a graduate seminar I team-taught starting in the fall of 2012 with Dr. Dan Leshem, Associate Director for Academic Outreach and Research of the Shoah Foundation, with the participation of Dr. Laura Pomerantz an independent scholar specializing in art and genocide, and incorporating the staff of the CSPG headed by Carol Wells, its Director. The students in this seminar were art history, archaeology, and journalism majors who, along with the various instructors, hailed from seven different countries: Finland, Serbia, Mexico, Italy, Israel, Argentina, and the United States. After a period of immersion in the literature of genocide and mass violence the group was faced with thousands of political posters. It was only after immersion in this visual culture of genocide that the class unanimously decided to focus the exhibition on mass violence violence against women.

This choice of the exhibition topic was colored by students' increasing understanding that, as a social and political phenomenon, violence against women crossed all national borders and affected all classes. It was important to incorporate this understanding into their project because as a group they came from so many parts of the world. Evidently it was a topic with which they especially empathized, everyone in the class being female. They undertook the exhibition, then, not only as an artistic project, but as a vehicle toward a greater political awareness, in agreement with the premise that "eliminating violence against women is a profoundly political challenge. . . because it requires redressing the unequal social, political and economic power held by women and men, and the ways in which this inequality is perpetuated through formal and informal institutions at all levels of society."[1] The university welcomed this course as an experiment in teaching art history and curatorship in an interdisciplinary way, with the intention of it being integrated into the larger Visions and Voices project, one carrying its own subtitle: "Artistic responses to Mass Violence."

Denouncing Violence Against Women was conceived (and specially funded) as the opening event in "Artistic responses to Mass Violence," a week of artistic projects, all designed to heighten the social and political awareness and memory of genocide and mass violence for students and faculty. "Artistic responses to Mass Violence" was the defining event of the annual "Genocide Awareness Week," a commemoration staged at various universities and colleges throughout the United States. In 2013, the emphasis of the whole week was on artistic responses for the first time. The aim of the "Week" is to make manifest through art, theater, and film, genocide's characteristics and effects, and thus to inspire an alertness to those characteristics and signs and making a contribution to its prevention in the future.

"Genocide Awareness Week: Artistic responses to Mass Violence" at USC in 2013 featured, in addition to our exhibition, a

1. Claire Courteille. "Eliminating violence against women is a profoundly political challenge", *Equal Times*, Opinions, March 7, 2013.

powerful activist performance by a survivor of the Rwandan Genocide of 1994; a theater piece that critiqued artistic representations of the Cambodian Genocide; and a film series by a granddaughter of Holocaust survivors recalling her maternal Jewish grandparents' protection by her paternal Protestant grandparents in Amsterdam during Holocaust. The weeklong series, generated as it was at USC by the Shoah Foundation, epitomized the foundation's mission to capture and preserve first the memory of the Holocaust, while increasingly to collect testimonies from other genocides, thereby revealing similar strategies that define all genocides. Our curatorial seminar—and the research it required, along with the curating of the exhibition itself—not coincidentally served the strategic vision of USC. That is, USC's strategic vision emphasizes the encouragement of pure research, especially when it functions in the interests of solving grave societal problems. This chapter is meant to give an idea of the process of this extraordinary project, to highlight the political awareness it fostered, and to suggest one model for other art and politics-based projects at the graduate level. Without question, our project served our mission to educate, to bring awareness, and to stir emotions even as we ignited the critical thinking that allows for the students to challenge any and all accepted ideas and received opinion with respect to the topic. We as a university hoped to contribute to an awareness in our student body of what constitutes "mass." In my art history course we hoped to do it through the production of an exhibition of political posters.

Why Political Posters in an Art History Course?

Political posters, it should be pointed out here, have been historically employed as tools of mass communication, not generally beginning as "art for art's sake." And, as such, they are most successful when disseminated in the public sphere. They do not normally begin their lives as artworks in museums. Indeed, traditionally, political posters are displayed in public spaces, often rapidly pasted or stapled on walls or trees or poles that people just as customarily pass rapidly by. Political poster artists need to assume that there will be little time to grasp or ponder their messages. To be successful, the image will be clear to its intended viewers, and, even if appearing to be a kind of coded communication to later generations, they will be discerned as calls to action by their contemporaries. The most successful political posters do not deal in nuance or subtlety. And, unlike, for example, the incomparable and deeply complex Mexican murals by Diego

Rivera, Jose Clemente Orozco, and David Alfaro Siqueiros (also political statements meant to be apprehended while people walked or drove past them; but made as "fine" art and with expectations of becoming a part of a catalyzing chapter in art history), political posters are not usually intended to be unique; nor are they principally intended to be precious or permanent or transformational moments in the history of art.

For the sake of our course the distinctions we made between "fine" art and political posters were that "fine" artists allowed for and encouraged ambiguity in their imagery—even if the subject matter was political—and that the very nature of their imagery required the viewer to participate in its reception with an effort to discern fully the message behind it. It should be noted that political posters have never been made exclusively by anonymous or unknown artists. Certainly, they are also sometimes made by world-renowned artists; and we need only to look at, for example, the Russian Avant-garde posters whose authors are celebrated and their work collected now in great museums everywhere. But, still, the normal hope and expectation for political posters—at the time of their making—has been that the public would come into contact with them differently than they come into contact with art for art's sake. The goal, when one creates a political poster is that the public will encounter it multiple times in an open civic space; and, furthermore, that it will have an impact on perceptions of a specific social situation—an impact that will increase political awareness and be a call to action. That is, true political posters are not, by definition, created as museum pieces or as art for domestic adornment. And, it was an enormous cache of political posters that the class mostly encountered at the CSPG. It was the political poster, as a genre, that provided the group with the artistic material it needed in order to be included in Genocide Awareness Week and to take part in its special event: "Artistic Responses to Mass Violence."

The Process

The eighteen posters the students ultimately put on display at the Fisher Museum of Art under the title *Denouncing Violence Against Women* were all chosen, then, from the Center for the Study of Political Graphics. The CSPG was the designated working laboratory, the site of the students' research into the visual culture at the heart of the project. At the CSPG the members of the class were given free access to steep themselves in the permanent collection of the archive. They began their research, though, by studying mass violence and genocide and only later in the semester began searching broadly for posters that they could imagine being under the aegis of "Imaging Genocide."

Once they did encounter the thousands of posters in the archive somehow or other related to genocide and mass violence, they realized they had to narrow their scope if they were going to tell a compelling and coherent story for a museum public. As a group they became increasingly interested in the subject of violence against women. It seems organic and inevitable in retrospect: there were an extraordinary number of high quality posters that described and protested that particular vein of violence; through their assigned readings the class as a whole came to perceive violence against women as an ongoing, persistent, pervasive, and global phenomenon, one affecting all economic classes, races, and ethnicities; and finally, as the class was made up wholly of women students, there was a critical mass of personal as well as scholarly attraction to the topic. Due to the combination of all of these factors, the class decided to work with this subject exclusively, and finally they titled their exhibition *Denouncing Violence Against Women.*

It should also be noted here that the class consciously avoided having to engage in the distracting politics around the naming or qualification of any particular mass violence as "Genocide"; and it was because of this decision that they chose to adopt the term "mass violence" instead of genocide in the title of their show. The students also chose not to use the term "femicide" because although much of this violence does involve murder, it also includes rape and other brutalities that sometimes fall short of murder (the usual meaning of femicide indicates the murdering of females) but are nevertheless profoundly traumatizing. In the end the students organized a carefully orchestrated and thematized range of images that protested a number of kinds of violence perpetrated on women everywhere. Furthermore, so as to maintain some chronological coherence, posters curated into the show were all produced from 1970 on and refer to a number of countries and different cultures. Of course, the posters chosen and the beginning date also reflect the holdings of the CSPG.[2] Finally, it was apparent that the students came to conceive of their art show as a political act itself, a visually based manifestation, a willful and willed concentration and demonstration of works of poster art that together resulted in an articulate, broad based, and deeply convincing act of resistance to violence against women.

---

2. Only one poster was about the Holocaust. It featured Anne Frank, but was created after 1970 and so was not able to be included.

But before our students researched their exhibition in the CSPG archives; before they were even faced with the power of the poster as a form of graphic art and call to action, they were required to saturate themselves with the literature of genocide and mass violence in the classroom. They read and debated the writings of witnesses and historians such as Elie Wiesel, Primo Levi, and Jean Amery;[3] while also reading foundational speeches by, for example, Hitler, Bernard Lewis, and Christopher Browning.[4]

Furthermore, they watched individual testimonies systematically recorded by the Shoah Foundation, the Institute for Visual History and Education's vast resources.[5] From this constant exposure to the written word and also the very different visual and oral testimonies, the class was able to extrapolate commonalities of genocide, including the genocides in Rwanda, Cambodia, and Armenia. They and we then brought in additional readings related to these genocides (and mass violence) that we read and discussed in class. They began to apprehend the immensity of the subject of genocide and mass violence. It was at that juncture that they realized the need to focus and started to apply that growing body of knowledge to their chosen subject: violence against women. Because this was also a museology/curatorial seminar, meaning that the students had to create an exhibition at the end of the year, they were also assigned a variety of readings in museum studies and curatorial practice.[6]

Finally, as a conclusion to the research phase, at the end of the semester, having decided to focus on art and violence against women, they each had to choose a sub-theme within that focus. Each student was required to produce a twenty-page research paper on their theme, taking into account the history, art history, and museology that they had also been studying throughout the semester. Those themes became the scaffolding of the exhibition that was mounted in the following semester.

---

3. Wiesel, "A Plea for the Dead" (1968); Levi, "Shame, or on the Subject" (1986); and Améry, "Torture" (1964).

4. See Lewis, "Anti-Semites" (1986); Friedlander, "The Setting" (1995); "Hitler's Reichstag Speech, January 30, 1939," in Gigliotti and Lang, ed., *The Holocaust*; and Browning, "From 'Ethnic Cleansing' to Genocide to the 'Final Solution'" (2000).

5. See http://sfi.usc.edu/aboutus for descriptions of the Shoah Foundation's core mission and its expanding activities to record history and to combat genocide and mass violence today.

6. Including my own *Beyond the Turnstile*, co-edited with Mari-Tere Alvarez.

The Exhibition

About half way through the first semester the class began to take shape at the CSPG. They were faced with thousands of political graphics. Their next task was to produce an exhibition that could be supported by the posters. They also now had to work with the Fisher Museum staff to physically produce *Denouncing Violence Against Women* in a given space and a determined time. They needed to give firm shape to the show by determining the specific materials that would be included. That is, of that mass of art available to them, a number of posters had now to be chosen that would reinforce that shape. Because they had already defined and elaborated their themes, what was excluded and what included became self-evident when they rigorously adhered to those themes—when they curated their exhibition. It was the scaffolding mentioned above that allowed the student curators to tell their story in a coherent way, a way supported by specific works of art.

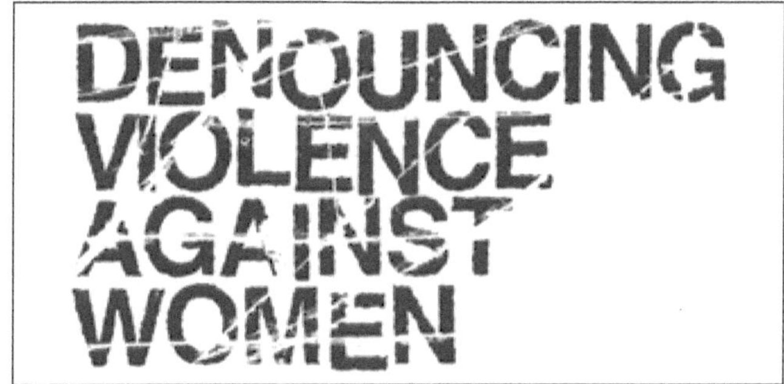

Figure 14.1. "Denouncing Violence Against Women", title sign wall created by the USC Fisher Museum of Art. Made in house. Various sized.

The themes the student chose as characterizing violence against women were "Dehumanization," "Breaking Bonds," "Individuality," and "Trauma." Once they had identified about fifty posters from among the myriad posters available to them, they needed to advance to the final step of curation: the consideration of the actual space of the gallery in which they would have their show. In doing this they also needed to allow room for the didactic panels that would contextualize the posters for the public. With the space for art and the attendant educational materials in mind, they then had to further essentialize their choices and curate their selections down to about two dozen posters. Then, in order to create those didactic panels, they had to distil their twenty-page long research papers into short "messages" of no more than 250 words. The text panels needed to telegraph the nature of their exhibition as a whole and the themes that supported it for unprepared visitors who could not be expected to spend more than a few minutes in front of any single piece in the show. In effect, they had to create verbal posters that would function as reliable abbreviated counterparts and contexts to the actual posters. I will partially quote the panels below to give an idea of the pithiness that was required of the students. Of course, each poster also had its own specific information next to it as well. This is known in the museum field as the requisite "tombstone" information. With the tombstone information they could compile their "checklist," the pragmatic record that would be needed should there be damage to any of the works, should the press need specific descriptions of the pieces, or should there be a need to apply for insurance if there were damage or vandalism during the course of the exhibition.

The introductory text panel to *Denouncing Violence Against Women*, written by Helena Liakanen, a journalism student from Finland, began with the quotation:

> violence against women is a manifestation of historically unequal power relations between men and women, which have led to domination over and discrimination against women by men and to the prevention of the full advancement of women, and that violence against women is one of the crucial social mechanisms by which women are forced into a subordinate position compared with men. [7]

It went on to state that "Violence affects millions of women and girls all over the world—from before birth to old age. Violence takes many different forms: physical, sexual, and psychological. . . The eighteen posters on display are distinct in their portrayal of visual resistance to violence against women. Some call for empathy, others demand justice or action. Nonetheless, they all denounce the diversified brutality against women, from domestic violence to genocide, from female genital mutilation to human trafficking."

After reading the introductory panel, museum visitors were directed into a small gallery where Liakanen had also produced a loop of women's testimony carefully culled from the Shoah archives. Fortuitously, two months after the seminar had begun the Shoah Foundation had announced a new initiative on sexual violence directed toward women in the Holocaust. Liakanen's panel prepared the visitors for what they were about to see and hear in these testi-

7. *The UN Declaration on the Elimination of Violence Against Women* (1993).

monies and read as follows: "In November 2012, the USC Shoah Foundation and 'Remember the Women Institute' organized an international symposium on sexual violence during the Holocaust. Approximately twenty academics and activists who participated in the event have all worked on this issue, which has been overlooked by most historians for nearly seventy years. The symposium focused on collecting new testimony to make victims' voices heard; discovering existing documentation; compiling already-published citations of sexual violence; and ensuring that sexual violence is included in the Holocaust narrative. This effort to bring recognition to sexual violence against women provided the focus for our exhibition." After viewing the haunting loop, the audience was then directed to the posters themselves.

The material below includes samplings of the text panels, all written by the students themselves, all reductions from their twenty-page papers and intended to contextualize the posters in the exhibition by their themes.

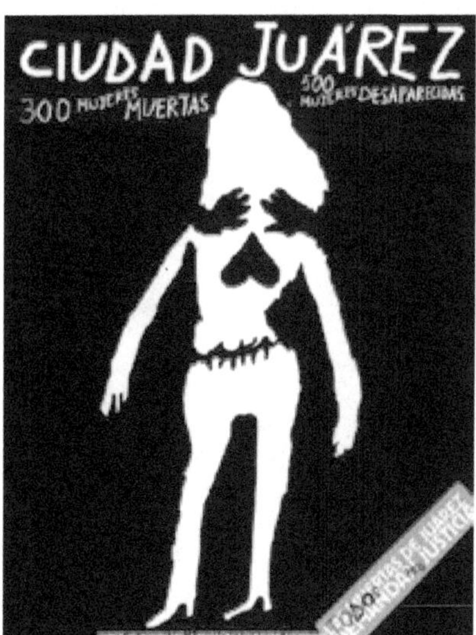

Figure 14.2. Ciudad Juárez 300 Mujeres Muertas 500 Mujeres Desaparecidas, *by Alejandro Magallanes from the "Dehumanization" theme, courtesy of the artist.*

Dehumanization

Ambra Spinelli, an Italian archaeologist in the seminar, began her text panel for the "Dehumanization" section by describing a deadly situation in Mexico that prompted this theme: "Since the first dis-

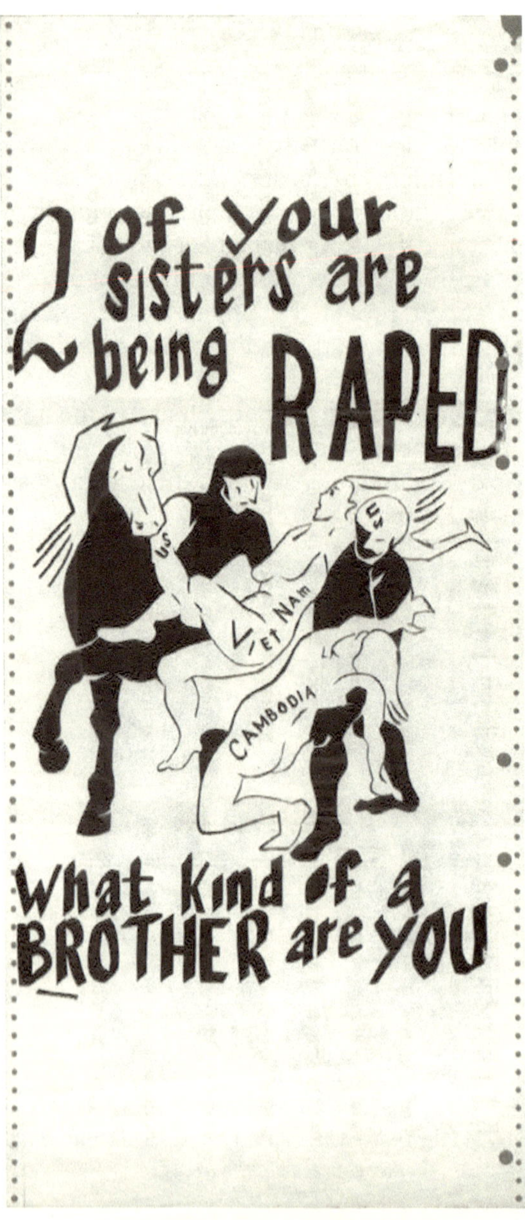

Figure 14.3. Two of Your Sisters Are Being Raped, *an anonymous poster courtesy CSPG, after diligent search for the artist.*

covery of nine young female bodies in June 1993, more than nine hundred women have been killed, kidnapped, and disappeared in Juárez, a city in the northern Mexican State of Chihuahua. The identities of the victims and perpetrators remain unknown. The police investigations of the 90's were conducted with superficial concern and underlined the prevailing gender prejudices: the murdered women were labeled as prostitutes. These posters are designed to provoke a reaction and inspire the viewer to demand justice. Some of the posters show the scope of the horrific massacres and visually display the quantity of anonymous women who have lost their lives. Others display the motivation of the crimes and how they are intrinsically tied to gender. They were designed by a group of Mexican artists and graphic designers in 2003, exactly ten years after the first officially documented female murders in Juárez. The posters were displayed in the subways of Mexico City with the aim to cast light upon this women-killing phenomenon, as well as to encourage the Mexican State to take care of its women and to protect their rights." (See figure 14.2.)

This group of posters is notable for its convincing communication of the dehumanization of the victims by the killers. There are no faces on these posters; the women remain unidentifiable: they are reduced dozens of legs without bodies, to lipstick canisters without the faces to put the lipstick on, to dolls in a shooting gallery. And the message—over and over again—is that the authorities of the city of Juárez, by never having apprehended the killers, were and are complicit in that particular violence against the women of Juárez.

Breaking Bonds

Helena Liakanen composed her introductory panel for "Breaking Bonds" by calling for attention to be paid to violence within the family, particularly domestic violence, rape, female genital mutilation, and trafficking in women.

The violence demonstrated here is very different from our other sections on mass violence, but the effects on a victim remain similar: loss of identity, helplessness in front of the torturer, betrayal, and mistrust toward the world. As the posters in this section demonstrate, family violence takes place all over the world, despite the religious, economic, or cultural group. Here, women are shown in a variety of powerful scenes: some of them are shown as passive victims while others are ready to fight back. Family violence can also be widely accepted in the community, hiding behind words like "traditions" and "religion." There is a poster denouncing female genital mutilation that is over thirty years old, nonetheless this "tradition" is still widely practiced in contemporary societies. And then, referring specifically to that poster on genital mutilation, Helena highlighted this quotation from the poster: "I don't remember screaming, I remember the ridiculous amount of pain, I remember the blood everywhere, one of the maids, I actually saw her pick up the bit of flesh that they cut away 'cause she was mopping up the blood." ("Jamelia," *The Observer*, July 24, 2010)

Notably, "Breaking Bonds" also includes the violence perpetuated by the United States in its wars in Southeast Asia. The students were thereby taking care to communicate that the exhibition was not exoticizing violence against women by suggesting that it is only perpetuated by people other than those in the United States. One poster (figure 14.3), crudely made in Berkeley, proclaims: "2 of your sisters are being raped. What kind of a brother are you?" This poster features a drawing

that directly refers to the iconic image of Peter Paul Rubens' *Rape of the Daughters of Leucippus*, with the words "Vietnam" and "Cambodia" inscribed on the bodies of the women being carried away to be violated. Unlike many posters that refer to a single event, this poster artist (anonymous and so far, unidentifiable) tried a different strategy. The artist is both universalizing the females being betrayed by referring to them as family members ("your sisters"), but is also particularizing them by pointing to the Vietnam War and the bombing of Cambodia being perpetrated by the United States, as the betrayers who break family bonds.

The other posters in "Breaking Bonds" included, for example, a denunciation on behalf of Aboriginal women in Australia of the rape of their women and children. Rather than asking for empathy, this poster calls for action, warning: "Aboriginal women are watching you? Strong Aboriginal women say: Stop the Abuse; Stop raping our women; Stop raping our children."

Individuality

Poster artists undertook "Individuality" that putting a human face on a poster Michele Crisosto who wrote in her text panel employs another effective strategy. Crisosto argues that an image of a recognizable individual appeals to the emotions and evokes empathy as powerfully as, but differently from, dehumanization. The posters in this theme direct attention to recognizable characters. Even when it

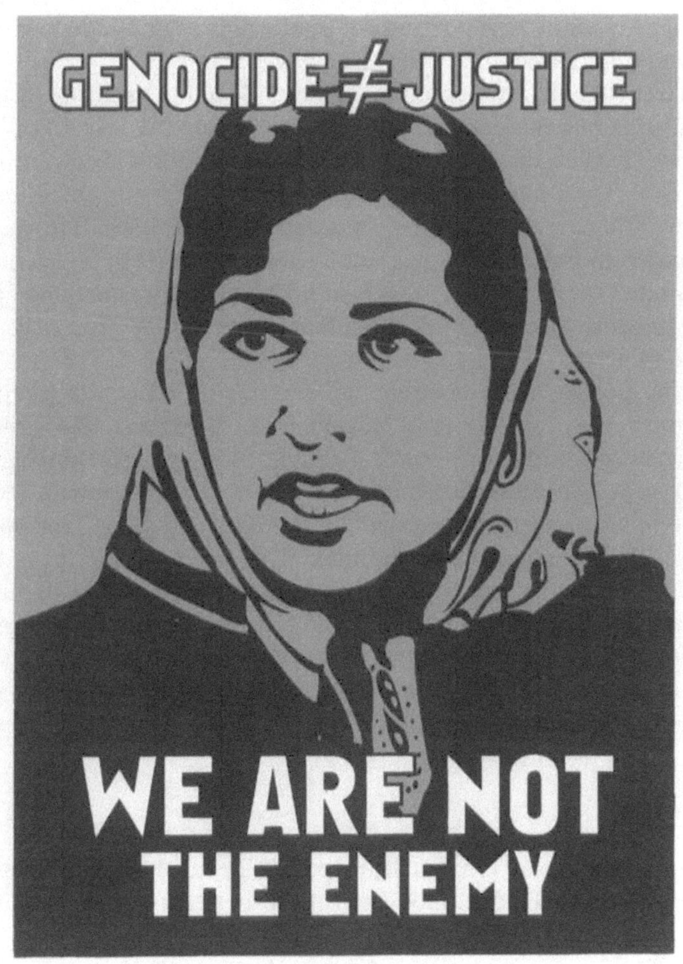

Figure 14.4. We Are Not the Enemy, *2001 by Favianna Giannoni Rodríguez. Courtesy of the artist.*

is quite clear that we might have never met these people personally, we immediately accept them as real people. Unlike the posters of the women of Juárez where the women are literally dis-embodied, the posters in the section dedicated to the picturing of the individual highlight recognizable portraits of public figures or allude to someone you might recognize as a neighbor or friend.

The Afghan woman and martyr, Meena Keshwar Kamal (1956–1987) is the central figure in the poster "We Are Not The Enemy." Meena, pictured in a headscarf and with a kindly, intelligent face, was a passionate women's rights activist and the founder of Revolutionary Association of Women in Afghanistan. She was assassinated in Pakistan by people who were believed to be agents of the Afghan secret police, the KHAD. The poster was created as an antiwar protest against the United States' call for war after 9/11. See figure 14.4.[8]

The poster "Miss Guatemala," not illustrated in this chapter, tells the very specific story of Rogelia Cruz Martinez (1940–1968), a university student and political activist who was kidnapped, tortured, raped, and murdered because of her association with members of a leftist party during the Guatemalan Civil War. This poster represents the discordant combination of a famous victim of that war in the foreground, carefully portrayed and identified as young and beautiful, waiting for her horrific future with more anonymous stereotyped indigenous victims assassinated in her orbit, in agony. And in the distance, two anonymous soldiers representing the government are seen skulking away.

Trauma

Trauma, the last section was the responsibility of art history doctoral student Lauren Dodds. Dodds wrote in her text panel: "Violence

---

8. The poem associated with the poster is titled "I'll Never Return"
"I'm the woman who has awoken
I've arisen and become a tempest through the ashes of my burnt children
I've arisen from the rivulets of my brother's blood
My nation's wrath has empowered me
My ruined and burnt villages replete me with hatred against the enemy
O' Compatriot, no longer regard me weak and incapable.
My voice has mingled with thousands of arisen women
My fists are clenched with fists of thousands of compatriots
To break together all these sufferings, all these fetters of slavery.
I'm the woman who has awoken
I've found my path and will return."

Meena Keshwar Kamal, published in RAWA.org, Revolutionary Association of the Women of Afghanistan.

leaves an enduring wound on its victims; the destruction of identity and human dignity creates lasting damage. For many who have gone through such deep suffering, it can present an impossible task to describe the experiences. A survivor of the Holocaust describes the life after the concentration camp: "*Everybody has a scar... it is a wound that is healing but underneath, it is still going on and we will have that for the rest of our life.*"

These posters, along with the video testimonies of the Holocaust survivors that were in the Reading Room, spoke to the way trauma represents violence against mind, memory, the body, and the future. They address issues from different locations of the world, reminding us that the experiences of violence and trauma are universal, although with varying consequences. Although including a more recognizable set of images including one of Anne Frank, Nancy Spero's silkscreen "Torture in Chile," included in this section, is distinct from all the posters in this exhibition. It was distinct in that the original artwork from which the poster was made is considered to be a work of fine art. "Can you tell why?" the text panel asks. Dodds was trying to get the viewer to think critically about what constituted a political poster and where it crossed the line into fine art. Dodds went on to write that, "Torture in Chile" is part of a larger series of Spero's works dealing with language and violence and that she was a well known political artist who relied upon testimonies of South American women recorded by Amnesty International to make her silk screen."

Lauren Dodds inserted her question in the text panel precisely because the Nancy Spero work does cross the line between poster and so-called fine art, a distinction described at the beginning of this article. In this case the positioning into the realm of fine art can be justified because of the work's pictorially ambiguous, less literal imagery than we have seen in the other political posters on display. Dodds wanted to use this fine artist's work to make the point about what political poster art normally is and what it usually is not. And, perhaps also, to challenge the categories that distinguish them by including the Spero work in the exhibition anyway. In Spero's piece the words included enter in and out of focus, change size, violate spacing norms, and sometimes become almost unreadable. This poster or work of fine art becomes more like a fever dream or persistent memory. It is therefore poetically rather than literally or descriptively referential to violence and thus different from the other posters in the exhibition. Spero seems to be making a poster that reflects the way she conceives of trauma, specifically the trauma in

Chile. She represents it as ungraspable, practically unreadable, and therefore narratively unrepeatable. Nevertheless, as an artist, Spero makes us understand that the trauma suffered remains in the psyche by virtue of its ghostly, punishing litany. Dodds posed her question because she wanted the visitor to think for herself and not be totally spoon-fed about what a political poster is or is not. Dodds' text panel concludes: "A poster on Darfur in this section shows three women covering their faces. Their bodily gestures indicate shame and pain, yet the imagery is made in such a way as to imbue them with both dignity and terror. In Darfur women have been subjected to sexual violence as a deliberate means of humiliation and degradation."

Beyond the Exhibition Itself

Watching the visitors to the exhibition, what stood out especially was the extended time they spent in front of each poster. This is unusual in an art museum, where it is generally accepted in the field of museum studies that audience members typically spend only several seconds in front of any given work of art. Yet our visitors were riveted.

To further deepen the experience for our visitors, our project included a roundtable on the evening of the opening of the exhibition. Organized by the students, it included a representative of the class, Helena Liakanen, the Director of the Shoah Foundation, Carol Wells, the Director of the CSPG, myself, and others who had taken part in the project. About two hundred people filled the galleries, and many in the audience were actively involved in the question and answer period that followed. We found the panel to be an indispensable complement to the exhibition itself.

As a whole, the seminar along with its attendant exhibition practicum provided extraordinary experiences for our students. They learned a great deal about art and society, but also about the art and science of curating. That is, they learned to confront reams of original materials in order to find the precise works that could form a meaningful and communicable narrative for the public; they learned to apply critical thinking with respect to a vast body of written and visual culture; and they developed an empathetic response to those who had endured unspeakable violence. Because they were successful in their project, many members of the public who came to participate in the "Genocide Awareness Week" also reported that they had a deep experience.

The public's experience came from visiting the exhibition and from the intellectual program that accompanied it. I would recommend this kind of collaboration in a university setting as a way to enhance resources and to encourage interdisciplinarity and collaboration, as well as to connect university research constructively to problems that plague the real world. It is important that we both prepare our students to grapple intellectually with history and its consequences, and to think about ways to confront those realities in life itself. With respect to the topic of art, it is clear that one can make a distinction between fine art and the art of political posters while recognizing that both are art. The students also grappled with this, coming to the conclusion that at times our art historical distinctions may be profoundly and usefully blurred, even by such politically committed "fine" artists as Nancy Spero, who themselves challenge the categories of "fine" art and political poster.

Finally, although in the conference "Beyond Guernica and the Guggenheim" we definitively delved into the subject of politics and art beyond the time of the painting of *Guernica*, it seems to me that we could still never be free of Picasso. He painted, arguably, the masterpiece of the twentieth century. *Guernica* is not a political poster: it speaks to every act of political violence and betrayal, to every unconscionable act of war, to every infliction of violence on the innocent. Even if it was born of a specific indefensible act of war, *Guernica* has traveled far beyond anything resembling a memorialization or better said, a condemnation of a specific action—even as it will also always function as such.

Bibliography

Améry, Jean. "Torture" In *Art from the Ashes: A Holocaust Anthology*, edited by Lawrence L. Langer. New York: Oxford University Press, 1995.

Browning, Christopher. "From 'Ethnic Cleansing' to Genocide to the 'Final Solution.'" In *The Holocaust: A Reader*, edited by Simone Gigliotti and Berel Lang. Malden, MA: Blackwell Publishing, 2005.

Friedlander, Henry. "The Setting." In *The Holocaust: A Reader*, edited by Simone Gigliotti and Berel Lang. Malden, MA: Blackwell Publishing, 2005.

Hitler, Adolf. "Hitler's Reichstag Speech, January 30, 1939." In *The Holocaust: A Reader*, edited by Simone Gigliotti and Berel Lang. Malden, MA: Blackwell Publishing, 2005.

Holo, Selma, and Mari-Tere Alvarez, eds. *Beyond the Turnstile: Making the Case for Museums and Sustainable Values*. Lanham, MA: Rowman and Littlefield, 2009.

Levi, Primo. "Shame, or on the Subject." In *Art from the Ashes: A Holocaust Anthology*, edited by Lawrence L. Langer. New York: Oxford University Press, 1995.

Lewis, Bernard. "Anti-Semites." In *The Holocaust: A Reader*, edited by Simone Gigliotti and Berel Lang. Malden, MA: Blackwell Publishing, 2005.

Wiesel, Elie Wiesel. "A Plea for the Dead." In *Art from the Ashes: A Holocaust Anthology*, edited by Lawrence L. Langer. New York: Oxford University Press, 1995.

Acknowledgments

I would like to thank Professor Zoe Bray for inviting me to contribute to this volume, to Dr. Stephen Smith, Director of the Shoah Foundation for including us in the Foundation's activities, and Carol Wells, President of the Center for the Study of Political Graphics (CSPG) for allowing us to work freely in the Center.

15

Reflections on a Feminist Model for the Field of Art: Montehermoso, 2008–2011

Xabier Arakistain

This chapter sets out the conceptual underpinning of the project of production, exhibition, and diffusion of contemporary art and thought that was carried out at the Cultural Center Montehermoso Kulturunea in the Spanish Basque city of Vitoria-Gasteiz during the four years from 2008 to 2011. For the first time in the Basque Autonomous Community and the rest of the Spanish state, women were incorporated into all the project's programs and activities equal to men. The project considered feminist thought as a crucial source of knowledge for understanding contemporary artistic practices and the societies that produce them. In fact, Montehermoso was the result of taking up the principal critical contributions made by feminism in the field of contemporary art since women had become massively and continuously involved in art practice and theory in the third wave of feminism, just forty years ago.

The ARCO Manifesto 2005

In February 2005, I invited a group of scholars, artists, curators, and institutional representatives of different generations and nationalities to a discussion forum on the intersection between art and feminism that I was directing for the second year running at the ARCO art fair, in Madrid. I did this with the awareness that in spite of possessing disciplinary and cultural specificities, the problem of sexism in art exceeds the field of art itself and also extends beyond national frameworks. In that edition, I proposed the title "Equality policies between men and women within the art world: Designing strategies," with the intention of promoting specific actions that went beyond the usual, though necessary, statistical elaborations that confirm the overwhelming evidence that women continue to undergo discrimination in the field of art even in the twenty-first century, or the equally usual, and necessary, task of recovering female artists forgotten by official Art History. For this, I invited speakers who would address the political dimensions from a feminist perspective. My proposal was initially based on two data: one being that women were (and are) a majority in Fine Arts Faculties and two, that in spite of this, the presence of female artists in the programs and collections of art centers and museums continued (and still continues) to be minimal. Moreover, I related these data to two other issues: firstly, that supranational bodies such as the EU and UN had been recommending member states to adopt measures aimed at correcting "gender" inequality for years—measures such as the application of gender quota policies that were producing positive results both in the political and business realms; and secondly, the fact that these measures were not being implemented in the field of art and did not even seem to affect it.

Both the speakers and the audience took part in a debate that soon polarized into two positions: On the one hand, the stance backing the idea implicit in the organizational proposal of the debate, demanding that public administrations establish policies such as gender quotas in programs and acquisitions of art works from art centers and museums as an adequate tool of ensuring equal opportunities for women in the field of art. It was alleged that most structures in charge of the production, exhibition, and diffusion of art in Spain are financed with public funds, and therefore those structures could be permeable to measures such as the application of gender quotas that had proven to be successful in other areas of activity. On the other hand, there were those positions insisting on the idea that quota policies would not solve the problem of women's discrimination in the art field, as this is a broader structural matter that requires a complete transformation of social and art institutions in order to eliminate their sex bias. The discussion was tough, mainly because a certain sector of feminism was highly critical of what some years earlier had been called the "institutionalization of feminism". In fact, the so-called gender public policies that had been implemented in the mid-1980s in Spain and in other countries were starting to be unfavorably evaluated. Certain non-English-speaking feminist theorists openly questioned the gender category itself as a valid analytical category within its own cultural contexts. Among the latter was the feminist anthropologist Lourdes Méndez who, in a work she published the same year, "Una connivencia implícita" (An implicit connivance), denounced how the "gender" category had been adopted by public institutions without further consideration, and how this was generating a number of "gender" studies and analyses that she considers were subjected to an "institutional reflexivity," unable to overcome the institutional framework in which they are produced and therefore incapable of eliminating the sexism that structures those same institutions. Méndez points out that in order to do so, the question should be approached from a standpoint of "epistemic reflexivity" in the same way some feminist studies do which enables them to analyze the issue of sexual difference in its real dimension. Méndez observes that "the illusion that the thorny problems regarding the difference/hierarchy between sexes and sexualities can be solved legally has become so deeply rooted that we tend to forget that the inequality which affects us as 'social' women—the same as that affecting gays and lesbians—is a basic pillar of a social, economic, and symbolic order reproduced by states, the laws they produce, and the scientific and social theorizations related to these issues, all of which are institutionally retained."1 In this sense, Méndez gathers in her text the voices of different feminist authors such as Françoise Héritier who reminded us in 1996 that "inequality between the sexes is structured by a sexual order that laws are unable to combat because it refers to a 'differential valence between the sexes' that interconnects and explains the functioning of the 'three pillars of the social tripod', which according to Levi-Strauss were the prohibition of incest, the sexual distribution of domestic work, and a recognized form of sexual union;"2 or others like Mary Douglas who stated in 1999 that "anti-discrimination laws are no use. . . campaigns dealing with battered women. . . [and] have no possibility of being effective. . . We need to change the institutions;"3 or yet another author who participated in the ARCO Forum, Francoise Duroux, who pointed out in 2004 that "equalizing measures or even affirmative actions will not prevent the 'odor di femina' from perfuming working and hiring places, premises of political parties, schools."4 (id: 211). On the other side of the feminist

1. Méndez, "Una connivencia implícita," 209. Note: I have translated the quotations to English from the original text in Spanish.

2. Quoted in ibid.

3. Quoted in ibid., 210.

4. Quoted in ibid., 211.

spectrum, among those who clearly stood for demanding that public administrations establish corrective measures and more specifically the implementation of gender quotas, was the feminist philosopher Amelia Valcárcel, who stated that, "It is necessary to illuminate the qualitative deficits. . . beyond the accumulation of skills and exceeding the quantitative margins of affirmative actions. It intervenes in the accumulation of authority and respect for the collective of women as an input with a value in itself. Nevertheless it must be illuminated in a quantitative manner. Quantity is closely related to quality. Parity means half . . . also regarding excellence which occurs for a good reason, i.e. the fact that women also possess it."5 Although, as this author had already reminded us back in her emblematic article "El derecho al mal" ("The right to evil"), published in the September 1980 issue of the journal Viejo Topo, true equality for women actually means having both rights, the right to excellence and the right not to be excellent: "We do not then assert our own evil -according to which we have been defined- or assert, either, the good which has been attributed to us. It is precisely your evil that we assert. This is a truly universal feminist moral discourse, which does not intend to show excellence but to assert the right not to be excellent. Just as your moral Logos has always operated."6 From this position, it was argued that, historically, institutions are pressured in a quantitative manner to achieve their subsequent qualitative transformation, and that the advances in women's living conditions, and those of other marginalized collectives in certain parts of the world achieved in the last century, responded partly to these dynamics. A distinction was also made between the terms "affirmative action" and "parity." The former refers to promoting people for the common good who lack the same skills and achievements they have been unable to acquire due to an unfavorable starting point, and the latter to the promotion of those who, possessing the same skills and achievements, cannot access certain areas due to ideological reasons—as is currently the case, for example, with women. And finally, according to this position the proposal was to write a manifesto—and it was done thus—which included the assumptions of the forum organizers as a gesture, which expressed existing discomfort, and denounced the situation before public authorities.

I should mention here that by the time the manifesto was finally signed, the debate had stagnated. The curator Ute Meta Bauer, however, managed to ease the situation by calling for "feminist

5. Valcárcel, *Feminismo en el mundo global*, 330.

6. Valcárel, "El derecho al mal," 165.

solidarity": "Approving this text, let's say 40% of it, I recognize the work accomplished by its promoters and I support it for the sake of feminist solidarity, and whenever I develop my disagreements in my own proposals I shall appeal to your feminist solidarity in order to get recognition for my work." Thanks to her invocation to feminist solidarity, and to the backing of participants such as Lourdes Méndez, who agreed to sign the manifesto as a "circumstantial strategy," the ARCO 2005 Manifesto was finally approved and signed by both the speakers and the majority of those attending the discussion on February 11, 2005. At the time, I considered that the three days of hard, intense discussion had resulted in various important conclusions, two of which I would like to highlight. First, it did not seem incompatible to work on two fronts at the same time, that is, institutional critique and internal reforms. Second, that establishing gender quotas was compatible with other feminist strategies.

The Nochlin and Pollock Perspectives

The complex political debate at ARCO 2005 referred to, ignored, and even contributed to the debate that has been developing at the core of feminist art history discipline since the early 1970s, when what was known in Europe as the third wave of feminism made it possible for the first time for women to become continuously and massively involved in art theory and practice. It was, in fact, another speaker at ARCO 2005, the art historian from the United States Linda Nochlin who, following the proposal about women and literature initiated by Virginia Woolf in *A Room of One's Own*, inaugurated in 1971 the feminist perspective in Art History with her now legendary article "Why Have There Been No Great Women Artists?" published in the journal *Artnews*. The question posed by her article, she said, "has led us to the conclusion, so far, that art is not a free, autonomous activity of a super-endowed individual, 'influenced' by previous artists, and, more vaguely and superficially, by 'social forces', but rather, that the total situation of art making, both in terms of the development of the art maker and in the nature and quality of the work of art itself, occur in a social situation, are integral elements of this social structure, and are mediated and determined by specific and definable social institutions, be they art academies, systems of patronage, mythologies of the divine creator, artist as he-man or social outcast."[7]

---

7. Nochlin, "Why Have There Been No Great Women Artists?" 158.

Nochlin's article revealed that art is one of the institutions that reproduce the long-lasting socio-sexual order that maintains and perpetuates the masculine hierarchy, which in those years was coined as patriarchy. Nochlin's article inspired a series of studies, publications, and exhibitions devoted to rescuing female artists who had been ignored or undervalued by the official art history, and was interpreted as the basis for a new model of historiographical and curatorial practice that, at the risk of excessive simplification, we could say consists of proposing a change of paradigm to include women and their work in the discipline, which has been seen from some sectors as ill-equipped to transform the history of art if we want it to include the knowledge and political and social agenda of feminism.

In fact, a decade later, in 1981, the British art historian Griselda Pollock, together with Rozsika Parker, published Old Mistresses: Women, Art and Ideology, in which they affirm that contrary to current popular belief, women have always made art, and that "it is only in the twentieth century that women artists have been systematically effaced from the history of art."8 Moreover, they add that art made by women has been categorized as minor through a stereotype in which women are negatively presented "as lacking creativity, with nothing significant to contribute, and as having had no influence on the course of art";9 and that although this female stereotype seems just to be a way of excluding women from cultural history, "it is in fact a crucial element in the construction of the current view of the history of art. . . [and] . . . art history as a structuring category in its ideology."10 Therefore, they reject presenting the history of women in art merely as a struggle for inclusion in institutions such as art academies. To them, "such an approach fails to convey the specific ways that women have made art under different constraints at different periods, affected as much by factors of class as by their sex." Moreover, they emphasize that if we only see women's history as a progressive struggle against great odds, we are falling into the trap of unconsciously reasserting the established male standards as the suitable norm. "If women's history is simply judged against the norms of male history, women are once more again set apart, outside the historical processes of which both men and women are indissolubly part."11

---

8. Pollock and Parker, *Old Mistresses*, xxvii.
9. Ibid., 169.
10. Ibid., xxvii.
11. Ibid., xviii–xix.

Finally, Parker and Pollock openly question the belief that women should fight to enter into the existing male-dominated field of art in search of recognition.12 In Old Mistresses, they set the basis of the question that Pollock would formulate alone in 1994, namely: Can Art History survive feminism? "To attempt to understand the nature and effects of feminist intervention, I cannot bend to the strict dominion of the history of art and its discourse in the context of Art History. The understanding of feminist effects lies beyond their critical and interpretation schemes. Knowledge is in fact a political issue, regarding positions, interests, perspectives and power. The history of art, inasmuch as it is a discourse and institution, maintains an order invested by male desire. We must destroy this order if we are to speak about the interests of women."13 In turn, Pollock's perspective has also inspired another historiographical and curatorial practice, which has exhibited and explained the work of women artists from positions and terms different from those of hegemonic art criticism. Pollock herself has continually developed this practice, to which it could be objected that the process of re-valuating artworks made by women may in some instances lead to a lack of critical observation of such works as a product of specific patriarchal power relations. In addition, although such practices may aim to destabilize the existing structural relationship between the valuation of art produced by women, and art produced by men (to date, with little success), it often appears not to have overcome the (essentialist) narrative of the feminine constructed by the patriarchy.

Montehermoso

The design of the project for the Cultural Center of Montehermoso came about as a result of the heated debate between feminists at ARCO 2005—as a need to test the possibility of bringing together the perspectives of Nochlin and Pollock in a single project, and has a specific meaning as a contribution to that debate. There is no doubt, however, that the legal umbrella offered by the new laws on gender equality, initially in the Basque Autonomous Community, and subsequently in Spain, made Montehermoso possible.

It was noteworthy that the Basque law of equality was passed by the Basque parliament five days after the signing of the ARCO 2005 Manifesto. This law only deals with culture in twelve lines in Article

12. Ibid., 169.
13. Pollock, "Histoire et politique," 69.

25, which merely refers explicitly to artistic activities in forbidding funding if there is discrimination on the basis of gender, with no further specifications. More remarkable was that a few months later, the manifesto was received by the Spanish Socialist party that was working on the Constitutional Law of January 2007 for the effective equality between men and women, and was mainly included in Article 26, in which the law deals with culture and art. Considerably longer than its Basque counterpart, this article suffers from the same main problem: it is merely a recommendation, thereby allowing its systematic violation.

Even so, the symbolic impact of the laws facilitated my winning a public competition for the launching of a cultural center whose programs would ensure the inclusion of women on equal terms to men, and include in its conceptual framework the "gender perspective" that, unlike the "feminist perspective," had been accepted by other EU member states. This competition also furthered the possibility of developing a specific project of a center for art and thought—Montehermoso—in the context of Vitoria-Gasteiz and the Basque Autonomous Community.

Thus in my application for the directorship of Montehermoso in 2006, I presented a project that retained three conclusions from the ARCO debate as well as my previous experience as a feminist curator: first, from my point of view, Nochlin and Pollock's positions, far from being obsolete, present two entirely relevant models for feminist intervention in the art world that, additionally, and as we will see below in the case of Montehermoso, can complement each other in one project. Second, the celebrations of isolated feminist events at institutions are still anecdotal, and fail to transform both the institutions that host them and the prevalent canons. And third, exhibitions that only show the work of female artists fail to avoid being seen as a subcategory within the art discipline, a subcategory that defines both the event itself and the artists it includes.

The project that I developed along with my colleague Beatriz Herraez for the Cultural Center of Montehermoso between 2008 and 2011 transformed the previous cultural center into a center for the production, exhibition, and distribution of contemporary art and thought. At the same time, it continued to be part of the Department of Culture of the city council of Vitoria-Gasteiz but was rearranged on the basis of the definition of culture stated in the Mexico Declaration of 1982 by UNESCO. Following this declaration, the center perceived art and culture as spaces for critical reflection in contemporary societies, and as stages and driving forces for the production of knowledge and processes for social and political transformations.

The project was originally devised around what has been defined in various realms as international contemporary art and/or a restricted field of art. In other words, it made up a series of art practices, which are produced, circulated, and consumed on an international circuit, which also generates and transmits the dominant art trends. However, our adoption of critical perspectives for analyzing and acting in the field of international contemporary art favored the study of systems of representation and their role in the construction and reproduction of symbolic imagery. This work made it possible on the one hand to examine issues such as the review of social values from the perspective of coexistence and, in a special way, perspectives referring to equality between the sexes. On the other hand, this work also enables the recovery of historic memory, lending visibility to the contributions by women in the territory of art and thought. With these aims the general project of the center was structured by applying policies of equality and seeing feminist thought as a crucial source of knowledge for understanding the current world. In fact, the feminist reinterpretation of the history of art, as well as that of the artistic practices of today and their analyses imply, as Pollock has pointed out "recognizing the hierarchies of power which rule the relationships between the sexes, lending visibility to the mechanisms on which male hegemony is founded, untangling the process of social construction of sexual difference and examining the role played by representation in that articulation of difference."[14]

The development of these policies and perspectives turned Montehermoso into the first center for contemporary art, culture, and thought to apply the references to art and culture as defined under the current equality laws of the Basque Autonomous Community. The center followed two strategies to guarantee the participation of women in parity without isolating them and their work as specific categories in the realm of art and intellectual activity: The first was to apply gender quotas in every activity and program to ensure that half of those taking part in the program were women; and to distribute the public budget on the basis of gender, and to lend visibility and promote the work of women. The feminist intervention upon the budget of the institution also included a consideration of the material conditions of artistic and intellectual production that generated a table of fees related to the salaries that we ourselves were receiving at the institution. The second strategy sought to apply feminist quotas, that is, to develop lines of artistic production and exhibition that promote feminist thought, focusing on the promo-

14. Pollock, *Vision and Difference*, 32.

tion of values such as equality, as well as the deconstruction of sex, gender, and sexual stereotypes.

Following the Nochlin and Pollock perspectives, the program of the center could be divided into two groups: First, the general program, which produced exhibitions that were inscribed within different international contemporary art currents, in which we applied gender quotas, and, at a different level, included the feminist perspective as one more among the perspectives that were informing the projects. In this sense, Montehermoso was a territory of possibility between two spheres/relational networks of the field of art that very rarely come into contact and almost never do continuously. The second group consisted of specifically feminist programs, like the curatorial and exhibition project Contraseñas/Passwords in which different feminists curators were invited from different cultural contexts to make a selection of "feminist art" pieces. The project was therefore produced and judged according to the criteria of different feminist discourses. Another example on this side was the course on feminist perspectives on art practice and theory that the feminist anthropologist Lourdes Méndez and myself codirected, in which we invited theoreticians from different disciplines and nationalities to insist on the social character of the production of art and to disseminate and continue to write a feminist art history.

The general program was structured around the "Art and Research" program, one of the central features of the center, which manifested and condensed a series of preoccupations/goals that, in a systematic, interconnected way, defined the cultural policy developed at Montehermoso. The open call for the projects, as well as their selection, exhibition, and dissemination, developed an art-research relationship focusing on art practices as a complex methodology for producing knowledge. Every year, eight artistic projects, one curatorial and three research projects, among which at least one was dedicated to the writing of the history of the relations between art and feminism in Spain, were produced and exhibited at the center as part of the "Art and Research" program. This and other programs connected a series of agents from the realms of education, criticism, art centers, and curatorial and art practice that wove a complex relational net.

The project of production, exhibition, and diffusion of contemporary art and thought carried out at the Cultural Center of Montehermoso during the four years from 2008 to 2011 was the result of taking up the principal critical contributions made by feminism in the field of contemporary art and was also the result of many years of my own and my colleagues' feminist work in this field. It was a contribution to feminist debates on art, but overall, Montehermoso proved that including women in parity in artistic and cultural programs is not only possible but also increases the quality of those programs. In this regard, the success of the project made it possible to place the Cultural Center Montehermoso within a network of renowned national and international institutions, at the same time as it broadened the relationships and strengthened the imbrication of the center with the local context, bringing contemporary art and culture closer to users. The project achieved a noteworthy popularity abroad. However, the institutional dimension of it has been ignored completely. This has particularly been the case in the Basque Country and the rest of the Spanish state.

I would like to conclude by stressing that Montehermoso was a project designed for a public institution, and that it was conceived as a means of applying the recommendations in the articles dealing with art and culture in current laws of equality in the Basque Country and Spain. Montehermoso was, and still is, a valid blueprint for transforming public institutions for art and culture from the inside so that they incorporate women in parity. It was this dimension of the project that was clearly obvious to the Socialist government of the city, and particularly appealed to Maite Berrocal, the city's councilor for culture, also a feminist who personally supported the project because she understood that cultural policies should also scrupulously respect one of the main horizons of contemporary democracy: equality between the sexes.

Bibliography

Méndez, Lourdes (2005) "Una connivencia implícita: "Perspectiva de género", "empoderamiento" y feminismo institucional." In *Antropología Feminista y/o del Género, Legitimidad, poder y usos políticos*, edited by Rosa Andrieu and Carmen Mozo. Seville: Fundación El Monte, Federación de Asociaciones de Antropología del Estado Español, Asociaión Andaluza de Antropología, 2005.

Nochlin, Linda. "Why Have There Been No Great Women Artists?" In *Women, Art and Power and Other Essays.* Boulder, CO: Westview Press, 1988.

Pollock, Griselda. *Vision and Difference.* New York: Routledge Classics, 1988.

———. "Histoire et Politique: l'histoire de l'art peut-elle survivre au féminisme?" In *Féminisme, art et histoire de l'art.* Paris:

Ecole nationale supérieure des Beaux-Arts, 1994.

Pollock, Griselda, and Rozsika Parker. *Old Mistresses: Women, Art and Ideology*. London: Pandora Press, 1981.

Valcárcel, Amelia. *Sexo y Filosofía. Sobre "mujer" y "poder".* Barcelona: Anthropos, 1991.

———. *Feminismo en el mundo global.* Madrid: Ediciones Cátedra, 2008.

16

"Newtopia": Artists Address Human Rights

Susan Noyes Platt

"We can at least dream of a new way for human societies to live together, caring for and respecting each other as brothers and sisters."
—Stéphane Hessel, 2012

In the fall of 2012 the city of Mechelen in Belgium hosted the exhibition "Newtopia, the State of Human Rights," curated by Katerina Gregos (see figure 16.1). Closely based on the Universal Declaration of Human Rights of 1948, this groundbreaking exhibition presents both historical and contemporary artists who are deeply committed to analyzing political process and social issues. Art works that address such topics as torture and immigration increase their impact when framed by human rights discourses. The exhibition places them in relationship to the four categories of human rights cited in the Universal Declaration, civil, political, social, and economic. In the process, "Newtopia" demonstrates the creative subtlety with which artists address these concerns. The affiliation with human rights provides a new direction for the analysis of engaged art, as well as new possibilities for more nuanced visual campaigns linked to activist issues.

While many treaties and covenants followed the original Declaration as a means of enforcing it legally, the principles laid out in the Declaration have continuously had enormous moral authority. They are constantly cited in movements across the globe as a means of shaming individuals and governments into action. Its articles were developed from June 1947 to December 1948 under the auspices of the newly formed United Nations and in the midst of the emergence of the Cold War, the partition of India and Pakistan, and the creation of the State of Israel.

The committee, chaired by Eleanor Roosevelt, received input from thinkers around the world, including Mahatma Gandhi, Chung-Shu Lo, a Confucian scholar, and Humayun Kabir, a renowned Bengali leader. They all stated that the principles of human rights, if not the term, existed in their cultures and ideologies.[1] At the same time, these rights, as thought through by the original writers from diverse backgrounds, are fundamental to human existence everywhere. Some recent writers have contested that rights are culturally contingent, and it is true that rights-based language has Western origins. However, the rights articulated by the Universal Declaration began by carefully incorporating non-Western conceptions of ethical responsibility, and they have evolved since their adoption through myriad social, legal, and political movements from around the world. Thus, rights such as that articulated by Article 3, "Everyone has the right to life, liberty and security of person," are expressed in rights-based terms, but have come to mean much more than narrow or Westernized articulations of "rights." Life is not a culturally contingent idea.[2]

Both the Declaration and "Newtopia" take the Holocaust during World War II as their foundation and point of departure. In the Preamble of the Declaration, the first statement of principle is the "inherent dignity . . . of all members of the human family . . ., whereas disregard and contempt for human rights have resulted in barbarous acts . . . it is essential . . . that human rights should be protected by the rule of law." Likewise "Newtopia" is a direct response to those same "barbarous acts" in both its location and purpose. Mechelen, Belgium is located half way between Antwerp and Brussels, and was a major center for the deportation of Jews, Roma, and others to Auschwitz during World War II. In November 2012, concurrently with the "Newtopia" exhibition, the City of Mechelen opened Kazerne Dossin, a Memorial, Museum, and Documentation Center of the Holocaust and Human Rights. The museum is directly opposite the army barracks in which people were gathered

1. Glendon, *A World Made New*, 73–74.

2. Gregos, "Righting Human Rights," *Newtopia*, 22–24 as well as Hessel, "Interview" with Stéphane Hessel, ibid., 103–4 discuss this question. Stéphane Hessel participated in the original process of drafting the Declaration in 1948. He had his roots in the French Resistance movement. His pamphlets *Indignez-Vous!* (Time for Outrage!) 2010 and *Engagez-Vous*! 2011 became worldwide bestsellers and handouts during the Occupy movement and beyond. He died in February, 2013, an outspoken activist to the end: Weber and de la Baume, "Stéphane Hessel, Author and Activist, Dies at 95," *The New York Times*, February 27, 2013.

for deportation. Commissioned as part of "Newtopia" is the artwork, *MenschenDinge* by the artist Esther Shalev-Gerz.[3] The artist presents interviews with professionals organizing Auschwitz as a memorial site. They are responding to the objects that survived at the camp after it was liberated. On other floors, the museum documents as thoroughly as possible, the names and faces of 26,000 of those who were deported.

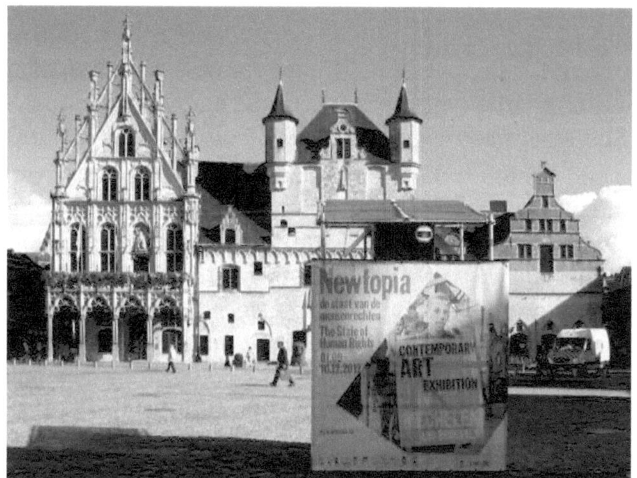

Figure 16.1. City Hall (Stadhuis) Mechelen, Belgium, photograph by Henry Matthews, reproduced with permission.

The Declaration and the exhibition are organized around the same groupings of human rights. In the Declaration the articles are conceptually ordered into individual rights, civil rights, political rights, economic, social, and cultural rights, and finally by the rights and responsibilities of the individual in society. In the exhibition, these ideas are ordered into four chapters: civil and political rights in chapter 1, and social, economic, and cultural rights in chapter 2. Chapter 3 addresses the same human rights from the perspective of changes in the world since 1948, including decolonization, globalization, global capital, and multiculturalism. Chapter 4 calls for a

3. According to the catalog, the word is invented by the artist. It can mean " 'the human aspect of objects'. The original German, however, is much wider, allowing for a variety of possible interpretations. The human and the object blend in the German word, the object becomes humanized, animated and the human objectified to some extent. These objects-by-humans, or human-objects can be perceived as a community of a kind, because they have shared the same dehumanized life." E(sther) S(halev), *Newtopia*, 237

new way to realize human rights in "Thinking beyond the Here and Now." It is described as "poetic, transformative leaps of the imagination," and "a diagnostic, programmatic of radical intervention in real life."[4]

As a curator, Katerina Gregos has already demonstrated her ability to take on art that addresses complex and controversial political issues in "Speech Matters," the Danish Pavilion at the 54th Venice Biennale in 2011. Although the controversy over the cartoon that depicted Mohammed published in Denmark in 2005 was one starting point for the pavilion, Gregos framed "freedom of speech" as a discursive issue with both historical and international significance. She assembled eighteen artists from diverse cultural backgrounds and explored the topic further with a thoughtful catalog.[5]

In the present exhibition she has followed the same model, but greatly enlarged the theme and the scope. The art in "Newtopia" demonstrates the ways in which artists offer dramatic alternatives to the usual photographs and videos sponsored by human rights campaigns. As Ariella Azoulay concisely states in her catalog essay: "Human rights discourse as embodied in photography has cultivated two major figures to date: the victim, whose rights have been violated, and the spectator who is supposed to recognize this violation."[6] The straightforward, and actually effective, purpose of these photographs is to generate guilt and pity in order to encourage us to give money to the non- profit to help the situation.

The fact that Amnesty International and Human Rights Watch are co-sponsors of "Newtopia" demonstrates that they are happy to embrace new ideas in their visual campaigns. Human Rights Watch, in particular, has already offered alternatives to traditional photographic approaches to visual imagery of human rights. The Human Rights Watch Film Festival shown annually in several cities states its commitment to bringing together creative thinking and human rights. [7]

---

4. Gregos, *Newtopia*, exhibition brochure, 49.

5. Gregos, ed., *Speech Matters*, Danish Pavilion, 54th Venice Biennale.

6. Azoulay, "The (In)visible Victim-Deconstructing the Spectator's Frame," *Newtopia*, 67.

7. Human Rights Watch Film Festival statement of purpose: "Through our Human Rights Watch Film Festival we bear witness to human rights violations and create a forum for courageous individuals on both sides of the lens to empower audiences with the knowledge that personal commitment can make a difference. The film festival brings to life human rights abuses through storytelling in a way that challenges each individual to empathize

Although photography is a dominant medium in "Newtopia," these artists re-negotiate the space between themselves, the subject, and the viewer in order to create new perceptions. As Katerina Gregos states "[art's] great power is that it is able to change the way people *think* about the world. Art may expand perceptual horizons."[8]

The benchmark artist of the exhibition, Alfredo Jaar, dramatically demonstrates that idea. In his early work, shown in chapter 1, Jaar presents us with the perpetrators of human rights violations, rather than the victims. As a Chilean, Jaar's subject is the CIA-engineered coup that killed Salvador Allende on September 11, 1973. In *Untitled (Handshake)*, he displays the covers of *Time* magazine with Henry Kissinger and Salvador Allende, as well as a newspaper photograph of Kissinger shaking hands with the dictator Augusto Pinochet, who came into power following the coup and perpetrated massive violations of human rights in every area of life.

In chapter 4, the utopian chapter, Jaar honors women who have stood up for human rights. *Three women (Aung San Suu Kyi, Ela Bhatt and Graça Machel)* includes three tiny photographs of the three heroes of human rights, in Burma, India, and Mozambique respectively. A forest of floodlights illuminates but almost renders impossible to see, the tiny photographs, suggesting the idea of their massive fame as well as the illumination and magnification of their enlightened ideas. Jaar frequently works with the primary source for a photograph, light and the absence of light, as a metaphor of the dialectic of enlightenment and ignorance. In highlighting heroes, Jarr parallels the exhibition catalog which features statements from six heroes as a major feature. The six heroes are two Pulitzer Peace Prize winners, Aung San Suu Kyi (Burma) and Shirin Ebadi (Iran), as well as Anna Politkovskaya (the murdered Russian journalist who was exposing human rights abuses in her country), Liu Xiaobo (an imprisoned public intellectual in China), Aman Mahfouz (the young woman who called people to Tahrir Square in January 2011), and Carina Govaert (representing a Peace Community of San José de Apartadó in Colombia).

---

and demand justice for all people." http://ff.hrw.org/about, accessed April 20, 2013. Another, less well-known example is the systematic photographic portrayal of human rights, as both absence and presence, in Kälin, Muller, and Wyttenback, eds., *The Face of Human Rights.* This book is based on a spiral of human rights with "The Right to Life" at the center, then moving outward to nine groupings of human rights that provide a concise summary of the longer Declaration. It includes five hundred photographs from all over the world that record abuses of human rights, those who work to keep those rights and those who enjoy those same rights.

8. Gregos, "Righting of Human Rights," *Newtopia,* 31.

"Newtopia" also sponsored a one-person exhibition of Jaar's work in Brussels, "Let There Be Light," focusing on his work in Africa including the *Rwanda Project.* In the immediate aftermath of the genocide that killed one million Tutsis by Hutus from April to July 1994, Alfredo Jaar went to Rwanda, perhaps because he had "seen" mass civilian death in Chile only through absences. He took thousands of photographs, made an obsessive report, but when he returned home he could not look at his work for two years.[9]

When Jarr finally did display his photographs, he put them into photographic black boxes stacked up in piles, so that the images were invisible. Instead of viewing a photograph, we read narratives written on the top of the box, based on the stories of specific individuals that Jaar had photographed. He wanted to avoid the superficial experience of the "other." He offers instead a graveyard that looks like a minimalist installation of black cubes.

Another Rwanda related installation, *The Eyes of Gutete Emerita*, gives us only the eyes of a woman whose entire family had been slaughtered in a church before her very eyes. Below is her narrative. The photograph of the eyes, enlarged, with each eye framed separately, draws us in. Her eyes saw the killings; they contain the killings; they live with the killings. One survivor's eyes connects to us more directly than statistics about death.

Krzysztof Wodiczko, another featured artist of "Newtopia," dramatically departs from traditional photographic representation in a different, though affiliated, way, as he addresses the human rights of refugees, and displaced persons, the right to work, and the many other rights that undocumented immigrants cannot access easily. His public installation, *The New Mechlinians*, was based on interviews with undocumented immigrants to Mechelen both recently and in the past. It was both intimate and public. Wodiczko worked with the immigrant rights group "Werkgroep Integratie Vluchtelingen" (Refugee Integration Working Group) to conduct the interviews. The refugees speak in several languages reflecting their point of origin and a few speak Flemish. They become the "face of the city": their eyes look down on us in a live projection (the eyes blink and move) as we listen to them speak about their nightmares,

9. He consciously "disappeared" (did not exhibit) the photographs that he took of ordinary people caught up in the mass murder. As he explained, "I have always been concerned with the disjunction between experience and what can be recorded photographically. In the case of Rwanda, the disjunction was enormous and the tragedy unrepresentable." Quoted in *Let There Be Light, The Rwanda Project 1994–1998*, unpaginated. This book includes a detailed discussion of all the formats of the project.

and their fears, one woman speaks about her absent husband, and questions us "how can a human being be illegal?" The artist points out that, in the Bible, the cities of Sodom and Gomorrah were destroyed because they mistreated newcomers.

In the installation, people hiding in the shadows hear their voices and see their eyes projected at the center of the main city square. The facade of the City Hall becomes their mask. The artist spoke of his hope that this transmission directly to the public might make a new consciousness possible that will change people's perspectives and make the work itself obsolete. Democracy is measured in part, according to Wodiczko, by its openness to strangers. These immigrants are now giving us the opportunity to properly welcome them

Other artists in "Newtopia" altered expectations with media such as posters, sculpture, painting, installation and found objects, For example, they create installations with objects that are signifiers of a social issue, not in themselves, but in the context in which they were found as in the example of Esther Shalev-Gerz mentioned above. Ziyah Gafić followed the same process in *Quest for Identity*, with his photographs of artifacts from the war in Bosnia. The International Institute of Social History assembled large constellations of posters from many protests, affirming the idea that collaboration, not individuality, is the way to a better world. Still others create multimedia actions like Satch Hoyt's *Say It Loud!*, a podium of one thousand books on the African diaspora and a free speech platform. Other artists participate in large public actions or document public theatrical gestures. There is nothing obvious in these works: even when artists adopt traditional media or aesthetics, they do so with odd scale, disorienting relationships, peculiar colors. In other words, the deformation, exaggeration, or deconstruction of traditional media and aesthetics are part of the social challenge.

At the entrance of the extensive chapter 1 in the Mechelen Cultural Center, Mona Hatoum's neon globe, *Hot Spot*, spills its neon red light into surrounding spaces. In a nearby gallery is her sculpture/found object, *Exodus II*. Two other works included in chapter 3, *Infinity* and *Conversation Piece II*, give the well-known Palestinian artist, who is doubly exiled from her homeland and from Lebanon, a strong presence. Hatoum adeptly manipulates our expectations with ambiguity and challenging imagery that at first appears straightforward, but with further viewing becomes layered references to urgent social issues. The stainless steel globe, glowing with red/orange neon, can refer both to the idea of the global and permanent wars of the planet, or to global warming and climate change, as our planet heats up. Of course those two ideas are interconnected, although that connection is rarely made; war is one of the biggest sources of CO^2 in the air, not to mention other types of pollution. Hatoum succinctly offers us the connection. Her *Exodus II,* with its two found suitcases connected by human hair also offers several possibilities for interpretation: exile, refugees, human trafficking, forced migration, and deportation. In *Conversation Piece II*, 2011, a circle of chairs connected by a wire spider web refers to multiple human rights concerns, the right to the privacy of your home, protection of property, and freedom of expression.

Chapter 1 ranged from personal liberties to participation in political life. It included references to the US Civil Rights movement, the Vietnam War, the anti-apartheid movement in South Africa, Tiananmen Square, the Bosnian War, and resistance to oppression in Latin America, Turkey, and in the post-Communist state of Belarus. Well-known quotes such as "A Right Delayed is a Right Denied" (Martin Luther King), and "If you don't stand for something you will fall for anything" (Malcolm X), appeared on the wall near Hatoum's globe.

Historically, the earliest works were by two printmakers, Belgian Frans Masereel and German Franz Meyer, both of whom fled the Nazis. Masereel worked in woodcut; as a conscientious objector, his art indicted the horrors of war. Almost all of his work was destroyed by the Nazis. Meyer published his linocut illustrations in Communist and other left-wing publications, survived only by chance and are shown for the first time in "Newtopia." Printmaking has always had a strong role in protest art most famously in Francisco de Goya's etchings of the *Disasters of War*. Because it is easy to produce in multiples, printmaking, ranging from woodblocks, engravings, and etchings to silkscreen, lithography, and digital prints, always plays a prominent part in protest art in all venues from the street to the gallery.

Leon Golub works in the traditional medium of painting on canvas, but his large, simplified imagery depicts paramilitary interrogation in Nicaragua in the 1980s, demonstrating that the right to a fair trial and the prohibition of torture have been violated for decades. The almost life size scale intentionally immerses us and implicates us in the action. These actions are now chillingly familiar to everyone as a CIA torture technique that was continued in the Iraq War.[10]

---

10. In *A Question of Torture,* McCoy explains these connections in detail. See also Mahmood, O'Kane, Madlena, and Smith, "General David Petraeus and 'dirty wars' veteran behind commando units implicated in

Some of the actions in Argentina protesting the thousands of disappeared during the military dictatorship were documented by Eduardo Gil. He presents a public project by the mothers of the disappeared (Madres de Plaza de Mayo) from 1982 to 1983, in which they created life-size silhouettes to represent some of the "desaparecidos." *El Siluetazo* made visible some of the thousands of people who were taken by the police never to be seen again.

David Goldblatt worked in apartheid South Africa, the state absolutely based on racial discrimination. In this series he created intimate and dignified portraits of individuals and families in their stores in an Indian community in South Africa about to be removed from an area declared to be White Only. The right to housing, and the right to work are about to be destroyed, but rather than show the actual destruction, Goldblatt gives us the people in their homes before that happens, still in the midst of what they have made of their lives.

Turkish artist Cengiz Çekil modified twelve Coca-Cola bottles to look like handmade Molotov cocktails in *Towards Childhood, Since Childhood.* Low lights cast a threatening glow. This work was a response to his childhood under martial law in Turkey from 1971 to 1973. His work combines a toy like feeling paired with a sense of threat and violence. The sense of constant danger within a seemingly harmless bottle also resonates with the sense of threat from homemade explosive devices that people in the wars in Iraq and Afghanistan and elsewhere deal with daily in the present.

Two African artists address the history of colonization and the current state of democracy. Sammy Baloji from the Congo photographs sites that were marked in a turn-of-the-century Belgian scientific expedition by Charles Lemaire. Comparing the "objective" early photographs and the contemporary site tells a story not of science, but of changing belief systems. Boniface Mwangi, based in Kenya, documented the 2007–2008 election between Mwai Kibaki (Kikuyu) and Raila Amollo Odinga (Luo) and the violent reaction to what was perceived as a rigged elections in Kibera, Nairobi, a huge slum outside the city center. All of these artists are addressing violations of political rights by the state.

Thomas Locher working only with words creates a transition between historical and contemporary human rights references. On large wall panels, he wrote in bold letters the text of Article 5 addressing torture in the Universal Declaration, Article 7 "All are Equal Before the law and are entitled without any discrimination to

---

detainee abuse," *The Guardian*, March 6, 2013.

equal protection of the law," and Article 14 "Everyone has the right to seek and to enjoy in other countries asylum from persecution." Amidst the quotations, he inserted his tiny questions typed or written in red and underscoring the theme of the contradiction of the state's actions with the ideals of human rights. The relationship of individual rights to community responsibilities, of the idea of freedom of the individual in relation to the benefits provided most effectively by the state is a central issue of human rights enforcement and has been debated since the very first discussions of human rights in the 1940s.[11] It is still at the center of political disagreements today.

Since 2008, Belarusian political activist and artist, Marina Naprushkina, has pursued multimedia resistance techniques addressing lack of freedom of thought and belief for individuals and the absence of freedom of expression, assembly, and movement for the collective public. She refers to her activities collectively as the "Office for Anti-Propaganda." It includes, in this installation, two videos, several drawings, and a wall chart that dramatically diagrams the lack of human rights in Belarus. Within the country, she also distributed, with the help of local activists, a self-published politically-charged newspaper *Self#governing*. According to the artist: "The second edition of the paper analyzes the patriarchal, masculinist system of government in Belarus. It shows how women themselves unwittingly perpetuate this model, and possibilities for changing the situation. Considering the recent wave of protest and resistance across the globe, *Self # governing* can be read—and used—as a guide for daring to think about political alternatives worldwide." In Naprushkina's video *Patriot II,* the artist carries a portrait of the president through the streets. The video is deadpan, humorous, ironic, and provocative. Naprushkina's formal approach sometimes echoes the colors and geometric abstraction of early Russian avant-garde art from the immediate post-Revolutionary era, an important reference point for political art. Her strategy is called radical "civil obedience": quoting or acting on the words of the documents that are intended to safeguard human rights, when in reality, these rights are constantly violated.[12]

U.S. artist Taryn Simon's large photographs of *The Innocents* points to the miscarriage of justice with photographs of people who served jail time, based on mistaken identity (through photographs), for crimes that they did not commit. Her unusual concept is to place

---

11. Glendon, *World Made New,* 39–40.

12. Sorokina "Between poetic justice and legal imagination," *Newtopia,* 82–84.

the freed prisoner at a scene related to the original crime or misidentification, a place the innocent men have never been to before. These poignant images are extraordinary testaments to individual survival in the face of state wrongdoing. They underscore the commitment of the exhibition to avoid simply documenting misfortune, but to present us with the strength of survival and resistance. The constant negotiations of individuals to assert human rights in opposition to state oppression is one of the central themes of chapter 1.

Chapter 2 in the Old Mechelen Meat Market considered social and cultural rights such as work, housing education, and women's rights. At the center of the space a small separate gallery held the work of self-taught Belgian artist Wilchar. Wilchar was detained in a concentration camp in Belgium during the war, and his art work is an ongoing and blunt criticism of the abuses and hypocrisies of the Catholic Church as well as other topics.

On the outside of this enclosure, the brilliantly colorful photographs of Ravi Agarwal, from India, seduce us into looking closely at globalization and its impact on ordinary workers. As is the case with David Goldblatt, Agarwal's photographs are intimate; they create a rapport between the viewer and the workers he photographs. In the series *Down and Out: Labouring under Globalisation*, he conveys human dignity in the face of unimaginable oppression of working conditions in the unregulated informal economic sectors. Agarwal follows these people as individuals, engaging with their work in various industries from diamond processing to construction. Because of his close connection to his subjects, he can photograph a young girl looking directly at him as she carries eight bricks on her head. The photograph conveys not helplessness but stamina.

Olga Chernysheva's simple black and white drawings of homeless people are not pitiful; they represent a human condition that violates a basic human right to housing. A tiny typed inscription reads "Person protected by a smoke." "Person protected by a Coat," the "bare life," means of survival in the absence of all else. The artist pairs these drawings with a video, "Festive Dreams," suggesting the dreams of plenty of the homeless. Sleeping in the street becomes normalized when the state fails to provide the human right to housing.

The right to housing, protection of private life, and the sanctity of the home are addressed in the installation of Palestinian artist Taysir Batniji. *GH0809 (Gaza Houses)* looks like a series of real estate advertisements, with a house and a text, until we realize that all the houses are ruined, and the texts describe the apartment or house before it was destroyed. The neutrality of the descriptions that ignore the current uninhabitable condition of the house underscores the violation of right to housing. In each case the (large) number of people who lived in the bulldozed house is listed. The Palestinian situation also violates the human right to a nationality. Batniji's conceptual photographs intentionally echo known references, as in his *Watchtower* series that recall the benchmark conceptual photography of Hilla and Bernar Becher of abandoned industrial towers in Germany. In this case, the towers are not abstract forms, but real towers occupied by unseen soldiers, who are enforcing military checkpoints. Creating the photographs of the towers was difficult. According to the catalog, the artist actually asked "a Palestinian photographer living in the West Bank to shoot the images for him . . . Under the conditions of occupied Palestine, the photographer did not have the time needed to find the perfect vantage point or ideal light conditions. Nevertheless, the images speak volumes of the oppression and surveillance suffered by the Palestinians under the Israeli military occupation."[13]

Women's rights are singled out in chapter 2 in the photomontages of Lynn Hershman Leeson in which women's limbs are merged with cameras. The result is the image of a woman who is both disempowered and resistant: sometimes the woman's face stares at us defiantly. Yet, they also suggest the way in which women's bodies are caught up in the technology of capitalism. Even more defiant is the video by Barbara Hammer, *Superdyke*, a fantasy of "Amazons marching through San Francisco, symbolically claiming public spaces." Hammer asserts the rights of women to freedom of movement, assembly, and equality.

Chapter 3, located in the Museum hof van Busleyden, focused on environmental and economic issues, sexual abuse, collective protest, and power. Tom Molloy's *Shake* and *Protest* approaches two aspects of public space: government leaders whose interchangeable photographs shaking hands flatten into a single elite image and the dozens of ordinary people protesting oppression all over the world. Their tiny photographs, taken from public media, and painstakingly cut out and assembled in long linear arrangements document the right of public assembly and freedom of speech, both rights frequently denied as in the violent suppression of the #Occupy movement in the U.S. photographs of which are included.

Another reference to collective public protest by Kader Attia, *J'accuse* (named, of course, after Emile Zolà's famous condemnation of the Dreyfus case in France), emphasizes immigration controversies in France, particularly focusing on veterans from colo-

---

13. Gregos, "Taysir Batniji," *Newtopia*, 160.

nized French Africa who fought for France in World War I and II. Attia takes an archival approach, filling a long wall with three rows of images. The top and bottom are historical posters, prints, and book covers with images of African soldiers who fought with the French, the center strip is a continuous enlarged contact print of black and white photographs taken by the artist as documents of demonstrations in the late 1990s by immigrant rights groups with whom he was working. After failing to get inside, the demonstration took place on the steps of the former Musée des Colonies in Paris (now the Musée des Arts d'Afrique et d'Océanie.) The protestors held large banners that read "They died for France, did they have their ID papers?" The French did not provide adequate veterans' benefits for these soldiers until 2006. The richness and extent of the colonial material underscores his point, that these soldiers played a major part in French history.

Sexual abuse in the Catholic Church is addressed by Lieve Van Stappen in her poignant installation of partially transparent glass christening robes that seem to move soundlessly toward an altar, like the innocent children abused by clergy in the Catholic Church. Van Stappen has paired the robes with a timeline that begins with the earliest proclamations of the church that condemns sex with young boys and continues to exposure of the extent of the sexual abuse that has taken place and the resignation of bishops in the last few years. The piece resonates with the contradiction of the delicacy of the sculptures and the appalling exploitation of innocence outlined in the impersonal black and white timeline.

Environmental degradation in chapter 3, a topic of grave concern in the present, is represented by Edward Burtynsky's large photographs of the construction of the Three Gorges Dam in China. Burtynsky's aerial view of the vast amount of human construction on the land, with hardly a trace of nature left, makes visible the scale of destruction of the natural environment currently being pursued in the cause of traditional energy production. Burtynsky has also photographed the tar sands in Canada and other environmental catastrophes. The writers of the Declaration of Human Rights did not address the planet, nature, or our responsibility to nurture the earth and not destroy it, but the articles that address treatment of humans might well also be applied to nature. The fact that only human rights are listed is indicative of the Enlightenment attitude to the earth in which humans are more important than the land or the animals. Edward Burtynsky's photographs present the absolute destruction wrought by humans on the land by adopting a large scale and the representation of deep space: there is barely a trace of the natural world left.

Paired with environmental concerns are two videos that address current economic abuses, Jan Peter Hammer's *Anarchist Banker* with its talk show format features a slick looking "banker" who declares that from his perspective, his freedom must be completely uncontrolled by interference from the government. Wooloo (a pair of Danish artists, Sixten Kai Nielsen and Martin Rosengaard) has produced a music video, *We need you now (more than ever)*, formatted to mimic fund raising videos by Human Rights groups; a dozen individuals (they were intended to be celebrities according to the nonprofit model, but the artists were frequently refused) ask the Catholic Church to turn over some of its enormous wealth to save Europe.

Finally chapter 4 suggests a way to move forward. Easily the most inspired work in this section was by Fernando Sánchez Castillo. In his video, *Pegasus Dance,* water cannon trucks normally used for riot control were choreographed to perform a type of balletic dance. The trucks created for oppression are freed to create poetry. This work captures the spirit of the purpose of the exhibition: the power of art to transform oppression.

Another work that offers solutions, but in a pragmatic way, is Thomas Kilpper's *Lighthouse for Lampedusa.* Kilpper proposes to specifically assist the thousands of immigrants who are crossing from North Africa by building a lighthouse with a powerful beam to guide them to the small Italian island of Lampedusa. He also proposes building an arts center as a place to "learn and listen" on the island, a resource for both the immigrants and local people.

Palestinian artist Khaled Jarrar's *State of Palestine* stamp project poignantly addresses the right to a nationality. He has created a passport stamp for the "State of Palestine" that he actually stamps in people passports. The risk that is incurred with Israeli border guards is real, although the stamp is an art work, and of course not part of a legal border process. Yet, the beauty of the stamp, and the artist's action in actually illegally stamping it into passports, makes clear the current Palestinian condition.

Seamus Nolan's objects align with the legal system as well. His multimedia installation, *Every action will be judged on the particular circumstances*, refers to a trial held in Ireland of Pitstop Ploughshares, a group who damaged a US plane on its way to the war in Iraq with pickaxes and hammers, as a protest against the Iraq war. Ireland was supposed to be neutral, but it supplied its airport for the US Army. At the trial they were charged with damaging property, but the defendants claimed they were actually protecting property, that of the people about to lose their homes in the war in Iraq. Nolan shows the actual pickax and hammers used in the protest, part of the evidence in the trial that were variously identified as weapons and antiwar protest tools. The installation includes many elements including a video of the action, and talk show responses to it. It addresses the human right of protest and the right to life and dignity for those caught up in the war. The oppressive role of the state as exempted from human rights in the "war on terror" is foregrounded here as peace activists try to stop killing.[14]

Finally, two artists are part of current conflicts. Ali Ferzat, the Syrian cartoonist, who has become famous worldwide for his caustic representations of Bashar al-Assad and the multiple violations of human rights in the Syrian civil war, had several biting cartoons.[15] Egyptian artist Ganzeer (Mohammed Fahmy) created the sardonic *Mask of Freedom*, a gagged and blindfolded man with the caption "Salute from the Supreme Council of the Armed Forces to the Loving Sons of the Nation." He posted it as stickers all over Cairo. Murals by Ganzeer, together with other artists, were an integral part of the Tahrir Square uprising. He was invited to create a mural in Mechelen, but was delayed by difficulties in getting a visa. He declared when he finally arrived:

> Hey! It's great to finally make it out to Mechelen. I had initially intended on creating a mural that would honor the efforts of revolutionary people across Europe's history such as Bakunin, Victor Dave, Ravachol, Jean Baptiste-Sipido, and Frank Van Dun for example via the creation of a fictional "revolutionary prophet" (Anarelic)—so to speak that—that would sort of represent all of these peoples' teachings. But after the sheer difficulty I've faced in being able to travel from Cairo to Mechelen upon the invitation from a "human rights festival," I've decided to do a little piece on freedom of mobility. Or rather . . . the lack of freedom of mobility![16]

14. Sorokina, 'Between poetic justice," refers to the "state of exception," in Nolan's work in her detailed discussion [80–82].

15. There is a long tradition of dissident art in Syria as described in cooke (sic.), *Dissident Syria*. Another current example is "Top Goon, Diary of a Little Dictator," a humorous puppet show with relentless attacks on the government. See Rives "Art and Revolution: The Syrian Case," *Near East Quarterly* Saturday, March 24, 2012, available as a downloadable pdf at www.neareastquarterly.com/index.php/2012/03/24/art-and-revolution-the-syrian-case/. Accessed April 22, 2013.

16. Statement on Newtopia blog www.newtopiablog.com/ganzeer-and-his-mural-for-newtopia/. Accessed April 20, 2013.

Like the people who created the original Universal Declaration of Human Rights, the artists selected for "Newtopia" are profoundly committed to social justice. They create art works that make visible the violations of human rights, the many forms of resistance to those violations, and transformative ideas for moving forward. These artists themselves are to be honored, in my opinion, as human rights heroes, for the dedication of their art to social justice. In doing so, they defy the traditional norms of the art world, which honor aesthetics more than content, and abstraction more than realism.

In the "Newtopia" exhibition, the City of Mechelen, with the collaboration of Curator Katerina Gregos, has indeed moved forward from its dark heritage to a new identity of enlightened sponsorship of artists who seek to make the world a better place. The exhibition clearly demonstrates the extent and sophistication of socially engaged art, its effectiveness, and the possibility that its cumulative presence in the world can deeply affect perceptions of human rights as moral imperatives. The age old model of conflict and conquer is clearly no longer viable. In these artworks, a new model emerges, that of art paired with human rights, a partnership that can change perceptions about the relationship of human beings to the planet.

Bibliography

Azouley, Ariella. "The (In)visible Victim-Deconstructing the Spectator's Frame." *Newtopia, The State of Human Rights.* Antwerp: Ludion, 2012.

cooke, miriam. *Dissident Syria, Making Oppositional Arts Official.* Durham: Duke University Press, 2007.

Glendon, Mary Ann. *A World Made New: Eleanor Roosevelt and the Universal Declaration of Human Rights.* New York: Random House, 2001.

Gregos, Katerina. *Newtopia, The State of Human Rights.* Antwerp: Ludion, 2012.

———. *Newtopia, The State of Human Rights.* Exhibition Brochure. Mechelen: Christel Kersemans, 2012.

———, ed. *Speech Matters.* Danish Pavilion, 54th Venice Biennale. Milan: Mousse Publishing, 2011.

Gregos, Katerina, and Elena Sorokina. "Interview with Stéphane Hessel." *Newtopia, The State of Human Rights.* Antwerp: Ludion, 2012.

Human Rights Watch Film Festival. At http://ff.hrw.org/about. Accessed April 20, 2013.

Jaar, Alfredo. *Let there be Light: The Rwanda Project 1994–1998.* 2 vols. Barcelona: Actar, 1998.

Kälin, Walter, Lars Müller, and Judith Wyttenback, eds. *The Face of Human Rights.* Zurich: Lars Muller, 2008.

McCoy, Alfred. *A Question of Torture: CIA Interrogation from the Cold War to the War on Terror.* New York: Henry Holt, 2006.

Mahmood, Mona, Maggie O'Kane, Chavala Madlena, and Teresa Smith. "General David Petraeus and 'dirty wars' veteran behind commando units implicated in detainee abuse." *The Guardian*, March 6, 2013.

Rives, Amélie. "Art and Revolution: The Syrian Case." *Near East Quarterly* (March 24, 2012), available as a downloadable pdf at www.neareastquarterly.com/index.php/2012/03/24/art-and-revolution-the-syrian-case/. Accessed April 22, 2013.

Sorokina, Elena. "Between Poetic Justice and Legal Imagination." *Newtopia, The State of Human Rights.* Antwerp: Ludion, 2012.

Weber, Bruce, and Maia de la Baume. "Stéphane Hessel, Author and Activist, Dies at 95." *The New York Times*, February 27, 2013.

Index

Page numbers followed by n indicate footnotes. Page numbers in *italics* indicate illustrative figures.

About the Contributors

Xabier Arakistain (Arakis) is a feminist curator and art critic.

Juan Arana is currently Teacher of Basque Language and Culture at the University of Liverpool, a position funded by the Etxepare Basque Institute. Arana has published articles on Oteiza and presented on this figure at the universities of Aberdeen, Birmingham, and Liverpool. Last year he published his first book *Oteiza y Unamuno: dos tragedias epigonales de la modernidad. Jorge Oteiza: Art as Sacrament, Avant-Garde and Magic* will be published this year.

Jesus Arpal Poblador was Professor of Philosophy and Sociology at the University of the Basque Country. He was 2012–2013 William A. Douglass Visiting Scholar at the Center for Basque Studies, together with Adelina Moya. Key publications include *La Sociedad Tradicional Vasca, Familia y Territorio en el Pais Vasco: de la Sociedad Tradicional a la Sociedad Industrial*, and *Las Ciudades: Historia y Sociologia*.

Aimar Arriola is a Curator and Researcher. He completed the MACBA Independent Studies Program (PEI) and the Curatorlab program at Konstfack University. He has carried out projects at museums and art centers such as CA2M, Moderna Museet, and Hangar. He is currently participating in the Museo Reina Sofia Residencies Program, and running the Marginalia project at Arteleku.

Zoe Bray is an artist and Professor at the Center for Basque Studies, University of Nevada, Reno. Her research focuses on identity politics and art, and painting and ethnographic methods. A second edition of her book *Living Boundaries: Identity in the Basque Country* was published last year. Bray's paintings can be found in collections and exhibitions internationally.

Txomin Badiola is an artist. He exhibits in numerous galleries in his home country and abroad and institutions. He curated *Propósito Experimental* and *Oteiza. Myth and Modernity* for the Guggenheim Museum in Bilbao and in New York, 2004 and 2005, and Reina Sofia Museum in Madrid, 2005. He is the author of numerous publications, including the *Catalogue Raisonné of Oteiza´s sculpture*.

Catherine Dossin is Professor of Art History at Purdue University, where she teaches Modern and Contemporary art in the USA, Europe, and Latin America. Her research encompasses the geopolitics of the art world, the history of art history, and cultural transfers in the second part of the twentieth century. She is coeditor of ARTL@S Bulletin, and President of European Postwar and Contemporary Art Forum. She has written for *Woman's Art Journal*, *American Art*, *Visual Resources*, and other edited collections. Her book *Geopolitics of the Western Art World, 1940s–1980s* will be published in 2014.

Fernando Golvano is a Professor at the University of the Basque Country. He is also an art critic and independent curator. He has published on artistic vanguards, the poetics/politics of memory, and the relations between art and democracy. His most recent curated exhibitions include *Oteiza: memoria y apropiaciones*, *Basterretxea y Ortiz de Elgea. En el curso del tiempo*, *Laboratorios 70*, *San Sebastián. De lo sagrado y lo profano*, and *Amable Arias. Dar forma al caos y al azar*.

Nathalie Heinich is a sociologist and Research Director at the French National Center for Scientific Research (CNRS); she works within the Ecole des Hautes Etudes en Sciences Sociales (EHESS, Paris). In addition to numerous articles in academic and cultural journals, she has published over thirty books, dealing with the status of the artist and the notion of author, contemporary art, the question of identity, the history of sociology, and values.

Selma Holo is Director of the USC Fisher Museum of Art and Professor of Art History at the University of Southern California. Her work examines how museums participate in the transition from dictatorships to democratic systems, and are thus not only preservers of the past but also engines of the future. Key publications include *Beyond the Prado: Museums and Identity in Democratic Spain* and

Oaxaca at the Crossroads: Managing Memory, Negotiating Change.

Ismael Manterola is a Professor at the University of the Basque Country. He is also an art critic and curator. He has published on Basque art at the beginning of the twentieth century. Key publications include *Hermes y los pintores vascos de su tiempo* and *Raemaekers' Cartoons: British propaganda in Spain and The Basque Country during the First World War.* His most recent curated exhibition is *Trama e hilos sueltos: Diálogo entre dos colecciones de arte vasco/Bilbea eta hari askeak: euskal arteko bi bilduma elkarrekin solasean.*

Adelina Moya Valgañon was Professor of Art History at the University of the Basque Country. She was 2012–2013 William A. Douglass Visiting Scholar at the Center for Basque Studies, together with Jesus Arpal. Key publications include *Nicolas de Lekuona. Orígenes de la Vanguardia Artística en el País Vasco* and *Jose Maria de Uzelay.*

Susan Noyes Platt is an independent researcher. Key publications include *Art and Politics in the 1930s* and *Art and Politics Now.*

Peter Selz is Professor Emeritus in the department of the History of Art at the University of California, Berkeley. He was Founding Director of its Art Museum. He was chief curator of Painting and Sculpture Exhibitions at New York's Museum of Modern Art. He is the author of twenty books on modern art. He recently co-organized two shows at San Francisco's nonprofit Meridian Gallery on the beat-generation poets and Irish painter Patrick Graham. He serves on the acquisitions committee of San Francisco's de Young and Legion of Honor museums.

Brett M. Van Hoesen is Professor of Modern and Contemporary Art History at the University of Nevada, Reno. She is writing a book on the legacy of Germany's colonial history in the arts and visual culture of the Weimar Republic. Recent publications are: "Carl Einstein and the Lessons of László Moholy-Nagy" in *Carl Einstein and the European Avant-Garde* and "Postcolonial Cosmopolitanism: Constructing the Weimar New Woman out of a Colonial Imaginary" in *The New Woman International: Photographic Representations from the 1870s through 1960s.*

Azucena Vieites is an artist. Her work is a conceptual approach to visual culture. She participates in numerous exhibitions and teaches at the Fine Arts College at the University of Salamanca. She is the co-founder of the Basque feminist artist group Erreakzioa-Reacción.

www.ingramcontent.com/pod-product-compliance
Lightning Source LLC
LaVergne TN
LVHW091024080826
845145LV00002B/353

* 9 7 8 1 9 3 5 7 0 9 5 6 5 *